Homeschooling

The History and Philosophy of Education Series

EDITED BY RANDALL CURREN AND JONATHAN ZIMMERMAN

PATRIOTIC EDUCATION IN A GLOBAL AGE
by Randall Curren and Charles Dorn

THE COLOR OF MIND: WHY THE ORIGINS OF
THE ACHIEVEMENT GAP MATTER FOR JUSTICE
by Derrick Darby and John L. Rury

THE CASE FOR CONTENTION: TEACHING CONTRO-
VERSIAL ISSUES IN AMERICAN SCHOOLS *by
Jonathan Zimmerman and Emily Robertson*

HAVE A LITTLE FAITH: RELIGION, DEMOCRACY,
AND THE AMERICAN PUBLIC SCHOOL
by Benjamin Justice and Colin Macleod

TEACHING EVOLUTION IN A CREATION NATION
by Adam Laats and Harvey Siegel

Homeschooling

*The History and Philosophy of a
Controversial Practice*

JAMES G. DWYER AND
SHAWN F. PETERS

THE UNIVERSITY OF CHICAGO PRESS   CHICAGO AND LONDON

The University of Chicago Press, Chicago 60637
The University of Chicago Press, Ltd., London
© 2019 by The University of Chicago
Published 2019

28 27 26 25 24 23 22 21 20 19   1 2 3 4 5

ISBN-13: 978-0-226-62711-3 (cloth)
ISBN-13: 978-0-226-62725-0 (paper)
ISBN-13: 978-0-226-62739-7 (e-book)
DOI: https://doi.org/10.7208/chicago/9780226627397.001.0001

Library of Congress Cataloging-in-Publication Data

Names: Dwyer, James G., 1961– author. | Peters, Shawn Francis, 1966– author.
Title: Homeschooling : the history and philosophy of a controversial practice /
    James G. Dwyer and Shawn F. Peters.
Other titles: History and philosophy of education.
Description: Chicago ; London : The University of Chicago Press, 2019. | Series: The history
    and philosophy of education series | Includes bibliographical references and index.
Identifiers: LCCN 2018050262 | ISBN 9780226627113 (cloth : alk. paper) |
    ISBN 9780226627250 (pbk. : alk. paper) | ISBN 9780226627397 (e-book)
Subjects: LCSH: Home schooling—History. | Education—Parent participation. |
    Education and state.
Classification: LCC LC40 .D994 2019 | DDC 371.04/2—dc23
LC record available at https://lccn.loc.gov/2018050262

Contents

Introduction

Threat to democracy, or bulwark against tyranny? Enslavement of the mind, or last refuge of human independence? Stunting of children's social development, or more natural and nurturing site of cooperative interaction? Violation of children's rights, or recognition of parental entitlement? Homeschooling—pervasive in colonial times, an anomaly a half century ago, today a national movement—now has this two-faced nature, one ugly and threatening as seen by critics, the other beautiful and wholesome in defenders' eyes. The reality is that today it is no one thing. Nearly two million children in the United States are now being homeschooled instead of attending what we will call a "regular school," private or public. That is 4 percent of all US children, about the same percentage as those attending Catholic schools. The overarching authority of the Catholic Church creates some uniformity among its parochial schools, whereas there is little standardizing of homeschooling, and so the latter takes on innumerable, extraordinarily diverse forms, reflecting the multiple reasons parents have for choosing it. Parents' motivations range from those everyone would grant are noble (even if detractors say they are misguided) to those everyone would grant are condemnable (e.g., the concealment of horrible child abuse). In addition, a significant number of parents simply do not send their children to any school and make no effort to provide homeschooling instead. They might be mentally ill, want the children working to earn money for the family, fear investigation by Child Protective Services or the Immigration and Naturalization Service, or have some other reason. And, in most states, permissive homeschooling laws enable these parents to do this with impunity, because the laws require no real oversight of homeschools; indeed, many do not even require parents to notify school officials of an intent to homeschool.

This is the paradox for legislators and state education officials: home-schooling can work very well, but authorizing it can also put some children in grave danger. Is it possible to facilitate good homeschooling without also enabling physical maltreatment and educational deprivation? Over-whelmingly, state legislatures in this country have chosen to give parents who wish to homeschool complete and unsupervised power and freedom, leaving children unprotected from the unknown number of parents who are seriously neglectful or abusive. Does this legislative choice arise from defensible principles or from political expedience and cowardice?

The complexity of the subject makes homeschooling intriguing for historians and challenging for philosophers. The historian aims to un-derstand and describe an infinitely varied phenomenon, and the phi-losopher seeks neat, normative conclusions about the permissibility of a practice whose consequences and underlying intentions differ consider-ably from one family to the next. This book is a unique pairing of these two disciplinary approaches to the subject. First, the historian (Peters) traces the evolution of homeschooling and the law relating to it, from be-fore America's founding to the present day, in the process uncovering the many arguments proponents and detractors have made for and against it. Then the philosopher (Dwyer) applies a moral framework constructed from the best account of what rights and duties the three players in the drama—the child, the parent, and the state (as *parens patriae* protector of the child or as agent for society as a whole)—possess, to analyze the com-peting arguments and ultimately generate a prescription for state policy. Is homeschooling today inherently deficient relative to regular schooling, as some assert, and if so should the state eliminate it as an alternative and insist that all children attend a regular school (itself a quite varied phenomenon)? Or can homeschooling actually be not only an adequate form of education but also even superior in some ways to regular school-ing, and if so should the state at least tolerate it and perhaps even en-courage and subsidize it? Ultimately, does it matter whether the rest of society approves of it and state education officials pass positive judgment on it, or are parents entitled, morally or constitutionally, to choose home-schooling for their children regardless of what anyone else thinks? Are homeschooling advocates justified in asserting that the state has no au-thority over children's education or that its authority is limited to guarding against serious physical abuse (somehow without intruding into family life)? Or are critics correct in maintaining that homeschooling, even if it can be adequate, makes children too vulnerable to educational and social deprivation and maltreatment, so close supervision or even prohibition of it is required? And do children themselves have any rights in connection with their education? If so, who gives content to those rights—parents or the state?

In practice, the state's answer to these questions has varied over time, as the historical account makes clear, and still today there is some variation in degree of regulation across jurisdictions. Does this reflect an inscrutability in the moral issues as a theoretical matter, or can careful philosophical analysis yield definitive answers to these questions? The task of this book is to shed new light by combining the historian's nuanced observation with the philosopher's normative analysis.

Given the complexity of the phenomenon, we adopt a fairly broad definition of "homeschooling." Throughout the book, we use the term to refer simply to parent-directed learning in the home that substitutes, partially or completely, for attendance at a regular school. This would encompass situations in which children learn at home by working their way through a packaged curriculum, so long as parents are overseeing this process. It would not include situations where children are left entirely to their own devices, because "school" as a verb is transitive, implying both a subject and an object. In those situations, we would say children are receiving no schooling. And when we use the term "homeschoolers," we will mean parents who are homeschooling their children and not also the children who are being homeschooled. This is simply for the sake of clarity and writing economy and is not meant to deny that many home-schooled children are more active participants in their learning than are typical students in a regular school environment.

The first three chapters of the book trace chronologically the history of homeschooling in America, from the colonial era (chapter 1) to the rebirth and remarkable spread of homeschooling in the half century after World War II (chapter 2) to the movement's maturation and steady growth during this past quarter century (chapter 3). This history reveals both common themes and different family-state dynamics across these time periods and highlights both shared beliefs and divergent ideologies across categories of homeschoolers—conservative Christians, leftist free thinkers, parents who homeschool out of practical necessity, and others. A transitional fourth chapter pulls together central facts revealed by the historical account, summarizes the many arguments and concerns that proponents and opponents have expressed, and then establishes some starting assumptions for the three normative and analytical chapters that follow.

Chapter 5 clarifies the state's role in connection with children's education, correcting widespread misconceptions about that, and analyzes what rights can properly be attributed to any of the three parties—child, parent, and state—in this context. Unlike other theorizing about children's schooling, the analysis here insists on adherence to a basic principle of moral reasoning—namely, that claims about rights should be articulated at the highest level of generality the subject matter allows, to guard against illicit prejudice regarding certain groups of persons, such as children. Even many philosophers have displayed uncharacteristic inclination toward ad hoc assertions about rights in connection with child-rearing, making little effort to develop or invoke general principles that might apply also to other types of human relationships.

Chapter 6 takes a hard look at various empirical claims people make on each side of the homeschooling debate, in an effort to establish an objective description of what, from the perspective of the state (which must ultimately decide what *the law* is going to be), are children's real needs in connection with schooling. Finally, chapter 7 applies the normative framework that emerges from chapter 5's analysis to the factual conclusions about children's needs arrived at in chapter 6, to draw conclusions about who is entitled to what and who owes what duties to whom. The upshot is a clear and confident position on what state law and policy should be, along with consideration of novel strategies for implementing them. The issue is so ideologically fraught at this point in American history that many people want to know only whether you agree with them on what the law should be, and are largely uninterested in how you arrived at your position even if you do agree with them. The authors came to the issue without preordained policy positions, eager to improve their own understanding of this increasingly prominent practice. One of the authors has seriously considered homeschooling his own children but thus far has decided not to do so. We believe everyone should find both the history and the philosophical analysis enlightening, even if these diverge at points from the reader's own prior views. Anyone who comes to the issue with an open mind and a sincere desire for clear thinking about it should be willing to engage with the analysis we present, step by step, which aims throughout to consider sincerely all reasonable viewpoints and should lead readers from all perspectives to see the practice and the policy issues in a new way.

CHAPTER ONE

Early Homeschooling

It is a challenge to find a culture or era in which family-based learning has not been an essential and irreplaceable element of the education of children. Indeed, in many cultural and historical contexts, families (both nuclear and extended) have provided the bulk of children's educational training. Sometimes this has been the only way for children to receive sustained instruction in the skills required to attain social status or long-term socioeconomic security.[1]

Children received home instruction for literacy from virtually the first moment of European settlement in North America. Whether the households were affluent or impoverished, ideological goals were paramount with this learning in the home. Parents taught the fundamentals of reading and writing so that children might be properly—and repeatedly—instructed in the tenets of religious orthodoxy. Children's book learning in the colonial period was not for the sake of acquiring critical thinking skills or developing core competencies of democratic citizenship. It was, rather, fundamentally religious training. If literacy was essential, it was to appreciate the enduring lessons of Christian scriptures, the only written texts of real significance in colonial homes.[2] In homogeneous communities with an economy that was, by modern standards, quite primitive, this, along with basic math skills acquired from everyday life, sufficed.

For the most part, parents directed this inherently nonsecular book learning; only the elite might have employed tutors. Children in colonial New England pored over catechisms and bibles in their homes, under the tutelage of their mothers and fathers. David Hall has suggested a peculiar division of literacy training between mothers and fathers, the former more often taking responsibility for reading, the latter for writing. "I learned to read of my mother," Increase Mather recalled. "I learned to write of

Father." Reading aloud, along with reciting and memorizing, were critical parts of parents' instruction.[3]

It would be a mistake, though, to equate this instruction in reading and writing in the home with schooling today, which constitutes comprehensive preparation for adult civic life and employment. In the colonial era, preparation for employment was mostly a matter of learning by doing in actual workplaces—that is, farms, craft shops, trading posts, and so on. Many children worked beside their parents and grew up in the "family business"—whatever the family did to make a living. Many parents, though, placed their children with other families or businesses as apprentices, to learn a trade, usually when the children were at an age not much higher than that for compulsory schooling today. There were not a great number of options for "careers," nor was there much of the individualistic sense we have today that every person should be free to pursue the occupation for which her or his talents and abilities are best suited. The focus was on survival, not fulfillment.

The at-home instruction, though, was viewed as of sufficient importance to the community that local authorities would mandate that parents keep the appropriate religious texts in their homes. In Massachusetts, officials periodically went from house to house to ensure families owned these texts. And parents who failed to train their children for a useful trade were likely to have the children simply taken away from them and placed by local officials in an apprenticeship with someone else.[4] In that era, none would have objected to such government oversight on the grounds that it was infringing parental prerogative; that notion would arise much later in our history. The prevailing conception of parenthood, reflecting both the monarchical cultures from which colonists came and the normative prescriptions of the Bible, was very much about duties rather than rights, with the duties being owed principally to God and the community. Jeffrey Shulman explains: "What is deeply rooted in our legal traditions and social conscience is the idea that the state *entrusts* parents with custody of the child, and the concomitant rule that the state does so only as long as parents meet their legal duty to take proper care of the child."[5] Thus, "the American colonies, and later states, developed a system of separating children from their undeserving parents"—that is, from those "not providing 'good breeding,' neglecting their formal education, not teaching a trade."[6] The great early nineteenth-century jurists James Kent and Joseph Story spoke clearly of parenthood as a sacred trust that the state has given to those whom it assumes will best fulfill legal child-rearing duties.

On the other hand, no one ever spoke of universal standards or core competencies (other than in scripture). In an era long before one could purchase ready-made curricula through the mail or glean information from homeschooling websites, there probably were as many approaches to teaching children in and around the home as there were parents doing it. Mothers and fathers simply did the best they could with what little free time and resources they could muster.

In the antebellum South, most African Americans received no book learning. Custom (and, later, law) prohibited enslaved persons from learning to read and write, because "access to the written word, whether scriptural or political, revealed a world beyond bondage in which African Americans could imagine themselves free to think and behave as they chose," according to historian Heather Andrea Williams. Many enslaved adults and their children nevertheless undertook clandestine and ad hoc efforts to obtain literacy skills. "I have seen the Negroes up in the country going away under large oaks, and in secret places," one enslaved person later told an interviewer, "sitting in the woods with spelling books." This piecemeal academic training became an important "symbol of resistance," as Williams puts it.[7]

In contrast to both African Americans and average white parents of that time period, Martha Laurens Ramsay approached the home education of her children from a position of privilege and in a systematic manner. The daughter of Henry Laurens, the wealthy South Carolina planter who at one point served as president of the Continental Congress, she took seriously her role as the primary educator of her children. One of her sons later wrote that she "studied with deep interest most of the esteemed practical treatises on education, both in French and English, that she might be better informed of the nature and extent" of her role as a teacher. Yet for Ramsay, too, one text was central to training children: "She taught them early to read their Bibles." This served the dual purpose of providing spiritual uplift and developing their literacy.[8]

Benjamin Franklin's formative intellectual experiences also took place largely outside of school. Franklin impressed his father by learning to read at an early age ("I do not remember when I could not read," he later wrote). With the hope that he would pursue a career in the ministry, he was initially dispatched to a grammar school for instruction in writing and ciphering, but after only a few years the school proved to be too costly. Franklin wound up apprenticing as a printer under his brother James. Outside the confines of a school, Franklin still managed to learn, borrowing texts from a bookseller and devouring them late into the night. This autodidactic training was famously successful, and Franklin almost wore his lack of formal schooling as a badge of honor, a sign that he had succeeded through grit and guile rather than privilege. Franklin's experiences also showed that genuinely independent thinking (and not simply religious indoctrination) could flourish outside of regimented school environments.[9]

Small-scale, makeshift home instruction continued throughout the nineteenth century, and sometimes the results were spectacularly successful. Thomas Edison, another famous polymath, succeeded without much formal school training. In the 1850s, Edison was abused both verbally and physically by his schoolmaster because, like many bored students before and after him, he doodled, daydreamed, and generally failed to cooperate with teachers. After only three months in school, he left for good when he overheard the man describe him as "addled." From there, Edison's mother took control of his education. Foreshadowing the post–World War II leftists who would rejuvenate homeschooling in the modern era, Mrs. Edison was, as one biographer put it, "determined that no formalism would cramp his style, no fetters hobble the free rein, the full sweep of his imagination." This approach clearly paid off, nurturing a singularly innovative mind.[10]

Dorothy Reed Mendenhall, the first woman to graduate from Johns Hopkins Medical School and later an esteemed pediatrician, experienced the opposite pattern—homeschooling first, then attendance at a regular school. A combination of family misfortunes (including her own early illnesses) prevented her from receiving any formal schooling outside the home until she was a teenager. Yet she never believed home education had hindered her. "I am unconvinced," she later wrote, "of the value of grade schooling." Mendenhall believed younger children would be better served if allowed to devote their energies to things like physical development and organized play.[11]

Illnesses such as those suffered by Mendenhall necessitated education in the home for many children. Theodore Roosevelt suffered from debilitating asthma and so received tutoring at home throughout his childhood and adolescence. Though he was instructed in a variety of subjects, including Latin and French, young "Teedie" (as the family called him) quickly developed a near-obsession with the study of natural history, and it remained a passion throughout the remainder of his life. (His family created an informal collection of specimens known as the "Roosevelt

Museum of Natural History.") The tutoring that young Roosevelt received at home was supplemented by his family's frequent trips abroad. His traditional schooling only began when he entered Harvard as an undergraduate.[12]

At the beginning of the twentieth century, Margaret Mead likewise found intellectual engagement at home rather than at school. In her formative years, the pioneering anthropologist attended kindergarten and high school, but during the intervening years she was schooled at home by her grandmother. Such was the elder woman's influence that Mead devoted an entire chapter of her autobiography, *Blackberry Winter*, to their relationship. In that work, Mead wryly observes that her grandmother kept her out of school because she wanted the young woman to receive an adequate education.[13]

In this earlier, formative period of American history, parents generally did not undertake home instruction with any sense of repudiating the state's authority or expertise in the realm of education. This was in part because in the prevailing view parents held authority themselves only by leave of the state, and in part because, in most places, the state's commitment to providing and regulating schooling was relatively tepid. In the hardscrabble world of many colonial settlements, the time and resources that might have been dedicated to educating children were instead diverted to keeping communities economically viable and secure from attack. Time spent ciphering in the schoolhouse would be time lost in the fields or the workshop.

Over time, more direct state control and coercion became prominent elements in the American educational landscape. Communities and colonies (and, later, states) gradually enacted laws mandating the construction and staffing of schools. There were some very early instances. In 1642, New Haven required "that a free schoole shall be sett vp in this towne." Massachusetts enacted general school laws in that year and again in 1647 that gave the colony a more direct role in providing that children be educated. The 1642 measure, lamenting "the great neglect of many parents and masters in training up their children in learning and labor," required parents to ensure that their children and apprentices were literate and understood the commonwealth's laws. The General Court appointed selectmen who were empowered to monitor these efforts. The 1647 law, memorably known as the "Old Deluder Satan Act," gave the state a more direct role in furnishing education, requiring towns of fifty or more families to hire a schoolmaster who would teach children to read and write (and thereby give them the intellectual tools necessary to understand the Bible and thus resist the devil). Although no one at the time understood it, here were the first moves toward universal compulsory education in the United States—and they were taken in response to the perceived shortcomings of parents as educators even when expectations were slight compared to those in the modern era.[14]

The state's interest in, and control over, education grew as immigration and industrialization began to transform American society over the middle part of the nineteenth century. Fleeing economic turmoil and ideological repression, waves of immigrants poured into the United States from places like Ireland and Germany as well as southern and eastern Europe. These hardworking newcomers fueled the new nation's breakneck economic expansion, but they also threatened the social and cultural hegemony that had reigned throughout the colonial period. A land that was once rural and Protestant became increasingly urban and Catholic. Schools were increasingly seen as a vital means of assimilating and acculturating immigrant populations as well as maintaining social order. They were places where immigrant children could shed the alien customs of their forebears and learn to become properly American.

A band of reformers led by Horace Mann came to view the schools as a bulwark against the changes that appeared to be recasting, if not outright threatening, the core values that defined American society. From his post as the chair of the state board of education in Massachusetts, Mann pushed for the establishment of a system of common schools backed by the full fiscal and legal authority of the state. The schools would work to the benefit of both society broadly and students individually. Mann insisted that it was a "great, immutable principle of natural law" that every person possessed an "*absolute right*" to an education. Along with this came the "correlative duty of every government to see that the means of that education are provided for all."[15] Thus, the earliest references to individual rights in connection with schooling in America were about the rights of children, not of parents.

The schools envisioned by Mann—staffed by well-trained, professional teachers—would provide consistent and rigorous academic training throughout the year. The results would be profound and far-reaching. Mann believed common schools could be a great equalizer, a "balance wheel of the social machinery."[16] No longer would affluent students be able to further their advantages in society by having exclusive access to the best schools. Now, everyone, rich and poor alike, would have the chance to learn. Moreover, the schools would build character and instill discipline. Moral education would be paramount.

The purported benefits of the common-school system were manifold. Children would be prepared for economic and social advancement in an increasingly fluid society that was becoming less agrarian and more industrial. Moreover, such well-educated citizens would be better equipped to participate effectively in the democratic system that governed the nation. Implicit in this argument for the common schools was the notion that many families—especially immigrant families—were largely incapable of providing such crucial training for their children. Indeed, few parents then would themselves have had more than the basic literacy that sufficed in the preindustrial economy. Mann touted the importance of common schools by insisting that in order "to provide surer and better means for the education of their children," parents had an obligation to send their sons and daughters outside the home for formal academic instruction.[17]

The common-school system Mann advocated took hold in the mid-nineteenth century and became more widespread in the decades after the Civil War. To be sure, meaningful reforms in schooling came more slowly in some places than others. Frontier communities often lacked the wherewithal to establish schools, and the attenuated nature of state power throughout the South often resulted in lackluster organization and administration of schooling. Nonetheless, in general, more and more children attended better schools and for longer periods of time.

Although their impact was often difficult to gauge, compulsory school attendance laws facilitated the growth of the common-school system advocated by Mann and other educational reformers. These measures, by which states assumed power to require families to send children to school for a prescribed number of weeks per year, did not have uniquely American roots. Martin Luther frequently called for compulsory schooling. "I maintain," he wrote, "that the civil authorities are under obligation to compel the people to send their children to school." This schooling was essential, according to Luther, because "we are warring with the devil, whose object it is secretly to exhaust our cities and principalities of their strong men." John Calvin was an equally staunch advocate of compulsory schooling and for similarly grave reasons.[18] Thanks in part to Luther's worried exhortations, a variety of Protestant states in Germany established school systems and then mandated attendance in them. Duke Christopher, Elector of Württemberg, is credited with establishing one of the first modern compulsory state-education systems, in 1559. (This

regime included close monitoring of attendance and punishment of tru-
ants.) Other German states soon followed suit. Calvinists succeeded in
pushing for the establishment of compulsory primary education in France
in 1571, and they prevailed in Holland in 1609.[19]

In the Americas, pioneers of compulsory school attendance included
the Aztec Triple Alliance, which in the fourteenth and early fifteenth
centuries governed what is now central Mexico. The educational system
there, which thrived until the arrival of the Spanish in 1521, required all
male children to attend one of two types of schools. One stressed military and vocational training, the other achievement in civic and religious
realms. This education was meant to imbue students with the core values
of the empire as well as promote loyalty and submission to authority.[20]

In its customary role in the vanguard of educational reform, Massachusetts took the lead in establishing compulsory school attendance
laws in the United States. An attendance measure enacted there in 1837
had, as was typical for such measures, complementary goals: to promote
education (and the myriad benefits thought to flow from it) and to curtail child labor. This first, tepid law did not include any provisions for
enforcement, and it merely required that children obtain a minimum of
three months' schooling in the year preceding their employment. The
state passed a more stringent law in 1842 that once again paired school
attendance with the regulation of child labor. It restricted the number
of hours that children under the age of twelve could work in factories
and required local school committees to enforce school attendance requirements. Finally, in 1852, Massachusetts passed the country's first bona
fide compulsory-attendance statute, one requiring school attendance for
at least twelve weeks per year for all children between the ages of eight
and fourteen.

Other states gradually followed Massachusetts' lead, though not always eagerly. By 1875, twelve other states had enacted compulsory school
attendance laws. (Every state would have one by 1918, when Mississippi
finally acted.) In general, these were not strict measures, and, at least
early on, many people doubted the laws had much impact. One observer,
surveying the first twenty years of the Massachusetts compulsory school
attendance statute, sniffed that "the history of the law is little more than
a record of failures."[21]

Part of the problem was that some ambivalent states dragged their
feet in enacting and enforcing meaningful school laws. Writing in 1921
on state regulation of school attendance and child labor in the United

States, Forest Chester Ensign explained why several states were slow to formulate and act on measures mandating school attendance. "Selfishness of employers and poverty of parents, unwilling to sacrifice their real and fancied interests to the social good, were for years relatively constant factors," he observed. "Social inertia long rendered adequate laws impossible. A few men with vested interests [i.e., factory owners] could easily prevent legislation, could usually divert attention away from the real issues." All too often, the rights and interests of children remained subordinate.[22]

Questioning the laws' efficacy, given parental resistance and the lack of facilities and trained teachers to educate all children, and fielding concerns about the laws' impact on the industrial-labor pool, authorities in Pennsylvania were slow to enact statutes requiring school attendance. The state supervisor of public instruction reported in 1881, long after many states had enacted similar measures, that he had "very serious misgivings as to the propriety of any strictly compulsory law" in a democratic society if it was not endorsed by most parents. But after becoming more familiar with the effects of child labor, he joined his predecessors who had pushed for universal schooling. When the state subsequently began making halting progress toward enacting school attendance laws, much of the impetus came not from educators but from state officials concerned about the myriad dangers posed by children's work in factories and farms. "If the privilege of education is refused," one state labor official said, "the general safety requires that it be made compulsory." Still, it took Pennsylvania lawmakers until 1895 to follow his advice and enact a school attendance measure.[23]

Slowly but surely, compulsory-education measures gained public acceptance among policy makers and the general public as an important means of ensuring that young people not only avoided the perils of industrial labor but also gained basic academic skills and citizenship training. "The arguments and discussions of thirty years or more have been gradually silencing opposition," the US Commissioner of Education notes in his report for 1894–95, "and public sentiment is slowly crystallizing in the direction of requiring by law all parents to provide a minimum of school instruction for their children. This tendency is unmistakable."[24]

Implicit in this emerging system of universal public education was not only solicitude for the welfare of children and the good of society but also a critique of the capacity of the typical family to fully educate and academically train its children as the economy and social interactions became more complex. Writing about the advent of compulsory education in England, Frank Musgrove contends that policy makers there "recognized the obsolescence of the educative family, its inadequacy in modern society in child care and training."[25] David Tyack observes that similar reasoning was applied in the United States, with advocates of compulsory schooling often arguing

> that families—or at least some families, like those of the poor or foreign-born—were failing to carry out their traditional functions of moral and vocational training. Immigrant children in crowded cities, reformers complained, were leading disorderly lives, schooled by the street and their peers more than by Christian nurture in the home. Much of the drive for compulsory education reflected an animus against parents considered incompetent to train their children.[26]

John Eaton, US Commissioner of Education from 1870 to 1886, asserted that parents all too often "have been found so indulgent and negligent of duty . . . , so regardless of the interests of their children, as to suffer them to grow up in ignorance and idleness." For Eaton, there was a ready cure for this neglect, and it involved the judicious exercise of state power. "To remedy this evil," he said, "I know of no better provision than the law of compulsory education."[27]

Schools, in short, could do what parents could not. And states, it was thought, bore the ultimate responsibility for children's positive formation. C. A. Black, Pennsylvania's superintendent of education in the mid-nineteenth century, expressed it thus: "The children of the Commonwealth are public property, and the government, as a faithful guardian, cannot discharge the trust without preparing them for the rights and duties of citizenship."[28] In addition to compelling attendance at schools, states in the late nineteenth century continued the practice of taking large numbers of children away from parents who were "neglecting their education suitable for their condition in life."[29] The prevailing conception of the parental role remained primarily one of duty holder more than right holder, readily supplanted when parents did not conform to the state's expectations.[30]

Compulsory-education laws were commonly viewed as having a broadly salutary impact that extended beyond schoolchildren themselves. A *New York Times* editorial asserted in 1875 that stringent enforcement of attendance laws would reduce the havoc idle youngsters wrought on city streets: "Vagrancy is rooted out; absence from school is checked; education becomes universal; the great source of crime in this city is attacked; and we enter upon a new era of improvement and intelligence."[31]

Whatever its implicit critique of the family, the common-school regime—given teeth by compulsory-attendance laws—was for the most part embraced by the American public. For immigrants, it appeared to offer the chance of economic success and political engagement. Schools seemed to offer a path toward respectability, Americanization, and long-term economic security. From a somewhat different perspective, white Protestants valued it for much the same reasons. While their own children acquired the skills necessary for advancement, immigrants would be homogenized and neutralized as a threat to order. Summing up the prevailing sentiment, one observer in 1878 wrote, "Free and universal education will flank the moral evils that are now invading the republic as the hordes of Huns and Goths and Vandals invaded the Roman Empire."[32]

In contemporary America, many people bemoan the lack of religion, especially Protestant Christianity, in the public schools. (Indeed, this is a main reason why some devout parents choose to homeschool their children.) In the nineteenth century, however, there wasn't much serious public debate over whether the common schools should attempt to inculcate its students with Christian beliefs. It was taken for granted that students in public schools would read the Bible and absorb its teachings. If there was controversy, it was over which *type* of Bible would be read in the schools: in some cities, Catholics objected to the use of the King James version, which was the standard for most Protestant churches. Disputes over such matters resulted in riots in Philadelphia in 1844.

As the "Bible riots" demonstrated, not everyone readily put their faith in state-run schools. Recognizing the sometimes overtly anti-Catholic tenor of the common schools, many members of the Catholic faith dispatched their children to church-run schools, where their religious beliefs and practices would be bolstered rather than subverted. Some wealthier parents believed private tutors were better suited to teach their sons and daughters at home. These included the parents of both Theodore and Franklin Delano Roosevelt, but also, somewhat paradoxically, Horace Mann, the great champion of the common schools, who did not send his own children to the schools that he battled so relentlessly to establish. Mann's children received tutoring at home from his wife, Mary. Jonathan Messerli, his biographer, wrote that Mann "fell back on the educational responsibilities of the family, hoping to make the fireside achieve for his own son what he wanted the schools to accomplish for others."[33]

Nor were compulsory school attendance laws, which undergirded the common-school system, universally popular. In her excellent study of the development of state authority over schooling in the early twentieth century, historian Tracy Steffes points out that the extension of state power over children through compulsory education "did not go uncontested." Some parents objected, often vehemently, because they believed their authority within the realm of home and family life was being abrogated. "Parents resisted the gradual extension of the state into decisions of the household," Steffes writes, "through legal challenges, organized protest, political lobbying, and, most often, through evasion and rejection of school policies in practice."[34]

The notion of a parental "right" to resist state authority had emerged at least by the end of the nineteenth century. Private schools mounted a variety of legal challenges against states' attempts to exercise control over not only the *amount* of schooling required of students but also the *type* of instruction they received. Ohio, for instance, mandated at least twenty weeks of teaching for children between the ages of eight and fourteen in a variety of subjects, including writing, geography, and arithmetic. The measure allowed for instruction in private or parochial schools, but Catholic educators resisted it anyway, claiming that its requirements for particular kinds of secular teaching overstepped the boundaries of legislative authority. Reverend Patrick Francis Quigley, a Catholic priest in Toledo, was charged under the law in 1891 for "neglecting, as principal of a school, to report to the clerk of the board of education the names, ages and residence of the pupils in attendance at his school."[35] On appeal he argued unsuccessfully that the state law violated Ohio's constitution. Quigley later penned a lengthy book recounting his legal battle, and in it states that his attorney argued that "the state has no right to control the education of the child, against the wishes of the parent, for that to the parent belongs the right to control the education of his children, [as] this is an inherent and unalienable right under and by virtue of the natural law." The compulsory-education statute violated the state's constitution, the attorney is said to have asserted, in part because it was grounded in the idea that "to the state and not to the parent belongs the right to control the education of the child."[36]

In his book, Quigley issues a dire warning about what such laws represent vis-à-vis state power. If the state could efface the authority of parents and dictate all aspects of education, he cautions, it might be emboldened to expand its power to the point where it ceased being democratic and became socialist, or even communist. After the state completely wrested control of education away from parents, it might "take control of any and every kind of business, and conduct it entirely under state management, and thus give us the socialist state in all its theoretical perfection."[37]

Quigley's failure in challenging the Ohio law was not uncommon: though they remained controversial, state laws mandating school attendance withstood legal challenges throughout the country. "There is no question," Wisconsin's labor commissioner stated in 1901, "that the supreme courts of every state would uphold and enforce the compulsory education law."[38]

Outside the courts, open assaults on the wisdom of the common schools and compulsory-attendance laws were infrequent but caustic. One sharp critique in the late nineteenth century flowed from the pen of a lawyer and publisher named Zachariah Montgomery. In 1886, the Kentucky native published a diatribe titled *Poison Drops in the Federal Senate: The School Question from a Parental and Non-Sectarian Standpoint.* For Montgomery, the common schools were not simply ineffective—they were in fact a grievous threat to the cornerstone of American society, the nation's families. In *Poison Drops*, he thunders against "an educational system which has broken down parental authority, sundered the sacred bonds of affection that bound together brothers and sisters, parents and children, and which has weakened and almost obliterated the human conscience." The failings of the public schools were so manifest that they could be held responsible for a "fearful increase of our insane, idiotic, blind, and deaf-mutes."[39]

Montgomery's screed failed to gain wide circulation, but later it often was described as a touchstone for the homeschooling movement that emerged a century after its publication. Of particular resonance were his vociferous claims that only parents possess the moral authority to direct the education of their children. The state's interests are, in this view, secondary.

Other critics took a gentler approach than Montgomery. In *A Mother's Letters to a Schoolmaster* (1923), Rita Scherman outlines her reasons for schooling her gifted son at home rather than at the local elementary school. Prefiguring a claim that would be made by subsequent generations of homeschoolers, Scherman asserts that her son Peter's intellectual development would be stunted by the standardized curriculum offered at the school. The local school was so lacking, she says, that "not fifty boards of education" could have compelled her to send Peter there. In her view,

the weaknesses of the schools are less ethical than pedagogical. Her pre-
cocious son simply learned more at home.[40]

Scherman's book also directly challenges one of the central tenets of
the common-school movement: the idea that public schools bolster democracy by training students to be effective citizens. She believed that the
schools were coercive, with teachers and administrators slavishly following "the doctrine of authority by force" and not concerning themselves
with students' intellectual development. No one could expect the principles of citizenship to be inculcated in such an oppressive environment.
As Scherman puts it, "it is plainly to be seen that democracy cannot be
learned in a place where it is not lived."[41]

By the end of the nineteenth century, establishment of common schools
and enactment of compulsory-attendance laws had allowed the state to
wrest much control over education of children away from parents. This
was indicative of a broader trend in which parental oversight of children's
development was diminished and the state assumed a more direct and active role in protecting the rights and interests of children. Put most simply,
as the state's power swelled, the authority of parents diminished. Children
benefited as they started to become recognized as legally distinct people
with their own rights—rights that the state had a duty to affirm and protect, particularly as new purported threats emerged, among them immigration, industrialization, and urbanization. With long-overdue help from
the state, children at last "emerged from hundreds of years of property
status," according to one expert on children's welfare, "to be considered
as persons."[42] That talk of children's rights was not mere code for state
power is evidenced by the fact that some of the earliest court decisions
invalidating excessive exertion of state authority (e.g., the commitment of
youths to residential training facilities) rested on children's liberty under
the Fourteenth Amendment of the US Constitution.[43]

In the late nineteenth century, states were also assuming a more active
role in preventing severe mistreatment by parents at home. Of course,
children have fallen victim to abuse and neglect by their parents since
the dawn of human civilization. Infanticide through exposure was so common in ancient Greece that Euripides, the great tragedian, wrote about
it at length in several works (including *The Phoenician Women*, which recounts the saga of the abandoned Oedipus). Children fared only margin-
ally better in Rome. There, fathers exercised absolute control over their
children, who essentially were chattel. The passage of legal reforms eventually criminalized infanticide, but the father "had the power to sell his

children, [and] he had the power to mutilate them," according to one history of childhood.[44] Matters scarcely improved in later centuries. Parents, possessing virtually unlimited power over their children, could abuse, mutilate, or abandon them, or sell them into slavery, all without fear of punishment. Reflecting on this bleak history in 1974, social thinker Lloyd deMause wrote, "The history of childhood is a nightmare from which we have only recently begun to awaken. The further back in history one goes, the lower the level of child care, and the more likely children are to be killed, abandoned, beaten, terrorized, and sexually abused."[45]

Part of this alleged nightmare involved long hours toiling. In the hardscrabble world of early America, as elsewhere, children often were valued primarily as economic commodities who could work. They were seen in agrarian communities as essential sources of labor, capable of working for hours in the fields or stables. State power helped to ensure that children worked: a Massachusetts law in 1641 announced that "it is desired and will be expected that all masters of families should see that their children and servants should be industriously employed so as the mornings and evenings and other seasons may not bee lost as formerly they have bene." Such measures reflected the belief, especially widespread among Puritans and Quakers, that work prevents idleness and provides essential training of children.[46]

The advent of industrialization in the nineteenth century moved children from farms and home workshops into urban areas and work in factories. For those managing the country's burgeoning industrial economy, children were ideal employees: they could be paid less than adults and were generally more compliant (and thus less likely to go on strike over their pitiful wages or miserable working conditions). Shockingly little thought was given to how the perilous work in textile mills or coal mines might affect children themselves, endangering their safety and retarding their intellectual and social development.

In this bleak milieu, children remained vulnerable to abuse by their parents. At the time, common law afforded children with few formal protections; legal safeguards did not yet extend to shield what later would be broadly recognized as the basic legal rights possessed by children. Furthermore, courts were reluctant to impose limits on parental exercise of discipline and parental control of children's behavior. In general, parents risked criminal prosecutions only when they engaged in especially heinous conduct that resulted in obvious physical harm. "Parents were considered immune from criminal prosecution," according to one account, "except when the punishment was grossly unreasonable in relation to the offense, when the parents inflicted cruel and merciless punishment, or when the punishment permanently injured the child."[47]

Over time, children benefited from the gradual and piecemeal emergence of legal principles meant to more formally regulate family governance. These included the notions that parental authority is limited and that parents have a legal duty to protect the overall physical and intellectual welfare of their children. Although they retained "a right to the exercise of such discipline as may be requisite to the discharge of their sacred trust," James Kent wrote in his *Commentaries on American Law*, parents were also "bound to maintain and educate their children."[48]

In the late nineteenth century, public authorities and private charitable organizations engaged in more concerted efforts to shield children from abuse, exploitation, and privation. While these efforts often lacked teeth, by 1900 most industrial states had enacted statutes prohibiting child labor. During this same era, reformers dedicated to "child saving" established institutions and aid societies to nurture youngsters whose parents were unwilling or unable to provide them with food, clothing, or shelter. By 1870, New York City alone boasted more than two dozen organizations helping needy children.

By the dawn of the twentieth century, most states had taken meaningful steps to formally safeguard children's welfare. Legislatures throughout the country enacted statutes proscribing a variety of crimes against children, including unnecessarily cruel punishment, abuse, neglect, and overwork. States also created juvenile court systems specifically designed to address the conditions that made youngsters either perpetrators or victims of crime. Not all of these efforts were successful. Too often, overworked juvenile courts and local "poor law" officials found themselves overwhelmed by the task of shielding large numbers of vulnerable children from so many potential threats. However, their piecemeal efforts represented real progress toward the long-overdue recognition that children are legal persons who possess rights. For all their failures, reformers in both the public and private spheres successfully "championed the idea that the state had a responsibility to ensure that all children had a childhood," as scholar David Tanenhaus puts it.[49]

In earlier periods, justification for the protection of children was couched primarily in terms of the state's "police power," by which the state acts as an agent for society collectively. For example, in *Blissett's Case* (1774) in Britain, Lord Mansfield upheld state-imposed limits on parental

authority on the basis of "the public right of the community to superintend the education of its members, and disallow what for its own security
and welfare it should see good to disallow," even if that meant encroach-
ing upon "the right and authority of the father."[50] But by the nineteenth
century, courts were increasingly likely to invoke the doctrine of *parens
patriae* (a Latin phrase meaning "parent of the country"), under which the
state acts as a protector of minors and incompetent adults. The roots of
the parens patriae principle can be traced at least as far back as medieval
and late medieval English chancery courts, which concerned themselves
with children mainly within the context of preserving feudal hierarchies.[51]
The principle became more firmly established in nineteenth-century jurisprudence. A celebrated legal case in England, one that arguably mis-
applied the doctrine, involved Romantic poet Percy Bysshe Shelley. The
iconoclastic Shelley lost custody of his children in 1817 when a court held
that the state had a duty to protect them from irreparable harm. The danger was not physical but rather moral and pedagogical: the court felt compelled to shield the children because it feared the poet would teach them
to be reformers, inveterate critics of the government, and, worst of all,
atheists. The poet's mistake was that "he avowed to raise his children as he
thought fit," according to one scholar's account of the dispute. "Shelley's
downfall was in thinking that the rights of a father included the right to
control the education of his children." The British court, invoking the parens patriae authority of the state, held otherwise as a means of protecting
the youngsters from "immoral and vicious conduct."[52]

American courts began to explicitly rely on the parens patriae doctrine
around 1840. The case *Ex Parte Crouse* involved a father who challenged
the commitment of his incorrigible daughter to a state-operated "house of
refuge." Ruling against the father in 1839, the Supreme Court of Pennsylvania directly addressed the state's role in safeguarding the best interests
of children, including their educational preparation, when their parents
faltered in protecting or nurturing them. "May not the natural parents,
when unequal to the task of education, or unworthy of it, be superseded
by the *parens patriae*, or common guardian of the community?" (i.e., the
state), the court asked. But the court also suggested a police-power rationale: "It is to be remembered that the public has a paramount interest
in the virtue and knowledge of its members, and that, of strict right, the
business of education belongs to it." In a similar case from Massachusetts,
that state's highest court held that a statute challenged by a parent "is a
provision by the Commonwealth, as *parens patriae*, for the custody and

care of neglected children, and is intended only to supply to them the parental custody which they have lost."[53]

Subsequent cases in a variety of jurisdictions further recognized the propriety of public authorities' intervening in behalf of youngsters when their parents failed to provide for "the nurture and education of the child," as one court put it. A 1905 decision of the Pennsylvania Supreme Court, in *Commonwealth v. Fisher*, reiterated many of the basic principles of *Ex Parte Crouse*, giving the state wide latitude in interposing itself between parents and children when the latter's best interests are in jeopardy. "To save a child from becoming a criminal, or from continuing in a career of crime, to end in maturer years in public punishment and disgrace," the court held, "the legislatures surely may provide for the salvation of such a child, if its parents or guardians be unable or unwilling to do so, by bringing it into one of the courts of the state without any process at all, for the purpose of subjecting it to the state's guardianship and protection."[54]

Decisions such as *Fisher* were particularly notable for what they did not privilege: the right of parents or children to due process of law. Courts in such cases often held that, when the state's intentions were benevolent and not punitive, it had no obligation to honor due-process rights; that is, it had no need to adhere to procedural niceties or regularities. When the state, acting as parens patriae, was "compelled to take the place of the father" for the purposes of protecting a child, it was not "required to adopt any process as a means of placing its hands upon the child to lead it into one of its courts," the state court held in *Fisher*. "When the child gets there and the court, with the power to save it, determines on its salvation, and not its punishment, it is immaterial how it got there." In this manner, American courts repeatedly held that the legal power of parents to control the upbringing of their children was neither absolute nor predominant.[55]

By the twentieth century's beginning, it was clear that parents would no longer have the de facto control over children's lives that they had in preindustrial society. The state would exercise its power not only to protect children from abuse and neglect in the home but also to compel regular schooling outside the home. As a result, the role that parents played in education changed. With the advent of common schools and the compulsory-attendance laws that aimed to keep them filled, parents were much less directly involved in providing formal academic training. Home and school, once indistinguishable, became separated.

Relationships between the school and the home were formalized and bureaucratized through the development of mothers' clubs and parent-teacher organizations. By design, these groups had limited influence, leaving parents in the sometimes awkward position of being "both insiders and outsiders at school," in the words of historian William Cutler. They could still play a role in the education of their children, but the role would be a supporting one. Professionally trained teachers and administrators would assume the lead parts.[56]

The National Parent-Teacher Association came into being as the National Congress of Mothers in 1897. The guiding principles laid out for parent-teacher associations (or PTAs) noted the need to "enable parents to learn what the schools are doing." However, the principles placed far more emphasis on providing instruction and training for overmatched and underprepared parents. They highlighted the need "to give fathers and mothers the opportunity to better educate themselves for intelligent home-making and child-nurture." Early on, PTAs prioritized the importance of establishing a more formal system whereby parents themselves could be trained and thus be equipped to provide instruction at home that would complement, and be consonant with, the instruction provided in the schools. As Hannah Schoff, an early president of the national PTA organization, puts it, the parent-teacher groups were established at least in part "to widen the scope of the educational system by making the schools serve a double purpose in education, by making it possible for parents to learn through them all that would enable them to be better mothers and fathers."[57]

Schoff was particularly interested in, as she puts it in a book published in 1915, "the wayward child," one who all too often committed crimes and wound up in a reformatory or a prison. She believed that much criminal activity was the result of bad parenting, and among the myriad "parents' mistakes" outlined in her book is their negligence in controlling the reading of impressionable boys. "One cannot regard too seriously the need for protecting children from sensational and impure literature," she warns. "It is one of the great factors causing runaway children, child burglars and the like." If parents want their children to avoid the perils of vice and crimes, they should ensure their youngsters the chance to "form wholesome tastes in reading." It was clear to Schoff that many parents simply could not find this material on their own and teach it to their children properly; they desperately needed help from experts.[58]

What eventually became known as the National Council of Mothers and Parent-Teacher Associations lobbied the federal Bureau of Education to acknowledge that, in Schoff's words, "parents are educators" who play an important role in shaping the intellectual and moral development of their children. Schoff and her colleagues were delighted when Philander Claxton, the federal commissioner of education, did precisely this in 1913. In a statement in which he pledged that his bureau would collaborate with the national parent-teacher group to support home education programs, Claxton said, "Rightly used, the home is the most valuable factor in the education of children."[59]

Claxton explained that the federal Bureau of Education would use its newly formed Home Education Division to work with the national parent-teacher group to provide structured support for parents. (In practice, the private groups did all of the heavy lifting; the federal government's chief contribution seemed to be simply lending its imprimatur to the enterprise, which was really run by Schoff.) The home education unit would produce "bulletins and literature, practical in their character, which will be available to every home," Claxton announced. It was hoped that these materials would assist parents in the "home education of their children" by providing information relating to such vital matters as "their early mental development" and "the formation of moral habits."[60]

To stress the importance of this new endeavor, Schoff mentioned in a public report how profoundly parents shaped the development of their children, as if this were not common knowledge. "The functions of the home in its educational capacity . . . exceed that of the school," she wrote. Yet parents, for all their influence, often lacked any kind of training that might help them perform their enormously important work as educators. The work of the Home Education Division thus was crucial, as "parents in most instances are without specific knowledge . . . of the methods that will bring the highest development of body, mind, and spirit." Sounding a familiar refrain, Schoff insisted that parents needed guidance if they were to adequately fulfill their duties as educators. They simply could not, in her view, do it effectively on their own.[61]

With a pronounced emphasis on what Theda Skocpol has called "maternalist social welfare measures," much of the material distributed by the Home Education Division was directed at mothers who sought help in caring for infants and toddlers. But the effort to bolster home education also targeted the intellectual development of older children. For instance, materials were distributed to help establish "home reading circles" in which parents and children could learn together about "Thirty World Heroes" (whose ranks included such diverse characters as St. Francis of Assisi, Molière, and Florence Nightingale) and American history (Dutch and Quaker colonies, the Revolution, Henry Clay). According to Ellen

Lombard, who eventually became the secretary of the Home Education Division, some eight thousand parents, children, and teachers were participating in these reading circles by 1918.[62]

While it encouraged teaching in the home, the Home Education Division never asserted that this instruction could, or should, supplant the teaching being done in the nation's schools. Parents, even when provided with resources from experts, were no match for trained teachers. "Schools have the best opportunity to create in boys and girls a desire for reading and to teach them to discriminate between good and bad literature," Lombard wrote in a pamphlet promoting home reading courses. "They set the standard." However, home instruction, conducted in a less hectic environment, could supplement and bolster the academic work being done in the schools. "More concentrated reading may be done in the home than in the school, where the attention is distracted by recitations and the confusion incident to school-room life."[63]

Press accounts of the Home Education Division's efforts picked up on the idea that additional instruction at home might supplement, rather than replace, the work done by students at their schools. The *Chicago Tribune*, in a 1920 article on a home-education reading course directed at boys, notes that "while in school, they have little time for general reading," as their days were crammed with lessons in math, history, science, and myriad other subjects. The home-study course (which featured works by Charles Dickens, Rudyard Kipling, Alfred Tennyson, and Mark Twain, among others) would flesh out a boy's learning, allowing him to "become familiar with a large part of the best literature of the world, fill his mind with helpful ideas and noble ideals, and gain much of the finest culture that the world can offer."[64]

Lombard did not try to oversell the extent or impact of the Home Education Division's initiatives. She knew that the Bureau of Education, working with the national parent-teacher organization, was shipping reams of instructional materials across the country, but it was difficult to gauge how many people had been inspired to actually use them or how, if at all, this had impacted the learning of parents and their children. Still, she was proud of the division's work, which was "but one of a number of evidences of the federal government's newly awakened interest in the long-neglected field of home education."[65]

At its core, the work done by the Home Education Division and its private partners represented a Progressive approach to educational reform. This was no retrograde movement intending to return education to its roots in the home and give parents plenary power to determine how, where, and why their children should be taught. Rather, it was an effort (albeit a hesitant one) to extend the reach of the state into the domestic sphere. With the help of experts, parents would provide more and better educational and moral training. They would complement and reinforce the work of the schools in these realms, not compete with or supplant public educational institutions.

For a variety of reasons, some parents managed to maintain roles as primary educators of children. Some children were too ill to attend regular schools. Some families lived in remote areas where shuttling youngsters back and forth to a schoolhouse was impractical. Many parents who found themselves in such circumstances in the early twentieth century turned to Baltimore's Calvert School for help in educating their children at home. Calvert's foray into homeschooling began in 1906, when a whooping-cough outbreak debilitated more than half the school's students. Virgil Hillyer, the school's headmaster, hit upon the idea of outlining lesson plans for the infirm students' parents to use while teaching them at home as they recovered. When the students returned to school, their teachers noticed they had not fallen behind the healthy pupils who had remained at Calvert. In fact, some of the homeschooled students appeared to have learned more at home.[66]

It dawned on Hillyer that there probably were myriad other homebound students throughout the world who could benefit from Calvert's curriculum (and whose parents could fill the school's coffers by purchasing it year after year). He soon began offering a series of home-instruction curricula for elementary-school students. By 1946, more than seven hundred children were being taught at home under the aegis of the school. They were a varied lot. Calvert's correspondence enrollees included the children of traveling rodeo cowboys, lighthouse keepers, diplomats, missionaries, and entertainers (Paul Robeson and Fred Astaire among them). An itinerant "boy preacher" who was on the road for much of the year and thus unable to enroll in a regular school took advantage of Calvert as well.[67]

Parents played a key role in facilitating the learning of Calvert's correspondence students. One account notes that "the mother can supply most of the supervision and encouragement" required to make the curriculum effective. However, it was understood that the students' teaching was really done by the instructors at Calvert, who formulated their curricula and evaluated the work that the youngsters regularly dispatched to Baltimore.

Most parents realized the benefits of this method. "Mothers have found," the news story notes, "that children usually work more carefully when they know that someone outside their own family will be correcting their lessons."[68] However capable a parent might be, the implication was that children perform at a higher level when they feel accountable to a nonparent authority figure, someone whose judgment is perhaps more objective and whose approval might be more difficult to secure relative to that of a mother.

Calvert's advertisements (which ran in such widely read periodicals as the *American Magazine* and *McClure's*) made it clear to parents that, whatever the nobility of their intentions or the intensity of their devotion to their sons and daughters, they needed structured help from experts if they were to provide adequate instruction for their children. If you want your child to be intelligent and cultured, "your love for them alone cannot make this possible," one ad admonishes. "You need to know the best methods of educating and training them." This is where Calvert came in, providing "a carefully prepared course of definite lessons for every school day, under the personal supervision of the lead child-education specialists in the world." If circumstances required it, parents could educate their children at home, but they would be lost without the guiding hand of professional educators virtually every step of the way.[69]

The parents who relied on the Calvert School often readily acknowledged their limitations as teachers. When her family made frequent moves for her husband's career, one mother turned to the school for help in schooling her young daughter. "I felt my own incompetence too keenly," she admitted, "to attempt to teach her at home myself." She marveled that the courses provided by the Calvert School were so carefully "planned and carried out" that her daughter could learn a great deal of material without either wasting time or feeling too rushed. Her own foray into home education a rousing success, the mother recommended Calvert to other parents who might be "stumbling along in the dark, uncertain just what to do and how to do it."[70]

This was, as the *Saturday Evening Post* puts it, a "funny way to go to school," but some educators saw the merit in the Calvert method, especially in cases where conventional schools were lacking. In 1915, a newspaper in Galveston, Texas, summarized the views of a local school's headmaster, who acknowledged that "the home is the natural place" for the training of children between the ages of six and twelve because "the mother is the natural teacher." Such schooling "has the advantage of personal, individual attention, care and watchfulness that more than compensate for the daily attendance at an inferior school." The schoolmaster added the important caveat that this home study had to be "planned and directed by experts." Parents might facilitate teaching but should not be in total control.[71]

Many stories on Calvert noted that the parents of sick children or children with permanent disabilities often had no choice but to educate their sons and daughters outside conventional schools. Calvert dispatched so many courses to hospitals that it eventually collaborated with the head of the pediatrics department of Johns Hopkins Hospital to craft special courses for hospitalized children.

Eventually, remote education by telephone became possible for some families with children confined to home. Iowa pioneered "teleteaching" in 1940. (The first student taught by this method was, appropriately enough, the bedridden daughter of a telephone lineman.)[72] In addition to sick children, there were those with physical disabilities that posed an obstacle to school attendance in a pre-accommodation world. Most public schools failed to commit significant resources to special education, but some school districts experimented with methods to reach "homebound pupils," including polio survivors and children suffering from severe congenital disorders. Thus, in the early part of the twentieth century, home-only education was mainly a matter of necessity rather than of choice for families finding themselves in unusual circumstances.

Notes

1. Knowles et al., "From Pedagogy to Ideology," 195–235.

2. Gaither, *Homeschool*, 17–19.

3. Hall, *Cultures of Print*, 58.

4. Jernegan, *Laboring and Dependent Classes in Colonial America*, 104, 149, 151, 161.

5. Shulman, *Constitutional Parent*, 3.

6. Rendleman, "Parens Patriae," 212.

7. Williams, *Self-Taught*, 7–20.

8. Ramsay, *Memoirs of the Life of Martha Laurens Ramsay*, 25–27.

9. Benjamin Franklin, *The Autobiography of Benjamin Franklin* (New York: Simon and Schuster, 2004), 5. Biographies of Franklin are numerous. One standard account of his education and upbringing is Edmund S. Morgan's *Benjamin Franklin* (New Haven, CT: Yale University Press, 2003). And of course there is Franklin's own *Autobiography*, available in myriad print and electronic editions.

10. Baldwin, *Edison: Inventing the Century*, 24–25.

11. Mendenhall, "Research Is a Passion with Me," 173–74.

12. The story of Roosevelt's early years has been told many times in such stellar biographies as Edmund Morris's *The Rise of Theodore Roosevelt* (New York: Random House, 2001).

13. Mead, *Blackberry Winter*, 45–56.

14. Perrin, *History of Compulsory Education in New England*; Monaghan, *Learning to Read and Write in Colonial America*, 21; Katz, *History of Compulsory Education Laws*, 5–32.

15. Mann is quoted in *Children and Youth in America: A Documentary History*, ed. Robert Hamlett Bremmer, vol. 1, *1600–1865* (Cambridge, MA: Harvard University Press, 1970), 451.

16. Horace Mann, "Education, the Balance-Wheel of Social Machinery, Horace Mann's Twelfth Report (1848)," in *American Public School Law*, 6th ed., ed. Kern Alexander and M. David Alexander (Belmont, CA: Thomson West, 2005), 29.

17. Mann quoted in Bremmer, *Children and Youth in America*, 451.

18. Jowett, *Dialogues of Plato*, 5:186; Rothbard, *Education*, 19–36. Luther's writing is quoted in Charles Glenn, *Contrasting Models of State and School: A Comparative Historical Study of Parental Choice and State Control* (New York: Continuum, 2011), 5.

19. Rothbard, *Education*, 19–36.

20. Tozer, Gallegos, and Henry, eds., *Handbook of Research in the Social Foundations of Education*, 53–54.

21. Ensign, *Compulsory School Attendance and Child Labor*, 52.

22. Ensign, 235.

23. Ensign, 178.

24. *Report of the Commissioner of Education for the Year 1894–95*, vol. 1 (Washington, DC: U.S. Government Printing Office, 1896), 1119.

25. Frank Musgrove, "The Decline of the Educative Family," *Universities Quarterly* 14 (September 1960): 377.

26. David B. Tyack, "Ways of Seeing: An Essay on the History of Compulsory Schooling," *Harvard Educational Review* 46, no. 3 (1976): 355–89.

27. *The Corporations Auxiliary Bulletin* (Cleveland, OH: Whitworth Brothers Company, 1902), 173.

28. Ensign, *Compulsory School Attendance and Child Labor*, 173.

29. 111 Pomeroy, Equity Jurisprudence §§ 1303–1310 (1883).

30. Rendleman, "Parens Patriae," 240, 246.

31. Unsigned editorial, *New York Times*, March 6, 1875.

32. Francis Abbott, *Compulsory Education*, 4.

33. Messerli, *Horace Mann*, 429.

34. Steffes, *School, Society, and State*, 121.

35. State v. Quigley, 11 Ohio Dec. Reprint 340, 341 (1891).

36. Quigley, *Compulsory Education*, 182.

37. Quigley, *Compulsory Education*, vii.

38. *Ninth Biennial Report of the Bureau of Labor and Industrial Statistics, State of Wisconsin, 1898–1899* (Madison, WI: Democrat Printing Company, 1901), 403.

39. Montgomery, *Poison Drops in the Federal Senate*, 35, 36.

40. Scherman, *Mother's Letters to a Schoolmaster*, 3.

41. Scherman, 19, 21.

42. Stuart N. Hart, "From Property to Person Status: Historical Perspective on Children's Rights," *American Psychologist* 46, no. 1 (1991): 53–59.

43. See Shulman, *Constitutional Parent*, 93–97 (discussing *O'Connell v. Turner* (Ill. 1870)).

44. Payne, *Child in Human Progress*, 212.

45. Payne, *Child in Human Progress*, 184–98, 209–22; deMause, *History of Childhood*, 1.

46. Massachusetts Bureau of Statistics of Labor, *Annual Report on the Statistics of Manufactures, 1898*, vol. 13 (Boston: Wright and Potter, 1899), 217.

47. Thomas, "Child Abuse and Neglect, Part I," 293, 304–5.

48. Kent, *Commentaries on American Law*, 2:218.

49. Peters, *When Prayer Fails*, 68–71; Tanenhaus, "Between Dependency and Liberty," 369.

50. Blissett's Case, 98 Eng. Rep. 889 (1774), 900.

51. In re Gault, 387 U.S. 1 (1967), 16–17.

52. Wright, "Policing Sexual Morality."

53. Ex parte Crouse, 4 Whart. 9 (Pa. 1839), 9–12; Farnham v. Pierce, 141 Mass. 203, 6 N.E. 830 (1886).

54. Milwaukee Industrial School v. Supervisors of Milwaukee County, 40 Wisc. 328 (1876), 338; Commonwealth v. Fisher, 213 Pa. 48 (1905), 53.

55. *Commonwealth v. Fisher*, 213 Pa., at 53.

56. Cutler, *Parents and Schools*, 6.

57. Schoff, "National Congress of Mothers and Parent-Teacher Associations," 139.

58. Schoff, *Wayward Child*, 42–43.

59. Schoff, "National Congress of Mothers and Parent-Teacher Associations," 145, 146.

60. Schoff, "National Congress of Mothers and Parent-Teacher Associations," 145–46.

61. *Report of the Commissioner of Education for the Year Ended June 30, 1914*, United States Bureau of Education (Washington, DC: Government Printing Office, 1915), 363.

62. Skocpol, *Protecting Soldiers and Mothers*, 480–81; Ellen C. Lombard, *Home Education* (Department of the Interior, Bureau of Education, Bulletin No. 3), (Washington, DC: Government Printing Office, 1919), 3–13.

63. Lombard, "Home Reading Courses," 267–69.

64. "Reading Course for Boys," *Chicago Tribune*, February 8, 1920.

65. Lombard, "Home Reading Courses," 267–69.

66. Magruder Dobie, "Funny Way to Go to School," *Saturday Evening Post*, August 12, 1950, 34–35, 98, 100.

67. Dobie, 34–35, 98, 100.

68. Dobie, 34–35, 98, 100.

69. Calvert School advertisement, *McClure's*, December 1919, 80.

70. Calvert School advertisement, *Cosmopolitan*, July 1921, 137.

71. *Galveston Daily News*, January 27, 1915.

72. Dorothy B. Carr, "Teleteaching—A New Approach to Teaching Elementary and Secondary Homebound Pupils," *Exceptional Children*, November 1964, 118–26.

CHAPTER TWO

The Birth of Modern Homeschooling

For the past century, the overwhelming majority of American children have been educated outside of their homes in public or private "regular" schools—state-accredited institutions staffed by professional educators who have received years of formal training. With school enrollments totaling in the tens of millions during the middle part of the twentieth century, homeschooling remained a novelty. There was a national consensus that the most worthwhile and profound educational experiences for young people were provided when, in the company of their peers, they attended schools staffed by certified teachers following a standardized curriculum.

More frequent and strident challenges to this dogma emerged in the decades following World War II. Academics, journalists, and professional educators penned a series of critiques insisting that the country's public schools were in fact spectacularly failing to educate the nation's young people. The year 1953 marked a watershed, with the publication of several notable books bemoaning the state of education in the United States. A characteristic jeremiad came in Arthur Bestor's provocative *Educational Wastelands: The Retreat from Learning in Our Public Schools*. The iconoclastic Bestor charts how education policy makers, "by misrepresenting and undervaluing liberal education, have contributed . . . to the growth of anti-intellectualist hysteria that threatens not merely the schools but freedom itself." These professional educators had effectively crippled the public schools by articulating "purposes for education so trivial as to forfeit the respect of thoughtful men, and by deliberately divorcing the schools from the disciplines of science and scholarship."[1] Even at this early point in America's modern history, some were blaming standardized testing for "dumbing down" the curriculum and inducing teachers to "teach to the test."[2]

Overheated warnings like Bestor's came at a time when the expectations for American schools were soaring rather than diminishing. The exigencies of the Cold War seemed to demand even more rigorous academic training, especially in the realms of math and science; adequate training in those fields would be essential if young Americans were to counter the advances of their peers in the Soviet Union. And yet there was a nagging sense that the nation's schools were not up to the task. Panic over the purported rise of juvenile delinquency in the 1950s was paired with a critique of the American education system. The schools apparently were failing to perform one of their essential tasks: training young people to be ethical citizens who understood and respected the rule of law.

Such damning analyses dovetailed with the broader indictments of state power that pervaded American public discourse in the postwar era. These condemnations emanated from across the ideological spectrum. Following the United States Supreme Court's landmark ruling in *Brown v. Board of Education* (1954), many whites—not all of them Southerners—were aghast that the courts would not only mandate an end to the segregation of public schools but also eventually countenance controversial measures meant to guarantee integration, such as busing. To some, this appeared to be an unfathomable abuse of state power. For critics on the Left, the debacle of the war in Vietnam epitomized the failings of a political and economic system that devoted enormous resources to military misadventure and imperialism while ignoring such urgent problems as poverty and racism. Conversely, conservatives insisted that the state was meddling too much in the latter matters and thereby squandering resources (as well as trammeling individual rights).

The courts also seemed determined to make the public schools more secular. In the early 1960s, the United States Supreme Court handed down two landmark rulings (*Engel v. Vitale* in 1962 and *Abington School District v. Schempp* in 1963) holding that school-sponsored prayer exercises and Bible readings violated the First Amendment's establishment clause. Although these rulings did not immediately put an end to religious exercises in public schools, they sparked considerable outrage among conservative Protestants who believed that God was being "removed" from the public schools. Their anger was further stoked by a perception that moral and religious training was being supplanted in the schools by sex education and the teaching of biological evolution. Summing up these perceptions, the *Christian Educator* would later complain that public schools had become "places where a carefully maintained atmosphere of materialism, humanism, evolution, relativism, and sometimes downright atheism is deliberately created for the impressionable student."[3] In short, the public schools were allegedly now anti-Christian by design.

No one bemoaned the supposed godlessness of American schools with more fervor than American theologian Reverend Rousas J. Rushdoony, a Christian Reconstructionist who penned several forceful attacks on the public schools in the 1960s.[4] *The Messianic Character of American Education*, his dissection of the progressive underpinnings of American public education, singles out for especially harsh criticism the likes of Horace Mann and John Dewey. Thanks to their pernicious influence, "the task of the schools has become religious conversion to a politico-economic statist order rather than education," Rushdoony wrote. As children were indoctrinated in this humanist order, he argued, it was inevitable that they would lose their faith in the teachings of the Bible. The implications of this were disastrously apparent in American life in the 1960s: social disorder, economic upheaval, and moral chaos.[5]

Soon enough, Rushdoony was offering an alternative: a thoroughgoing "Christian curriculum" grounded not in humanism but in a decidedly fundamentalist reading of the Bible. Instead of being subjected to the "devastating and enslaving forces of amoral statism and anarchistic individualism" that were being purveyed in the public schools, students would approach every subject through the prism of scripture. Of course, the teaching of evolutionary theory had no place in this scheme, nor did anything that challenged a rigidly conservative conception of God's law.[6]

Rushdoony hoped that such principles would help to spark and then guide the growth of nonsecular schools. And, indeed, a new breed of religious schools offered one alternative to parents who were appalled by the apparent decline of the intellectual and moral training provided by public schools. Roman Catholics, of course, had a long-established (if increasingly fragile) system of parochial schools in most areas of the country. Conservative evangelical Christians got a somewhat later start in the realm of creating their own schools, and their efforts—which often came in the form of small academies catering to a handful of students—generally lacked the overall coordination of the Catholic schools.

Despite their relatively late start, so-called Christian "day schools" experienced explosive growth in the late 1960s and early 1970s. Schools reflecting the approaches of Rushdoony and others for whom the public schools were anathema were founded, and grew, at astonishing rates in this period. According to one estimate, enrollment in them expanded by over 200 percent between 1965 and 1975, with overall enrollment in such institutions approaching half a million people by the end of that period. As the historian Adam Laats has noted, that number would essentially double by 2002 as evangelical and fundamentalist K–12 schools continued to grow. Evangelical leader Jerry Falwell, who opened the Lynchburg Christian Academy in 1967, lauded the rapid emergence of the Christian day-school movement as "the hope of this Republic," a bulwark against the baleful influences that permeated the nation's public schools and threatened to undermine the nation's core Christian values.[7]

The phenomenal expansion of Christian day schools was notable for several reasons. First, these nascent religious institutions represented, as a study in the *Journal of Thought* marvels, "the fastest growing segment of formal education in America today." At a time when the nation's public schools appeared to be foundering, the new religious schools rapidly became an extraordinarily popular alternative form of schooling. Second, these conservative Christian schools represented a distinct and significant departure from the public schools—something not seen on a large scale in the United States for many decades. This was, according to the journal's analysis, "the first widespread secession from the public school pattern since the establishment of Catholic schools in the nineteenth century." If nothing else, the proliferation and popularity of the new schools demonstrated that the long-established public-school regime could be challenged by those who were troubled by its apparent shortcomings.[8]

Several interrelated factors spurred parents to abandon public schools and enroll their children in Christian day schools. As Jerry Falwell made clear on numerous occasions, the perceived secularization of the public schools in the 1960s and 1970s—best exemplified by the US Supreme Court's rulings relating to prayer and Bible study—made them increasingly inappropriate for families in which parents hoped to expose their children only to conservative Christian values. It horrified Falwell and other conservative Christians to perceive that instruction in sex education and on evolution had replaced religious exercises and moral training in public schools. Christian day schools, with pedagogy and curricula firmly grounded in the lessons of the Bible, offered an alternative to what one Christian school guide laments as "the growing trend toward secularization" in public schools. The new religious institutions would be, in effect, havens for families seeking to shield their children from prolonged ideological corruption at the hands of public educators.[9]

Demographic changes in some public-school districts also prompted some parents to seek alternative forms of education in the 1960s and 1970s. Undoubtedly, desegregation, coming in the form of court-ordered school busing, outraged some white parents who imagined that their children, and their children's schools, were being threatened by undisciplined and potentially dangerous minority students. Predominantly white Christian day schools provided a welcome refuge for some of these families, although it is probably unfair to label them, as some did, as merely "segregation academies." Several surveys of parents who had switched their children out of public schools and into religious ones indicated that they were primarily motivated by a distaste for (at least as they perceived it) the ideological bent of public schools. One study noted that many parents who abandoned public schools viewed them as being a "vehicle of a godless humanistic philosophy" that lacked appropriate "moral values." The new religious day schools, in sharp contrast, were designed to promulgate Christian beliefs and practices.[10]

The new Christian schools eventually banded together into several large associations that helped the institutions coalesce into a broad and formidable movement. Organizations like the Association of Christian Schools International (ACSI) and the American Association of Christian Schools (AACS) provided their member institutions with a variety of valuable services, including legal and legislative advice as well as support for administrators and teachers. By the end of the 1980s, ACSI had grown into a formidable organization boasting a membership of over 2,000 schools (which had enrolled more than 340,000 students). AACS was somewhat smaller, with a membership of 1,200 schools (and 187,000 students) in 1991, but it too wielded considerable clout.[11]

An increased availability of specially tailored educational materials made it relatively easy for Christian day schools to get up and running. Many of the fledgling institutions relied on the Accelerated Christian Education (ACE) curriculum, a popular and easy-to-use program designed by a Bob Jones University graduate named Don Howard. Like many alternative curricula, ACE was decried by many established educators as being unproven, misguided, and woefully inadequate in providing substantive and structured learning for children. One scathing scholarly assessment of ACE claims that its content was "so skeletal that real understanding of cause and effect of events seems impossible in most cases."[12] Whatever its failings, the ACE program's unmistakable ideological orientation resonated with educators in Christian schools. They embraced materials that were, in the words of one historian, "permeated with Bible teaching and pro-capitalist ideology." A characteristic passage in an ACE eighth-grade-history textbook says of the founding of Jamestown,

"Captain Smith wisely dropped the communistic system and established Scriptural principles."[13] Howard made no apologies for furnishing such pro-Christian and anticommunist materials, arguing that they were essential to counter the influence of the secular propaganda being forced on students in public schools. In one typical complaint, he stated that most American history textbooks were "socialist and contain the philosophy of the humanistic left."[14]

Its ideological orientation aside, the ACE program was also notable for a pedagogical approach that did not stress direct instruction from adults. Students who followed Howard's curricula were granted an extraordinary degree of autonomy. Instead of sitting en masse in a conventional classroom, students independently pored over ACE workbooks without much direct instruction from an adult. "Children using ACE," Howard wrote, "are learning how best to learn because the responsibility for learning is placed upon them." Instruction under the ACE program was so lax that children were said to be learning, in the words of one account, "without [the] benefit of a teacher."[15]

Indeed, in both rigor and organization, Christian day schools operating under the ACE model were vastly different from traditional K–12 institutions. Pastors only needed to complete a two-week training course (and pay a hefty fee) before they could start operating their schools. Staffing was minimal, as students were dispatched not to traditional classrooms overseen by accredited teachers but to individual carrels, or "offices," where they worked alone on readings and assignments. When students got stuck, they summoned a "supervisor" (in many schools a parent volunteer) to answer their questions.[16]

Whatever its shortcomings, ACE provided a low-cost and flexible model of how K–12 learning could be furnished outside a traditional public-school setting. Thanks to ACE and similar plans, parents who were unhappy with what their children were being taught and exposed to in the public schools could turn to an alternative that was consonant with their ideological perspective—an alternative that did not require the credentialing of teachers or the erection of new facilities.

With the explosive growth of such alternative approaches to public schooling came bitter and prolonged controversies over the extent to which they should, or could, be regulated by states. "The dispute between Christian school educators and the state," scholars James Carper and Neal Devins wrote in 1985, "pits the educators' belief that education is inherently religious against the state's contention that its regulatory scheme is a necessary means to ensure that every child in the state receives an adequate education." Throughout the 1970s and into the 1980s, advocates for Christian day schools insisted that state oversight of their institutions, which was never especially robust, amounted to a governmental effort to exert control over religious practice, which is prohibited by the free exercise clause of the First Amendment. State education officials contended that their regulatory reach extended to all children and all schools, secular or religious.[17]

Legal challenges brought by Christian day schools involved several areas of regulation—zoning and fire-safety codes, teacher certification, textbook selection, even simply the requirement to report enrollment. Regulators denied a license to operate to some day schools that failed to comply with such mandates. In a few jurisdictions, authorities prosecuted parents for violating compulsory school attendance laws that mandated enrollment at accredited schools.[18]

Nebraska is one of several states where religious educators and state authorities have battled over the regulation of Christian day schools. The most prominent dispute in that state involved a church school that opened in Louisville, Nebraska, in 1977. The pastor of that church rejected state authority altogether, refusing to have the school accredited by the state and to employ certified teachers. (He even balked at providing regulators with a list of pupils enrolled at the school.) Invoking the protections of the First Amendment, he asserted that the state had no "right to inspect God's property." The Nebraska Supreme Court ultimately found in favor of the state, holding that the church had made an "arbitrary and unreasonable attempt to thwart the legitimate, reasonable, and compelling interests of the State in carrying out its educational obligations, under a claim of religious freedom." The school's operations, in the court's view, fell under the purview of state regulation, even though the school had an unmistakably religious orientation.[19]

This ruling, however, did not end the dispute. After church leaders and parents continued to periodically defy authorities and operate the school without state approval (an act of resistance that landed the church's pastor and several parents in jail), legislators and education officials in Nebraska worked out a compromise that essentially allowed religious schools to operate with only a nominal amount of state oversight. In a nod to compulsory-attendance laws, parents whose children were enrolled in such institutions were required to provide the state with a brief "information statement" attesting to the child's attendance and enrollment in core subject areas. But otherwise nothing was required of them. There was to be state oversight of Christian day schools, but it would be negligible.[20]

Attempts to operate Christian day schools outside the purview of state control in Ohio created similar turmoil and led to similarly ambiguous results in the realms of law and public policy. In 1973, children attending the Tabernacle Christian School, which was neither state approved nor chartered, received warning letters from local public-education authorities stating that they were "failing to attend a school which conforms to the minimum standards prescribed by the State Board of Education, as required by law." When the children continued to attend the school, more than a dozen Tabernacle Christian parents were charged for violating Ohio's compulsory school attendance statute.[21]

The arguments aired in the subsequent legal battle were characteristic of cases adjudicating the parameters of state power over private schooling in the 1970s and 1980s. State officials insisted that they were merely attempting to ensure that all children receive adequate schooling at a legitimate institution providing competent instruction. As one prosecutor put it, "We're not concerned with their religion, we're just interested in seeing that the parents send their children to an accredited school." Parents and church leaders saw the dispute through a vastly different lens. According to one parent, the state was going so far in its effort to enforce regulations on Tabernacle Christian that it was violating individual rights protected by the First Amendment. This overreach threatened "the freedom of the Christian church and parents to be able to guide their children the way they think they ought to, under God."[22]

The Supreme Court of Ohio determined, in a 1976 ruling in *Whisner v. Ohio*, that the religious and parental rights of Tabernacle Christian parents had been violated because the state had failed to demonstrate a sufficiently compelling interest in regulating religious schools. For backers of religious schools, the ruling appeared to be a boon, seemingly freeing the nonsecular institutions from state oversight. According to one careful study of the decision, "In effect, Christian schools in Ohio were free to operate without a charter or regard to the state's minimum standards." And, although the ruling's scope was limited to Ohio, *Whisner's* shield against state regulation was invoked by advocates for Christian schools in other states as they fought their own battles against oversight. It was described as a "rallying point" for the broader Christian day-school movement.[23]

However, as in many other jurisdictions, in Ohio the legal boundaries of permissible state regulation of religious schools remained somewhat ill-defined. In a later decision in an analogous case, the state's high court seemed to backtrack, signaling that it would uphold legislation designed to provide basic state regulation of religious schools. This muddle in Ohio was illustrative of a broader national confusion surrounding regulation of religious schools. Between (and sometimes even within) jurisdictions, there seemed to be no uniform approach to determining what was, or was not, legally permissible oversight by the state. Surveying the chaos in 1983, legal scholar Neal Devins wrote, "The courts thus far have been unable to provide consistent guidance either to the states or to the fundamentalist schools involved in state regulation lawsuits. In fact, many of the existing decisions are totally at odds with each other. And this includes decisions from the same state court and decisions involving identical regulations— all applying the 'same' legal standards."[24]

Lawmakers and state education officials in the early 1980s were thus scrambling to figure out how (or even if) the proliferating Christian day schools could be regulated. Advocates for close monitoring by the state seemed to be fighting an uphill and losing battle. In numerous states— for example, Vermont, Alabama, Nebraska, and Iowa in 1981 and 1982—legislators were considering bills that would do the opposite, exempting religious schools from state oversight. Lawmakers in Illinois passed such a measure, only to have Governor James Thompson veto it. Although there was a great deal of uncertainty surrounding such efforts, a few things seemed apparent: State education officials, ostensibly working to shield the interests of children, would continue trying to regulate the religious schools and thereby ensure that children were receiving bona fide academic instruction (and not merely religious training). The administrators of those institutions, in tandem with parents who had abandoned the public schools, would resist measures that appeared to encroach on their rights. Meanwhile, legislators and the judiciary were caught in the middle, attempting to balance the state's long-recognized authority to regulate education against legitimate concerns for safeguarding both religious liberty and what was now more widely viewed as an entitlement of parents—that is, control of children's intellectual and moral development.[25]

Christian day schools represented just one emerging departure from public schools. Others were urged by the likes of Raymond Moore, reformers who highlighted the weaknesses of the public schools and touted potential alternatives to them. In the 1960s, Moore, a Seventh-day Adventist who had earned a doctorate in education from the University of Southern California, conducted a comprehensive survey of hundreds of studies on early childhood education's impact. Moore concluded that sub-jecting young children to institutionalized schooling actually hindered their intellectual development. Touting the "dangers of early schooling," Moore's study appeared in *Harper's* in 1972 (and then *Reader's Digest* the following year) and attracted widespread notice.[26]

Moore differed from Rousas Rushdoony in actively promoting school-ing at home as the best alternative to the failed public schools. In his study, Moore concludes that "warm and consistent proximity" to parents is a far more important predictor of long-term academic development than ex-posure to the mechanistic world of the classroom. And of course the best way for children to remain close to their parents is for them to stay home for schooling. Moore also suggests homeschooling has the pedagogical benefit of allowing for subject matter of more immediate relevance. "No schoolroom can match the simplicity and power of the home in providing three-dimensional, firsthand education," Moore wrote. "The school, not the home, is the substitute, and its highest function is to complement the family."[27]

Religious training formed the core of Moore's vision of homeschool-ing, however. Such were Moore's ideological leanings that James Dobson, the prominent evangelical Christian broadcaster, invited him on several occasions to appear on the syndicated *Focus on the Family* radio program, which was wildly popular among conservative evangelical Christians. Dobson's platform was priceless for Moore and the homeschooling move-ment that emerged in the 1970s and 1980s. The broadcasts reached many thousands, including Michael Farris, then a young attorney living in Wash-ington State, who would later become the founder of the Home School Legal Defense Association (hereafter HSLDA). Hearing Moore on Dob-son's program inspired the lawyer and his wife to begin homeschooling their second-grade daughter, Christy. Another HSLDA founder, Michael Smith, also learned about homeschooling after hearing Moore extol its vir-tues on Dobson's program.[28]

Moore was part of a cadre of educational reformers who came to prom-inence in the late 1960s and 1970s. While some in this vanguard reflected a conservative religious outlook and traditional values, others articulated a leftist critique of institutionalized learning. According to one account, many of the alternatives to public schools that flowered in the following decades, including homeschooling, could trace their origins to "the influ-ence of the educational reformers who published in the late 1960s and early 1970s, a turbulent period that initiated considerable questioning about the status, goals, educational practices, and achievements of public schools." Iconoclastic thinkers like Everett Reimer, Allen Graubard, and Paulo Freire challenged normative assumptions about pedagogy and touted the potential of alternative educational environments. (For instance, Freire's 1970 masterwork *Pedagogy of the Oppressed* famously criticizes the "banking" concept of education, which views children as receptacles into which information is deposited, one of the underpinnings of traditional schooling.)[29]

Other dissenters also pushed for fundamental changes in how children are educated and socialized. Paul Goodman's *Growing Up Absurd* (1960) and *Compulsory Mis-education* (1964) argue that schools are little more than training grounds for conformity and intellectual orthodoxy. Edgar Friedenberg's *Coming of Age in America* (1965) describes how high-school students primarily learn how to submit to the arbitrary authority of teachers and administrators. Jonathan Kozol's bestselling *Death at an Early Age* (1967) details his disheartening experiences teaching in Boston's crumbling public schools. By highlighting the immense and seemingly intractable flaws of schools—among them underfunding, systemic racism, and rigid approaches to pedagogy—from a liberal, secular perspective, such works, too, "provid[ed] the ideological underpinnings for educational innovation," in the words of one study of the period.[30]

Kozol was so disturbed by his experiences as a teacher that he worked to establish free, independent, and community-run schools in disadvantaged neighborhoods. Describing these institutions in *Free Schools*, published in 1972, Kozol offers an impassioned plea for innovation in education as a means of freeing children from the thoroughgoing oppression of the public schools. And the impact of these liberating free schools would resonate beyond the children themselves, as committed parents and teachers banded together and challenged local institutions and political leaders to respond to the formidable economic, social, and cultural needs of their communities. Kozol pairs these broad ambitions with a narrower advocacy for intensive and rigorous academic training for students. There would be no long-term liberation for inner-city youth, he believed, if they lack core literacy and numeracy skills.[31]

To have any hope of legitimately liberating students and their communities, these free schools would have to be racially and socioeconomically diverse. Some of the sharpest passages of *Free Schools* are directed at breakaway schools that served the privileged—that is, white middle- and upper-class children who already enjoyed myriad advantages. Kozol, in one especially caustic outburst, excoriates schools that amount to little more than "a sandbox for the children of the S.S. guards at Auschwitz."[32]

The types of innovations championed by Kozol were part of a liberal wave of alternative-schooling proposals to emerge during the period. Some took shape in the form of "free" or "open" schools that were modeled on Summerhill, a British boarding school founded by A. S. Neill. The Summerhill model—popularized in America by the publication of Neill's book *Summerhill: A Radical Approach to Child Rearing* in 1960—stressed self-governance and minimal coercion by adults. (It should be noted that Kozol loathed Summerhill itself, calling it "one of the most racist schools in England.") Following such models, alternative schools made students' attendance voluntary. Furthermore, children learned by following informal curricula that stressed the value of practical, real-world experiences. Leadership emanated from parents and local communities, not educational professionals. These schools were almost by definition idiosyncratic, but they shared a fundamental aversion to the strictures and mandates that were the hallmarks of traditional schools.[33]

According to Allen Graubard, there were probably fewer than two dozen of these revolutionary schools in the United States in 1967. That number skyrocketed over the next five years, reaching roughly two hundred by 1972. The schools tended to be small—two-thirds enrolled fewer than forty students—and student-teacher ratios averaged 1:5. The size and scale of the schools were crucial to creating the kind of learning environments that reformers desired. "Obviously, the warm intimate atmosphere where everyone knows everyone else," Graubard observes, "is vital to the style of learning and governance which free schools espouse."[34]

Ron Miller, in his excellent study of the free-school movement, notes that its "ideology was explicitly countercultural; that is, it sought to educate children and young adults according to a set of attitudes, values, and beliefs in direct opposition to those of the predominant culture." Mainstream American practices and institutions—among them corporate capitalism and the pervasive state power that buttresses it—were rejected in favor of a utopian vision in which communities would be rebuilt to reflect more inclusive values. In this framework, the schools, instead of serving the interests of the state, would empower individuals to flourish on their own terms.[35]

To be sure, not all of these liberal experimental schools thrived. Activist Bill Ayers (later known for his role in the revolutionary group Weather Underground) helped to lead a "free school," called the

Children's Community School, in the mid-1960s in Ann Arbor, Michigan. "We felt that too many schools were highly competitive and destroyed people's learning," Ayers later said. "We thought that students had an inclination to learn, but that most schools stifled their creativity." Believing "that learning should be organic, that children should learn subject matter in real-life contexts when they are ready," students were, for instance, challenged to write, revise, and share their own life stories to build their literacy skills. But the school, which was designed in part to serve African American families in Ann Arbor, floundered and eventually closed. There were many reasons for the failure, including harassment from local authorities, but, according to one account, one of the main factors was pedagogical: "no one learned to read there."[36]

Amid this clamor on the Left for educational reform, it was a disillusioned schoolteacher named John Holt who catalyzed the liberal branch of the modern homeschooling movement. In two landmark books published in the mid-1960s, Holt offers a forceful critique of the public schools, insisting that they stifle learning by trapping children in regimented and repressive environments. *Why Children Fail* (1964) and *How Children Learn* (1967) describe a bleak educational landscape in which fearful children mainly learn to obey orders and are all but barred from thinking for themselves. With no thought given to nurturing their intellectual curiosity, Holt argues, most children in the public schools merely master the art of taking tests and charming teachers. "What impedes learning today is teaching, too much of it," he told a reporter in the late 1970s. "The teacher takes all the fuel that makes the learning engine run and turns the students into passive laboratory rats."[37]

As his critiques gained wider circulation in the 1960s, thousands of parents and educators reached out to Holt and praised him for his blunt, unsparing diagnosis of what was ailing the public schools. Their letters and phone calls confirmed for him that public schools had become, in effect, educational factories that were failing in their primary mission—fostering human growth and learning. There was, he realized, a widespread and fundamental dissatisfaction with how professional educators approached learning; they seemed primarily concerned with churning out docile students who pass tests. Instead of being organic and personalized, this learning was mechanized and standardized.

Initially, Holt was more of an educational reformer than an outright revolutionary. He clung to the belief that schools could and should be overhauled and transformed into sites of authentic learning. However, his perspective changed over time, in part because of the influence of Ivan Illich, whose 1971 book *Deschooling Society* questions the entire idea of institutionalized education. Asserting that "universal education through schooling is not feasible," Illich's book argues that the nation's system of compulsory education should be supplanted by "learning webs" in which all members of a community use advanced technology and serve both as instructors and pupils throughout their lifetimes.[38]

Illich, like Holt, bemoaned compulsory education as a counterproductive exercise of state power. In his view, it had engendered widespread passivity and provided but a thin facade of real learning. Compulsory education had served to create "a dazed population, a 'learned' population, a mentally pretentious population, such as we have never seen before," Illich commented. Its chief accomplishment might have been creating millions of compliant consumers of television.[39]

Illich's critique of schools was grounded in part in his distrust of the technocratic assumptions that undergirded them. It was a fundamental premise of schools that, as one scholar has put it, "self-development must occur in specially designed and administered places" where individuals surrender much, if not all, of their autonomy. So ingrained was this thinking that even many radicals had come to view their "'liberation' as the product of an institutional process," Illich wrote. But authentic deliverance could only be attained by "liberating oneself from school."[40]

Nudged in a more radical direction by the likes of Illich, Holt eventually concluded that schools, at least as they were presently constituted in the United States, were broken beyond repair. His book *Instead of Education* (1976) offers an unmistakably stark assessment of how dysfunctional they had become:

> Education, with its supporting system of compulsory and competitive schooling, all its carrots and sticks, its grades, diplomas, and credentials, now seems to me perhaps the most authoritarian and dangerous of all the social inventions of mankind. It is the deepest foundation of the modern and worldwide slave state, in which most people feel themselves to be nothing but producers, consumers, spectators, and "fans," driven more and more, in all parts of their lives, by greed, envy, and fear.

Holt no longer saw the point in trying to reform such a pernicious system. He thundered that he hoped it would be eliminated altogether and replaced by alternative, and superior, forms of schooling. These would surpass the "education" being foisted on millions of young people every school day, which was little more than "learning cut off from active life and done under pressure of bribe or threat. . . ."[41]

As he later told the story, Holt had an epiphany while talking to a young mother who was involved in starting up an alternative school in her community. Holt knew that this would be an enormously complex undertaking: the parents would have to secure a facility, hire teachers, agree on a curriculum, obtain necessary accreditation from the state, and so forth. It occurred to Holt that this route of alternative schooling might be unnecessarily complicated and burdensome if the parents were primarily concerned with educating their own children rather than building institutions. "Why not just take your kids out of school and teach them at home?" he asked the woman. "It can't be any harder than what you are doing, and it might turn out to be a lot easier."[42]

Convinced that attempting to change the schools was a fool's errand, Holt began to encourage parents to devote their energies to educating children at home. The home was an ideal place for genuine learning, he explained, because "it is a natural, organic, central, fundamental human institution, one might easily and rightly say the foundation of all other institutions." It was thus well-suited to nurture the kind of self-motivated "doing" that Holt believed was the essence of real learning.[43]

This notion was not new to Holt, as he readily acknowledged. When skeptics challenged homeschooling as being an untested and theoretically suspect practice, Holt sometimes invoked the ideas of French philosopher Jean-Jacques Rousseau as well as those of John Dewey, the great American philosopher and educational reformer. Both had championed the importance of learning by doing. Holt insisted that this kind of deep, experiential education—with its emphasis on the child and the process of gaining meaningful knowledge—had become all but impossible in the ossified atmosphere of the public schools, where rote learning prevailed.[44]

From the start, Holt encountered many objections when he promoted the idea of homeschooling, the same sort of objections one hears today. Some related to pedagogy—people doubted that untrained parents could teach as well as professional educators. Others focused on socialization— skeptics worried that children educated at home would be too isolated and thus denied beneficial interactions with peers. Holt countered that, judging from what he had observed in traditional classrooms, home-schooled children would not be missing out on much. He found that in public schools "the social life of the children is mean-spirited, competitive, exclusive, status-seeking, snobbish, full of talk about who went to whose birthday party and who got what Christmas presents and who got how many Valentine cards and who is talking to so-and-so and who is not."[45]

Holt was not solely an educational theorist. He was also a tireless evangelist who devoted his prodigious energies to spreading the homeschooling gospel. He spoke widely and fervently and published materials accessible to a broad readership rather than a few elite peers. To that end, he began publishing *Growing without Schooling*, a newsletter devoted to the nascent homeschooling trend.

Another emblematic text to appear in homeschooling's formative years was Harold Bennett's *No More Public School*. Bennett sought to "make it possible for people with little or no previous experience to build realistic alternatives to the public school system," including homeschooling. An inveterate pragmatist, he offered practical tips for parents on such potentially tricky matters as evading the compulsory school attendance laws that had been so foundational to American education for more than a century. (This often involved filing phony or misleading paperwork with school authorities—or simply no paperwork at all.) Bennett seemed to relish subverting the bureaucratic structures that were, in his view, undermining the education of millions of children.[46]

The antiestablishment ethos of Holt and Bennett fit the times. The conflicts experienced by American society in the 1960s—the war in Vietnam and the civil rights movement among them—left many questioning the very foundations of the nation's cultural, social, and economic order. This trend hardly abated in the 1970s, particularly after the Watergate scandal exposed the apparent corruption of the country's political elites. It was a time for questioning authority and challenging long-established traditions, and few people did that more brazenly than John Holt. While others merely talked of various iterations of "revolution," he devoted his career to sparking one in the realm of education.

Intrepid parents like Patricia Heidenry were, in the late 1960s, among the first to follow Holt's prescriptions in educating their children at home. Inspired and emboldened by Holt's *How Children Learn*, Heidenry decided to homeschool her children when they reached school age. This was no lark for her. "My desire to educate the children at home," she wrote, "is based essentially on my belief that it is almost immoral for the children to spend a large portion of their youth in one building with more than a thousand other children and teachers in an environment that is lifeless and not life-giving." She allotted time each day for traditional subjects like reading and math, but there were unconventional twists as well, including yoga sessions led by Patricia's husband. An hour per day was devoted to art. For some years, this occurred while the family led an itinerant lifestyle in Europe and Mexico.[47]

The Heidenrys' foray into homeschooling was illustrative in several ways. It lasted only as long as the family could afford not to have Patricia employed outside the home. When she found full-time work as an editor, all four children enrolled in public schools, where they faced considerable trouble fitting in with their classmates. And they quickly discovered that their scholastic preparation, despite their mother's best efforts, had been uneven. "Academically," Margaret Heidenry later wrote, "my siblings were all over the map." But she was also quick to point out that none of the children appeared to have suffered any long-term damage. (Only one of the four did not graduate from college, and he became a successful real-estate developer nonetheless.)[48]

Robert Sessions decided to homeschool his son Erik in the 1970s because, as he put it, "schools isolate kids from the real world" and stifle their creativity. The elder Sessions was difficult to dismiss as a crackpot when it came to education, as he was employed as a professor of philosophy at Luther College in Decorah, Iowa. Though he taught in a traditional education setting, Sessions came to believe placing his son in such an environment at an early age was not the best way to cultivate his intellectual curiosity. In schools, children did not engage in deep learning; rather, they were "taught to read a book and take a test on it," said Sessions's wife, Linda. Erik's home education was markedly different; his inclinations dictated what he studied. He read books that held his interest, played the violin, and wrote. "I really don't have classes all day," Erik explained. "I do what I am interested in. Right now I'm interested in walking in the woods, reading books, milking the cows, harvesting the garden, studying Indians and myths. I practice my violin for as long as I want."[49]

Today, with homeschooling so widely discussed and increasingly common, it is difficult to perceive just how radical the Heidenry and Sessions families would have seemed to their contemporaries in the 1970s. They were, after all, doing something of dubious legality and challenging some of the public's bedrock assumptions about how children should be educated. According to one account, homeschooling in this period "was seen primarily by the public and media as a subversive educational activity carried out by idealists, often surreptitiously or underground." Americans had become familiar with countercultural experimentation by adults on many levels, but the nation's kitchen tables and child-rearing seemed like unlikely or inappropriate venues for profoundly revolutionary activity.[50]

There seemed to be as many approaches to homeschooling as there were families practicing it. Some parents formulated and followed relatively traditional curricula that essentially mirrored (albeit on a smaller scale) the type of instruction provided in schools. A typical school day might be divided into set periods in which a child moved between traditional academic subjects. Other families, however, gravitated toward the looser practice of "unschooling," in which children were given the freedom to pursue their interests without being bound by conventional notions of schoolwork or even subject matter. Patrick Farenga has noted that unschooling parents and children "live and learn together, pursuing questions and interests as they arise and using conventional schooling on an 'on demand' basis."[51]

Homeschooling parents often marveled at the benefits of this joint learning. One mother explained that, before she began homeschooling, her math skills were embarrassingly poor. However, they grew "by leaps and bounds" after she began teaching math to her two daughters. The act of teaching brought her a deeper understanding. What she once feared, she now came to love. "So homeschooling has been a blessing to me," the mother stated.[52]

The nascent movement comprised "odd bedfellows," as John Holt said in 1979. "It has fundamentalist Christians, some of whom don't have much schooling themselves. It has back-to-the-landers, college-educated people who grow their own food and have babies at home. It has people representing all classes and all sections of the country." Holt noted that these seemingly disparate approaches have some significant things in common, most notably "old-fashioned independence, a skepticism of experts, and a willingness to trust themselves."[53]

More families were brought into the homeschooling fold after a convergence of events gave the movement widespread publicity in the late 1970s and early 1980s. In December 1978, *Time* magazine published an article on Holt and the "growing if still small number of converts" he had brought into the homeschooling cause. The piece explains why people were repudiating conventional schools: "More and more parents are becoming disenchanted with rigid programs, school strikes and the reluctance of teachers to accept responsibility for students' failures to learn."[54]

The *Time* article led to appearances by Holt and by homeschooling families on Phil Donahue's syndicated television talk show in 1978 and then again in 1981. When asked why he had taken his daughter out of public school, one of the parents, Peter Van Daam, explained that "her sense of freedom was taken away from her" and that she essentially was "incarcerated." Donahue was characteristically tough ("Who's watching you?" he asked one of the parents), but he did seem sympathetic to the homeschoolers' critique of conventional education. At one point he asked in exasperation, "Why should learning be such a crock for so many kids?" The programs served both to promote and legitimize homeschooling. (It was reported that Holt received several thousand letters from curious parents after the shows aired.)[55]

Early homeschoolers' claims about the perilous state of American education received added weight from the work of President Reagan's National Commission on Excellence in Education. Its 1983 report, *A Nation at Risk: The Imperative for Educational Reform*, offers an indictment of the nation's school system that is as wide-ranging as it is withering. The panel's widely-noted report asserts that "the educational foundations of our society are presently being eroded by a rising tide of mediocrity that threatens our very future as a Nation and a people." It documents this threat by charting declining average math scores on the Scholastic Aptitude Test (SAT) and noting how poorly American students performed on other tests, particularly in the natural sciences, when compared to their international peers. Summing up this increasingly desultory performance, the commission famously asserted that "if an unfriendly foreign power had attempted to impose on America the mediocre educational performance that exists today, we might well have viewed it as an act of war. As it stands, we have allowed this to happen to ourselves."[56]

The reality was less bleak than the report and its heralds suggested; the basis for alarm was primarily math and natural-science test scores, and that in part reflected a dearth of qualified teachers in those subjects, owing to the relative attractiveness of nonteaching careers for those who possessed the expertise.[57] Other studies showed a remarkable rise in the aggregate IQ scores and cognitive ability of students in the United States and all other countries as a result of mass school systems, especially in the post-Sputnik era when the cognitive demands of schoolwork increased dramatically.[58] And the report was meant to be a clarion call for nationwide school reform, not the abandonment of schools. But its general thrust—America's schools were failing—served homeschoolers well when they argued that students could benefit from being taught somewhere other than dysfunctional schools. Christopher Klicka of HSLDA

has pointed to the release of *A Nation at Risk* as being particularly cata-
lytic for Christians concerned with how their children were being educated. For many such Christians, the message of the report was clear: the
public schools are in trouble, not only morally but also academically. This
made schooling at home an appealing alternative.[59]

For many years, it was not entirely clear that those who chose to school
their children at home could do so legally. Statutes governing school attendance varied by state, and the United States Supreme Court never ruled directly in any case whether states constitutionally must allow homeschooling. However, in a line of decisions dating back to the early twentieth
century, the high court had given some guidance as to the power of states
over children's education. In *Meyer v. Nebraska* (1923), the Supreme
Court held that states may not prohibit instruction in a foreign language,
and in *Pierce v. Society of Sisters* (1925), it held that states must permit
private schools to operate as an alternative to public schools. In neither
case were parents parties to the litigation; the challenges to state law were
brought by teachers (*Meyer*) or school operators (*Pierce*). In both, the
Supreme Court analyzed the challenges through the lens of the Fourteenth Amendment's due process clause, resting its holding primarily on
economic rights—that of trained teachers to pursue their profession and
that of private parties to operate a business (a school). But in both cases
the court suggested that parents have some prima facie right under the
federal Constitution to direct their children's upbringing. The *Pierce* majority wrote,

> The fundamental theory of liberty upon which all governments in this Union
> repose excludes any general power of the State to standardize its children by
> forcing them to accept instruction from public teachers only. The child is not
> the mere creature of the State; those who nurture him and direct his destiny
> have the right, coupled with the high duty, to recognize and prepare him for
> additional obligations.[60]

At the same time, however, the Supreme Court affirmed the legitimate power of the state to ensure that all children receive what the state
believes to be an adequate education. *Meyer* averred that "the power
of the State to compel attendance at some school and to make reasonable regulations for all schools . . . is not questioned." The court applied
what would today be termed "rational basis review," the lowest level of
judicial scrutiny in the sense of being the most deferential to legislatures,

putting the burden on persons challenging a law to show it bore no rational relation to any legitimate state purpose. The court's ruling against the state therefore rested on a determination that the laws at issue in those cases in fact did nothing whatsoever to serve children's well-being or educational interests. The outcome should have been different if the challenge were to laws the state could have shown to be protective of some secular interests of children. In fact, the great Justice Oliver Wendell Holmes dissented in *Meyer* and in its "companion case" of *Bartels v. State of Iowa*, which also addressed an "English-only" school law, on the grounds that "if there are sections in the State where a child would hear only Polish or French or German spoken at home I am not prepared to say that it is unreasonable to provide that in his early years he shall hear and speak only English at school."[61] Also notable in the *Meyer* decision was a line indicative of how well-entrenched the idea had become that children must attend a school in order to be properly educated: "Practically," the Supreme Court observed, "education of the young is only possible in schools conducted by especially qualified persons who devote themselves thereto."[62]

A third case from this era also involving school regulation, *Farrington v. Tokushige* (1927), reached a similar result. In *Farrington*, the Supreme Court struck down as unconstitutional a Hawaiian territorial law that aimed to micromanage foreign-language schools and impose an extraordinary compliance burden, a law that seemed motivated by animosity toward and suspicion of Japanese-speaking residents. Again, the court appeared to apply rational basis review. As it characterized the statute and implementing regulations,

> They give affirmative direction concerning the intimate and essential details of such schools, entrust their control to public officers, and deny both owners and patrons reasonable choice and discretion in respect of teachers, curriculum and text-books. Enforcement of the act probably would destroy most, if not all, of them. . . . Apparently all are parts of a deliberate plan to bring foreign language schools under a strict governmental control for which the record discloses no adequate reason.

The court declined to determine the constitutional validity of each provision in the law separately; it looked at the regulatory scheme as a whole and found it excessive. In this litigation as well, parents were not parties, and the holding rested on the economic rights of the entities operating the schools.

Yet once again the court spoke of a "right of a parent to direct the education of his own child without unreasonable restrictions" imposed by the state.[63]

The upshot of this trio of Supreme Court decisions in the 1920s, as concerns constitutional protection of parents' preferences regarding children's education, was therefore that parents have *some* substantive right under the due process clause to make decisions about their children's schooling. That right clearly includes the power to select a private rather than public school and to choose a school in which some instruction occurs in a foreign language. But that right clearly does not preclude the state from requiring that children attend some school or from imposing reasonable regulations on any private schools in order to ensure they fulfill children's educational interests as the state sees them.

In none of the 1920s cases, though, did the Supreme Court consider a parental claim to free exercise of religion. It first did so in the 1940s in a case, *Prince v. Massachusetts*, that did not involve school law but rather child-labor law. Massachusetts had a statute providing that "No boy under twelve and no girl under eighteen shall sell, expose or offer for sale any newspapers, magazines, periodicals or any other articles of merchandise of any description, or exercise the trade of bootblack or scavenger, or any other trade, in any street or public place." That law is still in the state code, but with the ages changed to nine and twelve for boys and girls, respectively. Sarah Prince, a Jehovah's Witness, was guardian of her nine-year-old niece Betty and brought Betty with her one evening to sell copies of the religious pamphlets *Watchtower* and *Consolation* on city sidewalks. Ms. Prince testified that both she and Betty were ministers, and that Betty had begged to go with her that day because "Betty believed it was her religious duty to perform this work and failure would bring condemnation 'to everlasting destruction at Armageddon.'"[64]

To the police and the trial court, Ms. Prince asserted that she was respecting Betty's right to religious freedom, but she also claimed that the ordinance violated her own rights under the First Amendment free exercise clause and the Fourteenth Amendment due process clause (as interpreted in *Meyer* and *Pierce*) because it interfered with her ability as legal guardian "to bring up the child in the way he should go, which for appellant means to teach him the tenets and the practices of their faith."[65] Thus, there was a parent's rights claim much like what one would expect in a case in which homeschoolers objected to state schooling regulations.

The *Prince* court reasoned that parental preferences should receive greater constitutional protection when firmly grounded in religious faith:

"The parent's conflict with the state over control of the child and his train-ing is serious enough when only secular matters are concerned. It becomes the more so when an element of religious conviction enters." It first noted that the prohibition against involving children in selling anything on the streets would certainly be constitutional as applied to instances when there is no religious element. It would be a reasonable exercise of the state's parens patriae authority to protect the welfare of children, which includes not only their safety but also their development toward autonomy: "It is the interest of youth itself, and of the whole community, that children be both safeguarded from abuses and given opportunities for growth into free and independent well-developed men and citizens."[66] The court then went on to conclude that, even though a religious-freedom claim raised the bar, the state's interest in child welfare is so strong as to override religious claims as well, and that it would do so in a wide range of contexts:

> Acting to guard the general interest in youth's well being, the state as *parens patriae* may restrict the parent's control by requiring school attendance, regu-lating or prohibiting the child's labor, and in many other ways. Its authority is not nullified merely because the parent grounds his claim to control the child's course of conduct on religion or conscience. Thus, he cannot claim freedom from compulsory vaccination for the child more than for himself on religious grounds. The right to practice religion freely does not include liberty to ex-pose the community or the child to communicable disease or the latter to ill health or death. The catalogue need not be lengthened. It is sufficient to show what indeed appellant hardly disputes, that the state has a wide range of power for limiting parental freedom and authority in things affecting the child's wel-fare; and that this includes, to some extent, matters of conscience and religious conviction.[67]

The Supreme Court has never backed away from this pronouncement, so common claims among homeschooling advocates today that any attempt to restrict or regulate homeschooling violates parents' constitutional rights are patently false.

Perhaps the most interesting aspect of the *Prince* opinion, though, is its repeated reference to children's rights. Justice Rutledge readily accepted Sarah Prince's assertion that Betty had a First Amendment free exercise right that the ordinance infringed, and simply found the state had offered sufficient justification for the infringement. Further, his opinion charac-terized the *Meyer* and *Pierce* decisions as, at least in part, children's rights cases:

The rights of children to exercise their religion, and of parents to give them religious training and to encourage them in the practice of religious belief, as against preponderant sentiment and assertion of state power voicing it, have had recognition here, most recently in *West Virginia State Board of Education v. Barnette*, 319 U.S. 624 [holding that public schools may not require a child to salute the flag and recite the Pledge of Allegiance]. Previously in *Pierce v. Society of Sisters*, this Court had sustained the parent's authority to provide religious with secular schooling, and the child's right to receive it, as against the state's requirement of attendance at public schools. And in *Meyer v. Nebraska*, children's rights to receive teaching in languages other than the nation's common tongue were guarded against the state's encroachment.[68]

Nearly three decades after *Prince*, though, with a quite differently constituted (and predominantly liberal) Supreme Court, an unusual group of parents claiming religious freedom scored a major victory in an education case—namely, an exemption just for that group from laws mandating school attendance past the eighth grade. In its decision in *Wisconsin v. Yoder*, the court was dismissive of any assertions by the state about rights of children. Yet the court's holding was explicitly very limited in scope. The court held that Wisconsin's compulsory schooling law was unconstitutional as applied specifically to *adolescents in Old Order Amish communities*. The children at issue had completed the eighth grade, and their parents believed further schooling would be counterproductive, given the parents' aims for the children. To reach its conclusion, the court, following *Prince*, applied a higher level of scrutiny to the law because of the religious element, and this time it found the law failed the test.

The Supreme Court began by reaffirming the legitimate ultimate authority of the state over children's education: "There is no doubt as to the power of a State, having a high responsibility for education of its citizens, to impose reasonable regulations for the control and duration of basic education." And later it added, "No one can question the State's duty to protect children from ignorance."[69] However, because the parents' objection arose from religious conviction and lifestyle, rather than from secular concerns, the court demanded a stronger showing of necessity for refusing to permit Amish parents to withdraw their children from schooling two years earlier than the law stipulated. The court explained:

Pierce, of course, recognized that, where nothing more than the general interest of the parent in the nurture and education of his children is involved, it is beyond dispute that the State acts "reasonably" and constitutionally in requiring education to age 16 in some public or private school meeting the standards prescribed by the State. However . . . when the interests of parenthood are combined with a free exercise claim of the nature revealed by this record, more than merely a "reasonable relation to some purpose within the competency of the State" is required to sustain the validity of the State's requirement under the First Amendment.[70]

Thus, "only those interests of the highest order and those not otherwise served can overbalance legitimate claims to the free exercise of religion."[71]

The Supreme Court granted that protecting children's welfare and developmental interests is in fact a compelling state interest: "To be sure, the power of the parent, even when linked to a free exercise claim, may be subject to limitation . . . if it appears that parental decisions will jeopardize the health or safety of the child, or have a potential for significant social burdens." But it found that the children of the Amish had little to gain and much to lose by being forced to attend high school: "It is one thing to say that compulsory education for a year or two beyond the eighth grade may be necessary when its goal is the preparation of the child for life in modern society as the majority live, but it is quite another if the goal of education be viewed as the preparation of the child for life in the separated agrarian community that is the keystone of the Amish faith." The court was emphatic that its analysis and holding were limited to the Amish because of their unique history in America and insular way of life, and it stressed that Amish youth were attending regular school up to eighth grade and then were receiving adequate vocational training for adulthood within the Amish community. It dismissed the state's argument that children of the Amish should be prepared to live in mainstream society if they should wish to do so upon reaching adulthood, faulting the state for failing to introduce any evidence of attrition in the community or that any persons who leave the Amish community "become burdens on society because of educational shortcomings."[72] Significantly, in America at the time of the *Yoder* decision, only half of the adults in mainstream society had a high school diploma, so persons raised in an Amish community would hardly have been unusual in lacking formal education beyond the eighth grade. Also significant is that, in closing, the court indicated that though Wisconsin could not require regular-school attendance for children of Amish parents once the children reached age fourteen, it could regulate the vocational training the Amish provided within their community. The court stated that "there is no basis for assuming that . . . reasonable standards cannot be established concerning the content of the continuing vocational education of Amish children under parental guidance."[73]

Also worth mention is a Supreme Court decision a few years prior to *Yoder* that had to do with state material support for private schools but expressed in passing the view that states constitutionally may ban homeschooling if they wish. In *Board of Education of Central School District No. 1. v. Allen*, the Supreme Court upheld New York's practice of lending textbooks without charge to students in religious and other private schools, against an establishment clause challenge. In rejecting the argument that textbooks, unlike bus transportation, would directly support some schools' pervasively religious instruction, the court asserted that religious schools typically provide secular as well as religious instruction, and had this to say about its 1925 *Pierce* decision:

> A premise of this holding was the view that the State's interest in education would be served sufficiently by reliance on the secular teaching that accompanied religious training in the schools maintained by the Society of Sisters. Since *Pierce*, a substantial body of case law has confirmed the power of the States to insist that attendance at private schools, if it is to satisfy state compulsory-attendance laws, be at institutions which provide minimum hours of instruction, employ teachers of specified training, and cover prescribed subjects of instruction. Indeed, the State's interest in assuring that these standards are being met has been considered a sufficient reason for refusing to accept instruction at home as compliance with compulsory education statutes. These cases were a sensible corollary of *Pierce v. Society of Sisters*: if the State must satisfy its interest in secular education through the instrument of private schools, it has a proper interest in the manner in which those schools perform their secular educational function.[74]

The case that the *Allen* court cited as an example of those "refusing to accept instruction at home" constitutes an interesting lost artifact in American constitutional history. It is *Turner v. People of the State of California*, a 1953 California state court decision upholding prosecution of a homeschooling parent for violating that state's compulsory school attendance law. In *Turner*, a superior court rejected both the defendant's insistence that the state statute should be interpreted to allow homeschooling and an argument that, if the statute does not allow homeschooling, it is unconstitutional, a violation of the parent's rights. The defendant appealed that court's ruling to the United States Supreme Court, which issued a summary dismissal.[75] Summary dismissals tend to get overlooked because they do not make for interesting reading; they consist of a single sentence, "The appeal is dismissed for the want of a substantial federal question." But the effect of such a ruling is virtually the same as if the Supreme Court affirmed the lower-court decision after issuing a full opinion.[76] Thus, in effect, the Supreme Court has actually ruled that there is no parental constitutional right to homeschool.

Despite *Allen*, *Turner*, and the Supreme Court's repeated statements that states may require that all students attend regular schools subject to state oversight, homeschooling activists took heart from the *Yoder* ruling, because it reaffirmed the willingness of the federal courts to resist excessive state control of child-rearing and apply a higher level of judicial scrutiny for laws interfering with religiously motivated parenting decisions. More specifically, although the Supreme Court emphasized the narrowness of its holding and affirmed the authority of the state to oversee all forms of private education, even Amish vocational training, it had deemed at least some specially positioned parents constitutionally entitled to be exempt from compulsory school attendance laws at some point in their children's development. Subsequently, however, when non-Amish parents asserted a free-exercise right to homeschool, lower courts consistently rejected the claim, as the California court had in the *Turner* decision that the Supreme Court affirmed. If they addressed *Yoder* directly, lower courts deemed it inapplicable because the Supreme Court's holding was limited to the Amish and to groups similar to the Amish in their history and reclusiveness (e.g., Mennonites).[77] Homeschooling parents generally also lost when they claimed a constitutional right to be free of regulation, such as teacher-qualification or testing requirements, regardless of whether they asserted a religious basis for their objection and regardless of whether courts applied strict scrutiny, with lower courts regularly citing the Supreme Court's repeated affirmation of the state's authority to oversee all schooling.[78]

In addition, in 1990 the US Supreme Court deflated the free exercise clause considerably in its *Employment Division v. Smith* decision.[79] That case did not involve education but is relevant because the Supreme Court held that, as a general matter, free exercise clause objections to generally applicable laws henceforth would not trigger heightened scrutiny. Only if a law specifically targets a particular religious group or religion more broadly should courts demand strong justification from the state.

The general holding of *Smith* appeared to implicitly overrule *Yoder*, yet in dictum Justice Scalia's majority opinion seemed to suggest that

cases like *Yoder*, in which litigants allege violation of an additional constitutional right (such as the parental due process right) as well as religious
freedom, might be different and trigger heightened scrutiny. Most lower
courts addressing parental objections to laws governing child-rearing after *Smith*, though, have dismissed this dictum as nonbinding and nonsensical.[80] Others have avoided the level-of-scrutiny question by finding that
the law in question would satisfy strict scrutiny anyway.[81] Still others have
required that the second right be a specific one already recognized, like the
right of the Amish to withdraw offspring from school after eighth grade
or the right to teach in a foreign language; it is not sufficient to allege a
broad right like parental control over education.[82] In the rare case when a
lower court has applied strict scrutiny on the basis of a hybrid-right claim,
it has required that the plaintiff show "a fair probability or likelihood, but
not a certitude, of success on the merits' on the companion constitutional
claim"—that is, that they would likely win even without the free exercise
claim.[83] (If that seems nonsensical to you, then you understand why most
courts have simply rejected or ignored the hybrid-rights theory.)

In the quarter century since *Smith*, the Supreme Court has not taken
a single parental-free-exercise case, so the level-of-scrutiny issue remains
somewhat muddled. The Supreme Court did take a parental-rights case
without a religious aspect in 2000, a case concerning court-ordered visita-
tion with grandparents, *Troxel v. Granville*. But that case resulted in a
"plurality decision"—that is, one in which there was no majority supporting any particular rationale for the outcome, so the case has significance
only for its specific holding, which was merely that state courts must apply
a *presumption* in such cases that the custodial parent's view of the child's
best interests is correct.[84]

On the whole, then, the current status of parents' constitutional rights
to control children's upbringing appears quite weak, regardless of religious
motivation, leaving states free to impose any rules and restrictions rationally connected to what they deem children's well-being. If states have
a reasonable basis for believing they will promote children's educational
interests or other aspects of children's welfare by requiring attendance at
a regular school or by conditioning any authorization of homeschooling
on compliance with rules regarding qualifications to teach, content of curriculum, or assessment, Supreme Court doctrine clearly permits them to
do so. No parent's religious objection to such regulations entitles them to
an exemption. At most, some courts might say the state must show there
are no less-intrusive means of protecting children's interests.

Homeschool advocates have nevertheless had extraordinary success in creating a congenial legal environment, principally through a state-by-state legislative effort, along with a few lawsuits seeking favorable interpretation of *state* law.[85] Throughout the first three-quarters of the twentieth century, most states' compulsory school attendance laws made no provision for homeschooling, making the practice seemingly illegal in most communities. John Holt, for one, realized early on that homeschoolers would have to carve out legal protections on an ad hoc basis; only by doggedly securing and then building on advantageous judicial decisions grounded in state law, in a piecemeal fashion, could they hope to succeed over the long haul. He explained that "when we write up home schooling plans, we are going to have to cite and quote favorable rulings. The more of this we do, the less schools will want to take us to court, and the better the chances that if they do we will win."[86] The judicial victories were dwarfed by the judicial losses, but homeschool advocates could cite whatever positive outcomes or supportive snippets of opinions were available while ignoring the rest.

One early success occurred in New Jersey in the late 1960s. A magistrate had convicted Barbara and Frank Massa of violating that state's compulsory school attendance law (and fined them $2,490) after they began homeschooling their daughter Barbara. When they appealed their conviction to the Morris County Court in 1967, the couple argued that their daughter was receiving an education equivalent to that furnished by the local county school system. To prove their case, the Massas introduced reams of evidence attesting to the rigor of their home instruction as well as test scores indicating that Barbara was performing as well as (or even better than) her peers in most subjects. Their arguments carried the day. The court found that they had in fact complied with the attendance statute by furnishing their daughter with instruction equivalent to that provided in the public schools. The holding stressed that the purpose of the attendance measure was that "all children shall be educated, not that they shall be educated in a particular way."[87] It rested, crucially, on the parents' having demonstrated that their child was being educated in a manner consistent with the state's aims for children's schooling. There is no mention at all in the court's opinion of any rights of parents to resist the state's requirements.

Early homeschoolers in Illinois turned to the courts several times as they endeavored to clarify their rights. In *People v. Levisen* (1950), a case involving pioneering Seventh-day Adventist homeschoolers, the state's supreme court found that, under the right conditions, home instruction was the equivalent of a "private school" within the meaning of state statutes. Parents would bear the burden, though, of demonstrating that they are competent to teach and that their children are receiving an education "at least commensurate with the standards prescribed for the public schools." Given its ruling favorable to the parents on statutory grounds, the court found it unnecessary to decide whether the parents had a constitutional right overriding the state's requirements, but said in dictum that no parent has a right to deprive a child of an education equivalent to that provided in public schools.[88] However, in a later case, *Scoma v. Chicago Board of Education*, following soon after the Supreme Court's *Yoder* decision, a federal district court in Illinois did address a constitutional claim and rejected a homeschooler's challenge to the state's compulsory school attendance law on Fourteenth Amendment due process grounds. The parents had not asserted a religious objection to school attendance, so the court stipulated that the state "must act only 'reasonably' in requiring children to attend school," and found that burden easily met.[89] The court quoted *Yoder* for the proposition that there is "no support to the contention that parents may replace state educational requirements with their own idiosyncratic views of what knowledge a child needs to be a productive and happy member of society."[90]

In Massachusetts in 1978, a lower state court agreed with homeschooling parents that the local superintendent's oversight had gone too far in requiring that homeschoolers have a social experience equivalent to that which children have in public schools. Judge Greaney acknowledged that there is no federal constitutional right to homeschool and that homeschooling is properly subject to many regulatory requirements, including demonstrated competence to teach, approved content and methods of instruction, and submission to periodic assessment. But because state courts had previously found a right to homeschool in *state* law, education officials were not permitted to impose requirements so burdensome as to make homeschooling practically impossible, as the judge thought true of this "equivalent social experience" requirement. The judge noted that "attempts by parents to deny that the state has any right to set educational standards for school age children have been consistently rejected by the federal courts," but agreed with the parents that the state may not "set standards that are so difficult to satisfy that they effectively eviscerate the home education alternative."[91]

The annals of the early homeschooling legal battles have an almost Old Testament flair, with tales depicting well-meaning families enduring

persecution at the hands of overzealous bureaucrats bent on strictly enforcing school-attendance laws. In these accounts, truant officers barged
into homes and demanded to take homeschooled children to school, social workers insisted on interviewing homeschooled children who allegedly were endangered, and devoted parents who simply wanted the best
education for their children were threatened with arrest.

The Van Daam family, which had been featured in one of the *Donahue*
broadcasts on homeschooling, waged a lengthy battle against authorities
in Rhode Island. At various points in the controversy, Peter Van Daam
was cited for contempt of court, fined, and even jailed for continuing to
homeschool without submitting the requisite paperwork (such as a program of study) to local school authorities. In words America's founders
would have found shocking, Van Daam asserted, "We do not recognize
the right of the state to regulate the behavior of the family." Contrast that
attitude with the prevailing view in our country's early years, in which, as
articulated by legal-treatise writer Christopher Tiedeman, custodial authority "is not the natural right of the parents; it emanates from the State,
and is an exercise of police power," and parental control is "in the nature
of a trust, reposed in [the parent] by the State . . . , which may be extended
or contracted, according as the public welfare may require."[92] But fired up
with modern anti-statist fervor, Van Daam's supporters repeatedly threatened the family-court judge who was presiding in the case, as well as the
judge's family.[93] Such episodes constitute a large part of the explanation
for the widespread legislative capitulation to homeschoolers that has occurred in more recent decades.

Probably the most dramatic—and most tragic—of these combative
confrontations involved a fundamentalist Mormon in Utah named John
Singer, who began educating his children at home in 1973 because he objected to the moral decay of the public schools (which in his mind was tied
to the fact that the schools were racially integrated). Singer and his polygamous family became embroiled in a byzantine and prolonged dispute
with local authorities over the legal permissibility of his homeschooling.
After he was convicted of child abuse and neglect, police officers on snow-
mobiles appeared on his property early in 1979 to take him into custody.
Singer allegedly pointed a weapon at the officers, whereupon they shot
and killed him.[94]

There was no grand, overarching strategy guiding the homeschooling
legal campaign. It was a piecemeal effort carried out in multiple jurisdictions by parents and advocates who hoped to gain the legal power to

keep their children out of school. John Holt, the father of the modern homeschooling movement, believed the American Civil Liberties Union (ACLU) should have been integral to this effort. Compulsory school attendance laws, he wrote, "constitute a very serious infringement of the civil liberties of children and their parents." Students' fundamental rights were further violated, he asserted, by the authoritarian operation of the schools themselves. For Holt, these depredations should have drawn the attention of the nation's oldest and most prominent advocacy group for civil liberties, but, at both the state and national levels, the ACLU failed to show much sustained interest in homeschooling. The national leadership seemed to view "the right of children to go to school as paramount over their right not to go," according to homeschooling advocate Pat Farenga.[95]

In the absence of the ACLU, several organizations stepped up and advocated for homeschoolers in courts, including the Rutherford Institute, a Virginia nonprofit that championed myriad conservative political causes over the years. (Indeed, it was often described as a conservative version of the ACLU.) Rutherford's founder, John Whitehead, penned an enormously influential book, *Home Education: Rights and Reasons*, that for many years served as an essential primer on homeschooling law and jurisprudence.

Another important player has been the Home School Legal Defense Association, which built on and complemented the efforts of Rutherford and smaller organizations devoted specifically to homeschool advocacy. Founded in 1983, HSLDA began providing legal representation to homeschoolers throughout the country. Many attorneys who worked for the organization joined the effort in part because they perceived that the government was waging a legal attack on parents who merely wanted to provide the best education for their children. For such attorneys, HSLDA was not merely a legal advocacy organization; it was part of a holy crusade. They believed they were doing God's work by helping create a legal regime that enabled parents to do something profoundly important: ensure their children received only Christian instruction, in an environment free of influence from nonbelievers.

Driving the work of HSLDA were, as law professor Kimberly Yuracko has noted, two fundamental claims. One was the assertion that parents alone should control the upbringing of their children, without interference from the state. Echoing the sentiments of many homeschoolers, Michael Farris, the organization's founder, went so far as to say parents possess an "absolute right" to control children's education. As explained above, this assertion is plainly false as a matter of constitutional law, so Farris can best be understood as asserting a moral right that he thought legislators should recognize. The other pillar of HSLDA's work was the belief that Christian families have a duty to safeguard their children from the malignant secular influences that pervade public schools. What these institutions taught or at least countenanced—evolution, education about sex, disregard for biblical teachings—was anathema to parents who hoped to raise their children in an authentically Christian environment.[96]

According to HSLDA attorney Scott Somerville, the organization had one major tactical advantage when it squared off with local school officials: its lawyers, living and breathing homeschooling as they did, were extremely well versed in whatever legal support there was for this relatively new practice. School-district officials in any particular locale, in contrast, typically had little experience in dealing with homeschooling and received little counsel, direction, or support from state-level superiors. Many beleaguered administrators simply felt overmatched and had little personal incentive to resist. Or, as Somerville characterized it, "In the face of HSLDA's extensive knowledge and single-minded purpose, most districts looked for ways to tolerate home schoolers instead of prosecuting them."[97] At the state level, the best explanation for HSLDA legislative success might not be any superior knowledge of the law but rather the organization's ability to foment outrage among homeschoolers in any state contemplating a regulation, causing any legislator who supported the regulation to become the victim of a relentless barrage of hostile communications—occasionally including death threats—by mail, email, and office visits. A legislative aide in Michigan said, "I've never seen a lobby more powerful and scary."[98]

In some places, state school officials did mount a defense of compulsory attendance. In the 1980s, the Texas Education Agency determined that homeschooling was illegal and urged the prosecution of parents who engaged in the practice. (Charges were filed in 150 cases.) However, the Rutherford Institute facilitated a class action suit in which parents argued that school authorities were discriminating against them by failing to recognize homeschools as permissible private schools. They succeeded. In *Texas Education Agency v. Leeper* (1991), the Texas Supreme Court treated homeschools as a species of private schools within the meaning of state statutes exempting private schools from state oversight, and held that imposing regulations on parents who choose private schooling within the home but not parents who choose private schooling outside the home violated an equal protection right of the former group of parents. *Leeper* instantly made Texas one of the most congenial states for homeschooling.[99]

Although HSLDA focused much of its attention on such cases, its influence was felt beyond the courtroom. In 1994, the organization mounted a campaign against a proposed change to the federal Elementary and Secondary Education Act, which HSLDA insisted would require that homeschooling parents be certified as teachers, a requirement generally loathed by homeschoolers as too restrictive. There was some dispute as to whether the proposed law would in fact have imposed any such requirement, but HSLDA pressed anyway and scored another triumph, persuading lawmakers to include language in the law that explicitly disavowed any federal control over homeschooling.

Increasingly, parents wishing to homeschool faced fewer legal hurdles, as states began to amend their laws to accommodate that wish. In one brief period, between 1985 and 1992, half of the states enacted statutes that explicitly exempted homeschooled children from compulsory school attendance requirements. HSLDA helped persuade lawmakers in many states to also soften or eliminate requirements regarding curricula, testing, and certification. In 1985 alone, seven states (Arkansas, Florida, New Mexico, Oregon, Tennessee, Washington, and Wyoming) enacted measures meant to facilitate homeschooling. Five other states (Colorado, New York, South Carolina, North Carolina, and Pennsylvania) followed suit in 1988.[100]

State education officials often vehemently resisted these legislative changes. In Iowa, Kathy Collins, an attorney for the state department of education, offered a trenchant critique of efforts to amend that state's compulsory school attendance law to accommodate homeschooling. "It has taken nearly two centuries to enact the many legal protections existing today for children," she wrote in 1987. "Abrogating the state's compulsory-attendance laws, or weakening them by allowing parents to teach children at home, is no less than a giant genuflection backward." When describing the potential for abuses by homeschooling parents if they were allowed "to teach their children without oversight or interference from the state," Collins laid out a parade of horribles: children could be locked in closets, or forced to babysit siblings or to staff family businesses. But Collins's efforts to prevent children from being relegated to the status of (in her words) "chattel" were in vain, as Iowan legislators capitulated to HSLDA and amended the state's school laws in 1991 to accommodate homeschooling.[101]

Michigan was the last state to insist on robust qualifications in order to homeschool. After a prolonged legal battle backed by HSLDA, the state supreme court held in 1993, in *People v. DeJonge*,[102] that Michigan's law limiting instruction in "nonpublic schools" to certified teachers violated the First Amendment free exercise clause as applied to homeschooling parents who demonstrated in court that they were providing "more than an adequate education" and "fulfilling the academic and socialization goals of compulsory education" but had a sincere religious objection to state certification. The state court misread the Supreme Court's decision in *Employment Division v. Smith* as having "ruled" that assertion of a free exercise claim in conjunction with a claim of parental substantive due process rights "demands the application of strict scrutiny," despite the fact that *Smith* was not a child-rearing case. And though the court acknowledged that the state's interest in children's education is a compelling one, it found the state failed to show that applying the teacher-certification requirement to these particular parents was necessary to serve that interest, given that the parents had presented evidence of their providing a good education to their children.

Significantly, in a companion case involving parents with solely secular objections to teacher certification for homeschooling, who invoked only the due process clause of the Fourteenth Amendment and not also the free exercise clause of the First Amendment, the same court ruled in favor of the state, and so established for a time a discrimination in favor of religious homeschools.[103] In that same year, however, the federal appellate court in the circuit that includes Michigan, the Sixth Circuit, rejected the hybrid-rights theory and held that only rational basis review applies to any free exercise challenge to a law of general applicability, thus eviscerating the legal foundation of the *DeJonge* decision.[104] In any event, the Michigan legislature soon thereafter made the question of the teacher-certification requirement's constitutionality moot by eliminating it for all homeschools, religious and secular.

A final state-court battle that stands large in the history of homeschooling litigation, a case known as *Jonathan L.*, occurred in California just a decade ago. An intermediate appellate court sent shock waves through the homeschooling world when it ruled that California law does not permit homeschooling. Legislative changes to the state education code since the 1953 *Turner* decision had seemed to liberalize the state's stance toward homeschooling, and probably hundreds of thousands of parents were homeschoolers. But when child-protective services became aware of severe physical abuse by a father in a homeschooling family (not for the first time), the mother's knowledge of that abuse and failure to protect the children from it, the sexual abuse by a family friend that both parents tried to conceal, and the unsafe condition of the house (which was filthy and contained sixty unsecured rifles and assault weapons), a trial court declared the children dependent. The mother, whose own schooling had ended at eleventh grade, was the sole instructor for her eight children. When the court ordered the return of the youngest children to parental custody, attorneys representing those children requested an order that the children attend regular school so that teachers might keep an eye on the children's physical well-being. In February 2008, a California intermediate appellate court held that the state statute, despite the post-*Turner* amendments, still did not permit homeschooling, and so the children should be in regular school anyway. A firestorm of outrage from homeschool advocates ensued, and six months later the appellate court changed its mind. In perhaps the most contorted exercise in statutory interpretation to be found in the history of homeschooling litigation, the judges concluded that statutory authorization for education in "a private full-time day school" as an alternative to public schooling encompassed homeschools.[105] Homeschool activists heaved a sigh of relief and returned to their mission of eliminating state oversight of homeschooling around the nation.

In no state was the triumph of homeschooling parents over regulation more complete than in Alaska. The state's frontier character made it a natural breeding ground for homeschooling; in many remote and snowbound areas, it was essentially impossible for parents to send their children off to schools each morning. Recognizing the apparent necessity of home education, in 1997 the state enacted what might be described as a wish list for homeschooling parents. As one advocate happily describes it, the measure required "no teaching qualifications for parents, no regulation at any level of government, no notice to anyone of the parents' decision to conduct the home education, no registration with the state, no reporting to anyone of any information about the home education program, no testing of the children, no required subjects, and no evaluation of the program by anyone."[106]

As a result of homeschool crusaders' relentless efforts, today in the vast majority of states there is no real legal obstacle to parents' withholding their children from school and doing whatever they want in terms of instruction at home, including doing nothing. Regulations on the books vary significantly from one state to another, but by virtue of slight or no accountability measures in the great majority of states and school officials' disinclination in other states to enforce any significant regulations, by and large states leave children to their parents' devices. A 2015 report by the Education Commission of the States noted that a threadbare "patchwork of provisions" governs homeschooling throughout the country.[107] As of 2017, a dozen or so states are like Alaska, requiring absolutely nothing of parents who keep their children out of school, not even a notification to local school officials that they are homeschooling. In another handful of states, nothing is required of parents so long as they "associate with" some organization or private school or submit a religious objection to schooling. An additional dozen or so states require only notification; parents have to submit a letter or an affidavit to the local superintendent, stating that their child will not be attending school, but never anything else. Thus, in a majority of states, there is no effort whatsoever to see that children whose parents keep them out of school are receiving any sort of education.

In most of the remaining states, ostensible efforts to hold parents accountable are minimal or easily evaded. In a few states, parents must submit a plan of instruction, but local officials have no authority to disapprove it. A few other states require preapproval of a homeschooling curriculum but give local school officials complete discretion in approving, so it is difficult to know whether this is a meaningful safeguard; presumably it varies by locality. Four states require parents to maintain records or subject their children to testing but do not authorize school officials to demand to see either. Three other states and the District of Columbia require parents to either maintain records of progress *or* submit to standardized tests in certain grades, but do not require parents to submit test results or a portfolio of work to school officials unless the officials ask them to do so. Among the small number of states that require submission of any evidence of performance, most allow homeschoolers to choose between standardized tests and a private evaluation of the child's progress by someone of the parents' own choosing. A mere ten states require that homeschooling parents have any education themselves, and what they require is just a high school diploma or GED (and a few of these states allow parents who lack even this to try to demonstrate capacity to teach in some other, unspecified way).

New York appears to be the only state today in which the law ostensibly requires all homeschooling parents to annually submit evidence of adequate academic progress to local school officials, and gives those officials legal power to order parents to enroll their child in a regular school if the child's progress is inadequate and remains so after a period of attempted remediation.[108] But even if school-district officials enforce these rules (and there is reason to believe they do not),[109] educational deprivation might not be detected until middle school. Homeschooling parents in New York must receive prior approval from school officials, based on their submission of a satisfactory "individualized home instruction plan" encompassing all subjects listed in the state statute, and thereafter they must submit quarterly reports and an annual assessment to local school officials. The annual assessment, however, can be a "written narrative" of progress by someone the parents choose. The superintendent must approve the parent's choice of evaluator, but this might be granted freely based only on superficial qualifications, without assurance that the evaluator will actually examine the child's work and give an objective assessment. Not until fifth grade must a homeschooled child take a standardized test, with results reported to school officials. If the written evaluation or the test score reveals a lack of adequate academic progress, parents are placed on probation and subjected to somewhat more stringent scrutiny for two years. If the homeschooling remains inadequate for the additional two years, then and only then might the state require that the child attend a regular school (public or private).[110] Thus, assuming parents can find and get the superintendent to approve a sympathetic private evaluator, deficient home education might not come to school officials' attention until the end of a child's fifth-grade year, and then the child might suffer an additional two years of educational deprivation (i.e., until the child is the age of an eighth grader) before the state can require that the child attend a regular school. This, it seems, is the most rigorous oversight of homeschooling in the entire country.

For many years, neighboring Pennsylvania was among the most exacting of states in terms of monitoring homeschooling. However, thanks in part to HSLDA's efforts, the state substantially reduced its requirements in 2014. Among other changes, homeschool families are no longer required to submit portfolios of children's work to the local school superintendent. Lawmakers also eliminated a requirement that families submit to school-district superintendents the results of standardized tests administered in third, fifth, and eighth grade. Even these changes were not enough for some homeschool advocates, one of whom said that he hoped for the state to adopt "a total hands-off policy" toward homeschooling.[111] Homeschoolers in Pennsylvania still must maintain a portfolio of student work and arrange for the administration of standardized tests in some grades, and they must have a state-licensed teacher, private-school teacher, or licensed psychologist of their choice annually review the portfolio and test results and certify to the state that the child is receiving an appropriate education.

In contrast, in most states there is no oversight, no evaluation by anyone of the academic program and of students' progress. In Virginia, there is a complete absence of oversight of parents who claim a religious motivation for homeschooling, even though from the state's perspective these parents (because some of them might reject secular education altogether) might pose a greater threat to children's education than parents who homeschool for secular reasons. Although Virginia does impose loose reporting requirements on homeschoolers generally—namely, notification of intent to homeschool, description of curriculum, and some evidence of yearly progress—it also provides a blanket exemption from compulsory schooling for families that assert a religious objection to public-school attendance. In 2015, the state completely exempted almost sixty-five hundred parents from all regulation and oversight. Homeschoolers zealously defend this statutory exemption, contending that it is necessary to safeguard the religious "liberty" of parents. When one Virginia county sought assurance that the liberty of adolescents was also being respected, by requiring that homeschool pupils aged fourteen or older provide a statement about their own religious beliefs, homeschooling parents were vehemently opposed and HSLDA came to their aid in pressuring the school board to back down.[112] Thus, no one knows if or how these children are instructed at home. Said a state education spokesman, "Once a religious exemption is granted, there is no follow-up reporting."[113]

One context in which a parent's desire to homeschool might be thwarted, despite very permissive state school laws, is where separated parents disagree about it. In custody battles between non-cohabiting parents, courts might disfavor a parent who wishes to homeschool a child, based on a general skepticism about homeschooling or on a conclusion that a parent's schooling at home has been deficient. Idaho loosened its compulsory school attendance law to better accommodate homeschooling in 1992, but a homeschooling mother named Sandra Mangus lost custody of her son Jason because a judge ruled that her instruction of him was woefully insufficient. The judge granted custody to Jason's father (who pledged to send him to a public school) because the teaching the boy had been receiving at home was "almost equivalent to no schooling."

The judge, after reviewing a battery of tests that had been administered to the boy, held that he "has not developed as he should."[114] More recently, a New Hampshire state court judge made national headlines by ordering the transfer of a ten-year-old girl's custody from a homeschooling mother to a father who would send her to public school, based on a judgment that the mother's instruction was too ideologically confining and was alienating the daughter from her father.[115]

Notably, not all homeschoolers endorse the trend toward absolute legal empowerment of parents to do as they please without oversight. The Coalition for Responsible Home Education, seeking to become a counterweight to HSLDA, has pushed states to adopt certain forms of regulation aimed at more rigorous and uniform assessment of students and more protection of homeschooled children's physical welfare. These basic reforms, according to the organization's cofounder, are necessary to ensure homeschooling is "a child-centered option, used only to lovingly prepare young people for an open future."[116]

As Joseph Murphy has observed, the gains made by parents who chose to educate their children at home in the early years of modern homeschooling were made possible in part by the emergence of "larger political, cultural, and social forces" that "combined to create a culture that is hospitable to the growth of homeschooling." With the election of Ronald Reagan as president in 1980, political conservatives had a platform to seriously challenge notions of the role of state power that had reigned in American public life since the New Deal. At the core of the "Reagan Revolution" was an ostensible animus toward state power. Regulation (at least outside the realm of reproductive rights) was anathema.[117] The state's legal empowering of parents to keep children out of school was simply not recognized as an exertion of state power, though in fact it is an extraordinary one.

The push for state abdication of oversight was profoundly influenced by the "Chicago school" of economics. A group of economists associated with the University of Chicago, among them Nobel laureates Milton Friedman and George Stigler, attacked the regulatory and coercive power of the state. During the Reagan era (and beyond), their advocacy of laissez-faire policies was echoed and amplified by such conservative think tanks as the American Enterprise Institute. Reagan championed their agenda and pushed for deregulation in transportation, finance, and agriculture, among other realms.

In fact, Reagan was so hostile to *federal* oversight of public schools that he pledged in his 1980 presidential campaign to abolish the US

Department of Education. That promise remained unfulfilled, but his administration slashed federal funding for education and pushed for "local control" of schools, with states and school districts assuming greater authority. This was justified in part as a way to ensure that parents—not bureaucrats in Washington—were directing children's education. Michael Reagan, the president's son, later touted the efficacy of applying free-market principles to education, arguing that alternatives to public schools were more cost-effective and successful in terms of educating students. He singled out homeschooling as "the most freedom-oriented approach of all," one that could deliver "a higher-quality education and higher-achieving students at a fraction of the cost of government schools"[118] (a calculation that implicitly ascribed zero value to mothers' time and opportunity costs).

The Reaganites' efforts to transform political discourse and public policy were bolstered by the conservative evangelical Christians who were altering the American religious and political landscape. Fundamentalism was hardly "new." Christians had been bemoaning the perceived pitfalls of modernism for close to a century. But it gained unprecedented prominence in the 1980s. In the name of arresting the nation's spiritual decline, organizations like the Moral Majority (headed by Jerry Falwell), the Christian Coalition (Pat Robertson), and the Family Research Council (James Dobson) engaged in political activism on a wide variety of issues, most notably a prolonged effort to curb abortion rights, but also education.

For Christian evangelicals and fundamentalists, the public schools had long been a moral and political battleground, a place where their religious beliefs and cultural values seemed imperiled by the combined forces of secularism and state power. As noted above, Supreme Court decisions in the early 1960s banning state-sanctioned prayer and Bible reading in public schools intensified their concerns, as did later decisions stopping public schools from teaching the biblical story of creation. There was a widespread perception among conservative Christians that God had been "taken out of the public schools" by the courts. To make matters even worse, many other topics had been allowed *into* the schools, including sex education and books of dubious morality.

For many religious and cultural conservatives, the social-studies curriculum "Man: A Course of Study" (widely known by its acronym, MACOS) was emblematic of this downward trend. Grounded in the theories of educational psychologist Jerome Bruner, MACOS stressed the acquisition of knowledge through inquiry. Instead of memorizing facts, students were encouraged to formulate and test hypotheses and then use analysis of evidence to draw their own conclusions. The curriculum also devoted considerable attention to study of non-Western cultures. Conservatives bemoaned MACOS as humanism run amok and criticized its alleged challenge of biblical values. As Stephen Carter has noted, the curriculum came under fire because of "its seeming depiction of human beings as just another animal, its purported moral relativism, and its insistence on treating evolution as a literal truth."[119]

A fractious dispute over public-school textbooks in Kanawha County, West Virginia, in 1974 showed how fervently some religious conservatives had begun to resist these changes in the public schools. When a new statewide curriculum led to the adoption of textbooks reflecting multi- and countercultural perspectives, many parents and religious groups protested vehemently, claiming that the schools were bent on exposing their children to the pernicious, immoral ideas that had ripped the country apart in the 1960s. One leader of the protests insisted that textbooks, rather than being subversive, should "recognize the sanctity of the home" and "encourage loyalty to the United States."[120] When thousands of families boycotted county schools, local coal miners staged a strike to show their sympathy. Emotions ran so high that several schools were firebombed, and a school bus was hit by gunfire.

As scholar Adam Laats argues in his excellent overview of the Kanawha textbook controversy, leaders of the opposition to certain textbooks that the school board selected for the elementary schools had developed a broad critique of the failings of the local public schools. Alice Moore, for instance, "fought against progressive education broadly understood," according to Laats. She opposed sex education and the teaching of evolution and believed teachers should use traditional methods of discipline to keep students from misbehaving. Moore, like many like-minded religious conservatives in the 1970s, had come to believe public schools had lost their way and were now eroding students' core religious beliefs and devotion to God. For proof, one need look no further than the textbooks being proposed for use in West Virginia.[121]

Such concerns resonated with Mel and Norma Gabler, conservative textbook activists from Texas. Starting in the 1960s, the couple waged a tireless battle against the expunging of Judeo-Christian values and beliefs from public-school textbooks. They decried the "humanist minority's takeover of the public school curriculum," evidenced in textbooks that, they said, routinely contained passages depicting violence, immorality, and sexual perversion. The books allegedly pushed moral relativism on students when they desperately needed to learn the bedrock values and traditions that had made America great.[122]

These critiques of the public schools did not exist merely on the fringes of American conservatism. No less a personage than Phyllis Schlafly, founder of the Eagle Forum and a key player in the defeat of the Equal Rights Amendment, issued a book titled *Child Abuse in the Classroom* that aims to document how public schools were failing to provide sufficient intellectual or moral training for America's youth. Summarizing her findings in a speech in 1987, Schlafly said millions of parents had come to believe they were subject to "a continuing attack on their religion, on their morals, [and] on their family" because of what was being taught to their children in the public schools.[123]

The explosive growth of religious television broadcasting in the 1970s and 1980s made it easier for critics of public schools, such as Schlafly and the Gablers, to air their views. By 1975, Pat Robertson had built the Christian Broadcasting Network into a media empire that reached an estimated 110 million viewers over more than a thousand cable-television systems. Jerry Falwell's *Old Time Gospel Hour* garnered a massive audience as well. The growth of cable television, with its myriad niche channels, brought Robertson, Falwell, and like-minded Christian evangelicals into the homes of millions of Americans. Rarely did they have a kind word to say about the public schools. Robertson, for instance, lamented the "gray mediocrity of present-day public schools" and claimed that they were "the most dangerous places in America."[124]

In this congenial environment, homeschooling boomed in the 1980s and 1990s. Estimating the number of children homeschooled in the United States has always been an imprecise exercise, but it seems unlikely their ranks ever numbered more than twenty thousand in the 1970s. The federal Department of Education estimated that this tally grew to as many as 244,000 students in the middle of the 1980s and to 355,000 by the end of that decade.[125] This exponential growth was evidenced in states like Maine; in 1981, state authorities received exactly four applications from parents looking to homeschool their children, but nine years later the number of applications had skyrocketed to 1,500.[126]

The emergence of a network of support organizations was crucial to the expansion of homeschooling in these years. It was easier for families to repudiate traditional schooling when they knew others had made a similarly dramatic choice. Parents felt more comfortable tackling the myriad practical and philosophical decisions involved in homeschooling when they could turn to peers for guidance.

John Holt's *Growing without Schooling* (hereafter referred to as *GWS*), which started publishing in 1977 and gained a thousand subscribers in its first year, facilitated the emergence of these networks. What the bare-bones newsletter lacked in style, it made up for in focus and passion. In addition to Holt's regular analyses, every issue of *GWS* was densely packed with a wide variety of practical information about homeschooling. Readers could learn about the formulation and implementation of homeschooling regulations in every state. The newsletter also carried blurbs about homeschooling books, testing strategies, educational games, teaching aids, and recordings. Event listings and want ads were featured too.

The pages of the newsletter brimmed with accounts of the challenges faced by families that chose to repudiate the schools. Some parents recounted struggles with school authorities who believed homeschooling was at best misguided and at worst downright illegal. Others described battles within their homes. There were successes, too: one mother happily announced that once she started homeschooling her son, he stopped wetting the bed, avoided the frequent illnesses that had plagued him at school, and grew two inches. There were many frank acknowledgments of their failings (both as teachers and as parents), but the prevailing ethos seemed to be triumphal: homeschooling was hard work but worth the enormous effort. And *GWS*, under Holt and under those who succeeded him at the newsletter after his death in 1985, rarely missed a chance to highlight the struggles and shortcomings of public schools.

Homeschooled children, undoubtedly prompted by their parents, also weighed in on the pages of *GWS*. Nine-year-old Shaina Dow explained that she left traditional school in first grade because "I wasn't learning and I was being treated badly." (Among her tormentors was a teacher who falsely accused her of stealing a classmate's toy car.) Taught at home by her mother, Shaina tackled social studies, science, math, and English while also having time to explore her neighborhood, play, and embark on field trips. She especially enjoyed reading; her assignments ranged from the works of Will Rogers and Laura Ingalls Wilder to the Bible. There were difficulties, to be sure, but she was thriving overall because "we don't do things like the school does."[127]

GWS was complemented by myriad homeschooling newsletters and publications in every state. Thanks in part to the bonds forged by such publications, by 1990 there were over sixty associations of homeschooling families in New York State alone. Parents and children in these groups met regularly for field trips and social gatherings. These events provided opportunities for homeschoolers to encourage one another as well as exchange information and ideas. Statewide and national conventions served a similar function, with homeschoolers sharing their experiences and resources. Attendees could sample curricula, learn about their legal rights, and even swap used books. Such events mitigated the isolation of homeschooling parents and bolstered their confidence.[128]

Statewide advocacy groups also fueled homeschooling's growth, particularly among conservative Christians. In Virginia there was the Home Education Association, which pledged to "help and encourage parents to fulfill their God-given rights and responsibilities to educate their own children." It was not uncommon for such groups to include in their mission statements explicit promises to promote narrowly literal interpretations of the Christian scriptures. In addition to providing spiritual uplift, these organizations served as clearinghouses for homeschoolers, distributing information and curricula. They lobbied lawmakers as well, pressing for changes that would lessen (or eliminate altogether) regulation of home education.[129]

It did not take long for savvy entrepreneurs to recognize the potential for profit in the homeschooling market. With his Christian Liberty Academy (CLA), Paul Lindstrom established a nonsecular equivalent to the Calvert School's correspondence curriculum. Lindstrom urged parents "to remove their K–12 children from public schools and, with or without local approval, simply teach them at home" with the unabashedly Christian curriculum sold by CLA. "Every subject," CLA stated in its promotional materials, "is to be studied with the purpose of discovering the God-given meaning contained in it."[130]

Christian publishers also entered the fray and dominated the homeschooling market in the 1980s with a wide array of educational materials. A Beka Book, founded in 1975, offered for purchase books and videos about subjects ranging from art and music to science and mathematics. The ideological orientation of these materials was difficult to miss. As one observer noted, "Every chapter in every book is written through a biblical filter." Indeed, a typical passage from a title in A Beka's junior-high science series reads, "The physical universe is God's machine; He designed it; He created it; and He established the physical laws by which it functions." In a section on budget planning, an elementary school math text published by Bob Jones University Press urged that at least 10 percent of an individual's or family's income be given "to the Lord." (After this allotment was made, money could be devoted to housing and savings.)[131]

How substantive and reliable were these materials? Critics argued that the science textbooks published by A Beka and Bob Jones University Press dismissed or simply ignored the prevailing consensus on evolution and any scientific findings that presupposed or supported it. (The offerings of both publishing houses promote a creationist perspective grounded in the book of Genesis.) In a California lawsuit challenging the state university system's rejection of courses using these texts as adequate preparation for entrance, former Stanford University president Donald Kennedy reviewed biology textbooks published by the two houses. He found that by "teaching students to reject scientific evidence and methodology whenever they might be inconsistent with the Bible," the books failed to "encourage critical thinking and the skills required for careful scientific analysis." Another expert in the same case concluded that the texts "reject the methodology generally accepted in science." The federal courts ruled in favor of the universities.[132]

Notes

1. Bestor, *Educational Wastelands*, 10, 11.

2. Schneider, *Beyond Test Scores*, 30.

3. Quoted in Guterson, *Family Matters*, 7.

4. Christian Reconstructionism is a fundamentalist Calvinist movement advocating restoration of Mosaic law. The movement declined considerably after 1990, but Christian Reconstructionist organizations such as the Chalcedon Foundation and American Vision remain active today.

5. Rushdoony, *Messianic Character of American Education*, 258.

6. Rushdoony, *Philosophy of the Christian Curriculum*, 12.

7. Hartman, *War for the Soul of America*, 85–86; Laats, *Fundamentalism and Education in the Scopes Era*, 195. Falwell is quoted in Leslie Francis and David Lankshear, eds., *Christian Perspectives on Church Schools: A Reader* (Harrisburg, PA: Morehouse, 1993), 274.

8. Carper and Devins, "Rendering unto Caesar," 99.

9. Hartman, *War for the Soul of America*, 85–86.

10. Laats, "Religion," 164.

11. Hunt and Carper, *Praeger Handbook of Faith-Based Schools*, 1:98.

12. Laats, "Religion," 170.

13. Laats, "Religion," 170.

14. Angulo, *Miseducation*, 170.

15. Howard is quoted in Diamond, *Spiritual Warfare*, 88; Carper and Hunt, *Dissenting Tradition in American Education*, 205.

16. Wilhoit, *Christian Education and the Search for Meaning*, 74.

17. Carper and Devins, "Rendering unto Caesar," 100.

18. Carper and Devins, 99–113.

19. Carper and Devins, "Rendering unto Caesar," 107; State ex rel Douglas v. Faith Baptist Church, 301 N.W.2d 571, 573–81 (1981).

20. Carper and Devins, "Rendering unto Caesar," 99–113.

21. Carper, "*Whisner* Decision," 283.

22. Carper, 284.

23. Carper, "*Whisner* Decision," 281–302; State v. Whisner, 47 Ohio St. 2d 181 (1976), 197–223; Carper and Hunt, *Dissenting Tradition in American Education*, 232–34.

24. Devins, "State Regulation of Christian Schools," 374.

25. Carper, "*Whisner* Decision," 281–302.

26. Moore and Moore, "Dangers of Early Schooling," 58–62.

27. Moore and Moore, 58–62.

28. Klicka, *Home School Heroes*, 27–30.

29. Knowles, Marlow, and Muchmore, "From Pedagogy to Ideology," 200; Freire, *Pedagogy of the Oppressed*.

30. David and Micki Colfax, *Homeschooling for Excellence: How to Take Charge of Your Child's Education—And Why You Absolutely Must* (New York: Warner Books, 2009).

31. Jonathan Kozol, *Free Schools* (New York: Houghton Mifflin, 1972).

32. Kozol, *Free Schools*, 11.

33. Knowles, Marlow, and Muchmore, "From Pedagogy to Ideology," 203; Jonathan Kozol, *Death at an Early Age: The Destruction of the Hearts and Minds of Negro Children in the Boston Public Schools* (New York: Bantam, 1968), 182.

34. Allen Graubard, "Alternative Education: The Free School Movement in the United States," *ERIC Clearinghouse on Media and Technology*, (1972): 6–7.

35. Miller, *Free Schools, Free People*, 3.

36. Kozol, *Free Schools*, 30–40, 62; Ben Joravsky, "The Long, Strange Trip of Bill Ayers," *Chicago Reader*, November 8, 1990.

37. "Teaching Children at Home," *Time*, December 4, 1978, 78.

38. Illich, *Deschooling Society*, xix.

39. Cayley, *Ivan Illich in Conversation*, 68.

40. Miller, *Free Schools, Free People*, 138; Illich, *Deschooling Society*, 47.

41. Holt, *Instead of Education*, 3–4.

42. Holt and Farenga, *Teach Your Own*, xxxiv.

43. Holt and Farenga, 238.

44. Holt and Farenga, 72.

45. Holt and Farenga, 33–34.

46. Hal Bennett, *No More Public School* (New York: Random House, 1972), unpaginated front matter.

47. Patricia Heidenry, "Parent and Child: One Couple's Experiment with Do-It-Yourself Education," *New York Times*, October 19, 1975.

48. Margaret Heidenry, "My Parents Were Educational Anarchists," *New York Times*, November 8, 2011.

49. Ed Nagel, "A School without a School," *Mothering*, Summer 1979, http://www.nalsas.org/article.html.

50. Knowles, Marlow, and Muchmore, "From Pedagogy to Ideology," 206.

51. Holt and Farenga, *Teach Your Own*, 238.

52. Unnamed parent quoted in "What Parents Learn from Homeschooling," *Growing without Schooling* 87 (n.d.): 3.

53. Bumstead, "Educating Your Child at Home," 97–100, 98 (quoting Holt).

54. "Teaching Children at Home," *Time*, 78.

55. "John Holt on the Phil Donohue Show Discussing Homeschooling," 1981, accessed February 7, 2016, https://www.youtube.com/watch?v=fXLWPpln0rQ.

56. National Commission on Excellence in Education, *A Nation at Risk: The Full Account*, 2nd ed. (Washington, DC: USA Research, 1983), 5.

57. See Lawrence Cremin, *Popular Education and Its Discontents* (New York: Harper & Row, 1989), 39ff.

58. See Ulric Neisser, *The Rising Curve: Long Term Gains in IQ and Related Measures* (Washington, DC: American Psychological Association, 1998). Fluid intelligence is defined as an ability to solve novel problems by planning approaches to complex tasks and employing working memory, effective information processing, and spatial relational understanding. It has been shown to rise in national populations (including that of the United States) in which the cognitive demands of schooling have increased. See James R. Flynn, "Massive IQ Gains in 14 Nations: What IQ Tests Really Mean," *Psychological Bulletin* 101, (1987): 171–91; James R. Flynn, "IQ Gains Over Time: Toward Finding the Causes," in *The Rising Curve*, ed. Ulric Neisser, 25–66.

59. Klicka, *Home School Heroes*, 4.

60. Meyer v. Nebraska, 262 U.S. 390 (1923); Pierce v. Society of the Sisters, 268 U.S. 510 (1925), 535.

61. Meyer v. Nebraska, 262 U.S. 404, 412 (1923).

62. *Meyer v. Nebraska*, 262 U.S. at 400. For insightful discussion of the social significance of the court's decisions, see Robert Kunzman, "Education, Schooling, and Children's Rights: The Complexity of Homeschooling," *Educational Theory* 62, no. 1 (2012): 75–89, 78.

63. Farrington v. Tokushige, 273 U.S. 284 (1927).

64. Prince v. Massachusetts, 321 U.S. 158 (1944), at 160, 162–63.

65. *Prince v. Massachusetts*, 321 U.S. 158, 160–63. Why the court used a masculine pronoun is unclear.

66. *Prince v. Massachusetts*, 321 U.S. at 165.

67. *Prince v. Massachusetts*, 321 U.S. at 166–67.

68. *Prince v. Massachusetts*, 321 U.S. at 165–66.

69. Wisconsin v. Yoder, 406 U.S. 205 (1972), 213.

70. *Wisconsin v. Yoder*, 406 U.S. at 233.

71. *Wisconsin v. Yoder*, 406 U.S. 205, 215.

72. *Wisconsin v. Yoder*, 406 U.S. at 233, 222, 224.

73. *Wisconsin v. Yoder*, 406 U.S. at 236.

74. Bd. of Ed. of Cent. Sch. Dist. No. 1 v. Allen, 392 U.S. 236, 245–47 (1968).

75. People v. Turner, 263 P.2d 685 (1953), appeal dismissed for want of a substantial federal question, 347 U.S. 972 (1954).

76. See Washington v. Confederated Bands & Tribes of the Yakima Indian Nation, 439 U.S. 463, 476 n.20 (1979) ("[S]ummary dismissals are of course, to be taken as rulings on the merits, in the sense that they rejected the 'specific challenges presented in the statement of jurisdiction' and left 'undisturbed the judgment appealed from.'"); and Mandel v. Bradley, 432 U.S. 173, 176 (1977) ("Summary affirmances and dismissals for want of a substantial federal question without doubt reject the specific challenges presented in the statement of jurisdiction. . . . They do prevent lower courts from coming to opposite conclusions on the precise issues presented and necessarily decided by those actions."). The Supreme Court has noted that a summary dismissal should not be viewed as adopting the lower court's rationale for its decision, but it does have the same precedential value as does an opinion of the Supreme Court after briefing and oral argument on the merits. Neely v. Newton, 149 F.3d 1074, 1079 (10th Cir. 1998) ("The Supreme Court has cautioned that for purposes of determining the binding effect of a summary action, the action should not be interpreted as adopting the rationale of the lower court, but rather as affirming only the judgment of that court."; "[I]f the Court has branded a question as unsubstantial, it remains so except when doctrinal developments indicate otherwise."). Hicks v. Miranda, 422 U.S. 332, 344 (1975).

77. See, e.g., Combs v. Homer-Ctr. Sch. Dist., 540 F.3d 231, 250–52 (3d Cir. 2008); Crites v. Smith, 826 S.W.2d 459, 466–67 (Ct. App. Tenn. 1991); State v. Riddle, 285 S.E.2d 359, 361–62 (W. Va. 1981); and In re Lippitt, No. 38421, 1978 Ohio App. LEXIS 9867 at *18–23 (Ohio Ct. App. Mar. 9, 1978). See also Grigg v. Commonwealth, 224 Va. 356, 361 (1982) (upholding the finding that children of homeschoolers were "in need of services" because of parental education neglect, given that parents were not state-certified teachers or tutors, and noting the unquestionable authority of the state to require this qualification); and Gaither, *Homeschool*, 177–78 (collecting cases).

78. See, e.g., Combs v. Homer-Ctr. Sch. Dist., 540 F.3d 231, 250–52 (3d Cir. 2008) (reporting and superintendent review requirements); People v. Bennett, 442 Mich. 316, 332, 501 N.W.2d 106, 114 (1993) (teaching certificate required); Clonlara, Inc. v. Runkel, 722 F. Supp. 1442, 1457 (E.D. Mich. 1989) (teaching certificate

required); Murphy v. State of Ark., 852 F.2d 1039, 1041 (8th Cir. 1988) (upholding several oversight measures for homeschoolers); Blount v. Dep't of Educ. & Cultural Servs., 551 A.2d 1377, 1385 (Me. 1988) (prior approval requirement); State v. Patzer, 382 N.W.2d 631, 639 (N.D. 1986); and In re Kilroy, 121 Misc.2d 98, 467 N.Y.S.2d 318 (1983) (home visits). One short-lived exception, People v. DeJonge, 501 N.W.2d 127, 140 (Mich. 1993), is discussed below.

79. Employment Division v. Smith, 494 U.S. 872.

80. See, e.g., Keeton v. Anderson-Wiley, 664 F.3d 865, 880 (11th Cir. 2011); Combs v. Homer-Ctr. Sch. Dist., 540 F.3d 231, 246–47 (3d Cir. 2008); Leebaert v. Harrington, 332 F.3d 134, 143–44 (2d Cir. 2003); Watchtower Bible & Tract Soc'y of N.Y., Inc. v. Stratton, 240 F.3d 553, 561 (6th Cir. 2001); Henderson v. Kennedy, 253 F.3d 12, 19 (D.C. Cir. 2001); and Douglas Cty. v. Anaya, 269 Neb. 552, 557, 694 N.W.2d 601, 605 (2005) ("Although Smith discussed prior decisions that involved not only the Free Exercise Clause but other constitutional provisions, the Court did not hold that a strict scrutiny review is required simply because more than one constitutional right might be implicated.").

81. See, e.g., Workman v. Mingo Cty. Bd. of Educ., 419 F. App'x 348, 353 (4th Cir. 2011).

82. See, e.g., Brown v. Hot, Sexy and Safer Productions, Inc., 68 F.3d 525, 539 (1st Cir.1995); Miller v. Reed, 176 F.3d 1202, 1207–08 (9th Cir.1999); and Swanson v. Guthrie Independent School District No. I–L, 135 F.3d 694, 699–700 (10th Cir.1998).

83. See, e.g., Brown v. Buhman, 947 F. Supp. 2d 1170, 1222 (D. Utah 2013).

84. Troxel v. Granville 530 U.S. 57. A majority of the court's members did in their opinions speak of parental control over children's lives, even when not tied to religious belief, as a fundamental right under the federal Constitution. But absent a majority opinion pronouncing that to be the case, such statements are not authoritative.

85. Gaither, *Homeschool*, 179ff.

86. Holt and Farenga, *Teach Your Own*, 272.

87. State v. Massa, 95 N.J. Super. 382, 231 A.2d 252 (Morris County Ct. Law Div. 1967).

88. People v. Levisen, 404 Ill. 574, 90 N.E.2d 213 (1950).

89. Scoma v. Chicago Board of Education, 391 F. Supp. 452 (N.D. Ill. 1974).

90. *Scoma v. Chicago Board of Education*, 391 F. Supp. at 460.

91. Perchemlides vs. Frizzle (CA-16641, Massachusetts Superior Court 1978).

92. See Shulman, *Constitutional Parent*, 3–4.

93. *The Day* (New London, CT), May 5, 1988; *The Intelligencer* (Doylestown, PA), June 21, 1981.

94. Bennion, *Polygamy in Primetime*, 229.

95. *Growing without Schooling* 1, no. 4 (May/June, 1978): 44; Scott Somerville, "The Politics of Survival: Home Schoolers and the Law," accessed February 3,

2014, http://www.hslda.org/docs/nche/000010/politicsofsurvival.asp; Holt and Far-enga, *Teach Your Own.*

96. Kimberly Yuracko, "Education Off the Grid: Constitutional Constraints on Homeschooling," *California Law Review* 96 (2008): 123–84.

97. Somerville, "Politics of Survival."

98. Jessica Huseman, "Small Group Goes to Great Lengths to Block Home-schooling Regulation," *ProPublica: Journalism in the Public Interest*, August 27, 2015, accessed October 2, 2015, https://www.propublica.org/article/small-group-goes-great-lengths-to-block-homeschooling-regulation.

99. Texas Education Agency v. Leeper, 893 S.W.2d 432 (Tex. 1994).

100. Stevens, *Kingdom of Children*, 14.

101. Kathy Collins, "Children Are Not Chattel," *Free Inquiry* 7, no. 4 (1987): 11.

102. People v. DeJonge, 442 Mich. 266 (1993).

103. People v. Bennett (After Remand), 442 Mich. 316; 501 N.W.2d 106 (1993).

104. Kissinger v. Bd. of Trs. of Ohio State Univ., 5 F.3d 177, 180 (6th Cir.1993).

105. Jonathan L. v. Superior Court, 165 Cal. App. 4th 1074, 1091, 81 Cal. Rptr. 3d 571, 584 (2008).

106. Klicka, *Home School Heroes*, 278.

107. Micah Ann Wixom, "State Homeschool Policies: A Patchwork of Provi-sions," *Education Commission of the States*, July 2015, accessed October 2, 2015, http://www.ecs.org/clearinghouse/01/20/42/12042.pdf.

108. Pennsylvania eliminated a similar requirement in 2014. Today, parents must instead submit a certification of "appropriate education" from a private eval-uator of the parents' choosing.

109. See Jennifer Miller, "Yiddish Isn't Enough: A Yeshiva Graduate Fights for Secular Studies in Hasidic Education," *New York Times*, November 21, 2014. (The article reports conversations with two school-district superintendents who indicated they were unaware they had a responsibility to enforce regulations gov-erning private and home schools, and quotes a letter from the State Board of Re-gents stating that nonpublic schools "operate outside the scope of state-mandated general education requirements and oversight.")

110. N.Y. Comp. Codes R. & Regs. tit. 8, § 100.10. See also Huseman, "Small Group Goes to Great Lengths," *Pro Publica*, August 27, 2015.

111. Motoko Rich, "Home Schooling: More Pupils, Less Regulation," *New York Times*, January 4, 2015.

112. See Melissa Hipolit, "Goochland Parents Upset about New Home School Policy," *WTRV News*, http://wtvr.com/2015/01/09/goochland-parents-upset-about-new-home-school-policy/.

113. Susan Svrluga, "Thousands of Virginia Students Aren't Required to Get an Education," *Washington Post*, September 11, 2012.

114. *The Spokesman-Review* (Spokane, WA), July 19, 1993.

115. See In re Kurowski, 161 N.H. 578, 582, 20 A.3d 306, 310 (2011). See also In

re Marriage of David H.B. and Linda E.B. (Ill. App. 2015) (transferring custody from father to mother because of the father's insistence on continuing with home-schooling that the mother asserted, and the court found, was deficient).

116. Huseman, "Small Group Goes to Great Lengths," *Pro Publica*, August 27, 2015.

117. Murphy, *Homeschooling in America*, 38.

118. Reagan, *New Reagan Revolution*, 189–90.

119. Moore, *Suing for America's Soul*, 65–66; Carter, *Culture of Disbelief*, 166.

120. Eugene Provenzo, *Religious Fundamentalism and American Education: The Battle for the Public Schools* (Albany: State University of New York Press, 1990), 23.

121. Laats, *The Other School Reformers*, 186–205.

122. Laats, *The Other School Reformers*, 193–97.

123. Schlafly, "Child Abuse in the Classroom," 94–104.

124. Robertson, *Collected Works of Pat Robertson*, 154, 157.

125. Murphy, *Homeschooling in America*, 8.

126. Sam Allis, "Teaching Kids at Home," *Time*, October 22, 1990, 84–85.

127. Shania Dow, "9-Year-Old's Opinion," *Growing without Schooling* 49, 8–9.

128. Cindy Soehner, "There Are Benefits in Homeschooling," *New York Times*, December 17, 1989.

129. Klicka, *Home School Heroes*, 25–26.

130. Gaither, *Homeschool*, 114–15.

131. Parsons, *Inside America's Christian Schools*, 42–43.

132. Ass'n of Christian Sch. Int'l v. Stearns, 679 F. Supp. 2d 1083 (CD. Cal. 2008), aff'd, 362 F. App'x 640 (9th Cir. 2010).

CHAPTER THREE

Homeschooling Comes into Its Own

The national media took note of homeschooling's coming of age. In some ways, it was an irresistible story: with the public schools seemingly beyond repair, some idealistic parents were taking matters into their own hands by providing old-fashioned instruction around the kitchen table. In 1990, both *Time* and the *New York Times* ran laudatory articles marveling at the increasing number of children who were being educated at home. "Home schooling—motivated by the notion that learning should be unpolluted by the classroom—is an eccentricity that has become a national movement," the *Time* article notes. This account and the one published in the *New York Times* feature glowing portrayals of homeschooled children and their parents. The youngsters in one family depicted in the *Times* story had become "independent thinkers" who had been given the freedom to pursue their curiosities.[1] Of another homeschooled child, reporter William Celis wrote, "He seems to be benefiting from personal attention and from being able to learn at his own pace."[2]

It was clear from these stories that some homeschooling parents were concerned with something besides providing their children with a learning experience and moral instruction superior to those found in public schools. Many mentioned an ostensible concern for physical health and safety. One Fundamentalist mother who homeschooled her four boys pointed out to *Time* that, as the article puts it, "there are no drugs in her bathroom, or switchblades in the hallways." Another parent, explaining in 1981 why she had decided to teach her children at home, stated, "Public schools are pushing us away with their drugs, their sex, their drinking, their smoking."[3] These parents insisted that the overly permissive public schools simply had become unsafe.

Indeed, for many parents who made the decision to educate their children at home, social and cultural concerns dwarfed worries about the supposedly ineffective pedagogy of the public schools. One homeschooling sourcebook bemoans the schools' "failure to provide an environment in which children can grow in moral strength and integrity. Most parents, whether or not they are teaching at home, are worried about drugs, violence, promiscuity, and teen pregnancy." The book compares the relatively benign hijinks of students in the 1940s (running in the hallways, chewing gum) with the much more dire transgressions of their counterparts in the 1980s (arson, murder, extortion, and gang warfare). The book's authors assert that such dangers are nonexistent in the traditional home, which promises a safe and secure environment.[4]

Beneath the surface of homeschoolers' discourse about "safety," some perceive implicit worries about racial integration. Certainly homeschooling has been particularly popular in communities where courts have ordered school districts to use busing plans to create more racially balanced schools. (Such plans proliferated nationally after the US Supreme Court's 1971 ruling in *Swann v. Charlotte-Mecklenburg Board of Education*, upholding such order.) In the Los Angeles area, an antibusing group created an educational alternative called the Home Tutorial Program in 1978. Eighty-nine percent of the participants in the program were white, and they stressed that they were motivated to keep their children safe from harm and within their neighborhoods. Three scholars who studied the program concluded that these rationales were essentially proxies for aversion to racial mixing.[5] In the end, some parents appeared really to be balking at sending their children to integrated schools.

The homeschooling movement continued to comprise two basic and quite divergent groups—"pedagogues" and "ideologues." The former category included the likes of those who, taking their cue from John Holt, sought out alternatives to traditional schooling because they believed it failed to deliver the kind of meaningful education that would help children fully develop their myriad creative and intellectual talents. Meanwhile, for ideologues, predominant were worries that the public schools represented a direct and dire threat to both their faith and their authority as parents.[6]

In 1990, Michael Farris of HSLDA joked that, of the parents who had joined his organization, "We have everything from Black Muslims to Jews and one woman who is a cross between a Zen Buddhist and Winnie the Pooh." However, it was clear by that year that the "ideologues" described by Jane Van Galen had come to predominate in not only HSLDA but also in the broader homeschooling movement in the United States.

One researcher estimated that, by 1990, an overwhelming majority of homeschoolers—roughly 90 percent of them—were conservative Christians. Their adherence to traditional gender roles helped to catalyze this growth: wives, not expected to work outside the home, could more readily make themselves available to direct the education of children.[7]

Parents were not shy in articulating their religious motivations for homeschooling. One mother in Texas told a newspaper reporter that her family had decided to teach their children at home after their public school put on a completely secular Christmas play. Another parent from Texas explained, "Our issue in home schooling wasn't purely academics. It was more out of religious conviction. We wanted to pass on to our children our Christian faith, our biblical values and standards. And that cannot be done in the public school anymore."[8] Of course, parents have ample time outside school hours to "pass on" their beliefs to their children, if by "pass on" one means convey or teach about, so implicit was a perception that public schools were not simply devoid of religious instruction but actually antithetical to faith and undermining parents' efforts to ensure their children would always hold the same beliefs. Research suggests that this worry is misplaced; one of the more reliable studies of homeschooling outcomes found that children with deeply religious parents display the same beliefs and behaviors regardless of whether they are homeschooled or attend public school.[9] But any parent can relate to this worry about bad influences in public schools. Also typically unarticulated, though, were the reasons why parents did not send their children to a religious school. Those reasons likely varied significantly from one family to another.

Kip and Mona Lisa Harding chose to homeschool their children—all ten of them—in part because of their strong religious beliefs. Like many parents who turned away from public schools, they found justification in specific passages of the Bible, including Deuteronomy 6:6–7, in which God advises, "Keep these words that I am commanding you today in your heart. Recite them to your children and talk about them when you are at home and when you are away, when you lie down and when you rise." For the Hardings, the import of these words was unmistakable. They wrote that they "do not feel that strangers should educate our children" and that "Christians do best to keep their kids with them as much as possible." The couple chose to homeschool because they felt "as Christians it is our God-given responsibility to keep our children home when they are young and impressionable." (The Hardings' approach proved to be extraordinarily successful: their seven oldest children all started college by age twelve, and their daughter Serreneh became a practicing physician at age twenty-two.)[10]

Many Christian homeschoolers believe that in order to properly superintend their child's spiritual and intellectual development, they must exert complete control over the vulnerable youngster's environment. Outlining their approach to educating at home, one family described their children as being "like tender young plants" whose nurture needs to be overseen by a skilled "gardener" (parent) in a "greenhouse" (home) where pernicious influences could be minimized. "The greenhouse allows the gardener to control all the elements of the environment," they wrote in a blog posting, "so that the plant grows into a sturdy, mature plant with deep, well anchored roots, and a strong supportive trunk." If all went according to plan in this ideal homeschooling environment, "by the time [the children] complete the high school years, they are finally anchored in GOD'S WORD, and have learned to stand against the world."[11]

Of course, given the number and diversity of Christian denominations, there have been myriad different practitioners of "Christian homeschooling." A great many are conservative evangelicals who provide for children an education grounded in a literal interpretation of the Bible on such matters as the creation of the universe and the origins of life. As Robert Kunzman describes it, "In the eyes of fundamentalists, the sanctity of sacred scriptures trumps all human sources of knowledge and understanding. For conservative Christian homeschoolers, this means that 'if it doesn't line up with the Word, throw it out.'"[12] Parents who follow other strains of non-mainline Christianity—among them Mormons, Jehovah's Witnesses, and Seventh-day Adventists—have turned to homeschooling as well. One Witness parent, describing her decision to homeschool, wrote that she and her husband "endeavor to raise our children to serve Jehovah to the best of their ability. Spiritual things come first, and then all other things, including education, wrap around that."[13]

The Christianization of homeschooling—driven less by a concern with *how* children are taught and more by worries over *what* they are taught—represented a marked shift from the movement's origins in the 1960s. In that formative period, most of the reformers advocating for educational alternatives had a largely secular orientation, and their overall ideological leanings were distinctly anti-authoritarian. They hoped to foster independent thinking and learning—the very things that would undermine strict adherence to any kind of dogma, religious or otherwise. This was a far cry from the orientation of those who later came to predominate in homeschooling. Charting this change, one careful study of the movement asserts that its focus shifted over time "from pedagogy to ideology."[14]

Milton Gaither, in his seminal history of homeschooling, observes that John Holt and Ray Moore were increasingly displaced as leaders in the 1980s "as a younger and more aggressive group of baby-boomer Christian leaders emerged." Their ranks included Gregg Harris, an evangelical Christian who had been inspired by hearing Moore on James Dobson's radio program. Harris was no pedagogue: he "believed home schooling could lead to a renewal of traditional Christian family living," according to one account. Harris worked for Moore but then moved on in order to promote homeschooling more directly as a Christian enterprise. His "Christian Life Workshops" reached thousands, as did *The Teaching Home*, a magazine focusing on evangelical homeschooling.[15]

The explosive growth of homeschooling, with its increasingly unmistakable ideological cast, did not come with widespread acceptance among professional educators. Indeed, some of the most vehement criticisms of homeschooling were articulated by the National Education Association (NEA), the nation's largest teachers' union. The organization began voicing its opposition to homeschooling in the late 1980s and has never tempered its critique. A resolution passed by the organization in 1988 (and reaffirmed several times since) baldly asserted that homeschooling programs were inherently inferior to traditional schooling because they "cannot provide the student with a comprehensive education experience."[16] What exactly is necessarily missing from homeschooling, the NEA did not say. Other portions of the resolution, as it has evolved—for example, contending that homeschooling parents should receive no financial assistance to improve their instruction and that public schools should not permit homeschooled youth to join athletic teams—appear to confirm the widespread perception that the NEA is at least as concerned with protecting its members' professional credentials as it is with the developmental needs of homeschooled children. If homeschooling is permitted, the NEA's position is that it should be subject to teacher-licensing and curriculum requirements.

But the real legal battles today are not over efforts to impose greater oversight of homeschooling; that seems to be a lost cause for the public education establishment. Instead, the clear trend, relentlessly pushed by homeschooling advocates, is toward further elimination of what little oversight exists, and indeed toward the channeling of state education funding to homeschoolers.[17] In recent years HSLDA has had significant success striking regulations in Pennsylvania, Utah, Iowa, New Hampshire,

Minnesota, West Virginia, and other states.[18] A number of states now have various schemes for financially supporting homeschooling, most taking the form of tax deductions and credits, and HSLDA and other homeschooling advocacy groups ensure that these states do not attach any accountability measures to the funding.[19] In Minnesota, for example, there is a refundable state-tax credit of up to $1000 available for homeschoolers, to reimburse them for the cost of educational materials and equipment (including computers and musical instruments), the receipt of which does not trigger any reporting or assessment requirement.[20] Some members of Congress have repeatedly tried to pass federal voucher legislation that would redirect federal education funds to private schools and homeschools. Although these funding mechanisms present a propitious opportunity for providing some protection to children whose schooling is now "off the radar," insofar as they are voluntary but create an incentive for participation, legislators do not seize that opportunity. HSLDA actually opposes government funding of homeschooling in overt forms such as vouchers, out of concern it could lead to regulation.

For those who have opposed such legislative succor, homeschooling's weaknesses are not limited to its baleful effects on children's intellectual development. Teachers' organizations have expressed concern that keeping youngsters out of traditional school impairs their social skills. Not only were they receiving substandard academic training, they also were failing to learn how to interact with others, including individuals from different backgrounds. As the executive director of the National School Boards Association put it, "We think that children should be in the traditional setting because home schooling takes away from a child's social skills and isolates children racially and ethnically."[21]

State and local education officials have sometimes seconded these objections. Numerous career educators were perplexed by the notion that parents—most with little or no formal training as teachers—would presume to supplant them. Michigan's state supervisor of public instruction, echoing the prevailing sentiment of his professional colleagues, mused, "If you need a license to cut hair, you should have one to mold a kid's mind."[22] It is hard to underestimate the disdain felt by these educators for homeschooling. A survey of public-school superintendents conducted by the *American School Board Journal* in 1997 found that nearly three-quarters of them did not believe homeschooling was sufficiently regulated by the states. More than 90 percent of them believed homeschooling to be the worst kind of education for children.[23]

Homeschoolers dismissed such criticisms as being primarily grounded in entrenched public educators' desire to maintain an immensely lucrative stranglehold on schooling; homeschooling came under fire because it represented a financial threat to teachers and school districts. With state funding for education allotted on a per-pupil basis, schools that lost students to home instruction saw their state funding diminish. As homeschoolers saw it, state education officials did not have the best interests of children at heart; they were mainly concerned about protecting their turf.

The parents providing instruction at home overwhelmingly were mothers. According to some estimates, they constituted 95 percent of homeschool teachers. The gendered nature of homeschool instruction dovetailed with the prevailing notion among conservative evangelical Christians that women should fully submit to a husband's authority. To do this, wives must devote themselves to the domestic sphere and child-rearing while their husbands pursue careers outside the home. "The wife's job is to stay home and home school the husband's children," said Rachel Coleman in describing the approach of her evangelical Christian parents, who homeschooled her. "That goes back to the 19th century, when men and women had separate spheres. The man does the public things. The woman is in the home."[24]

As Jennifer Lois has chronicled, the demands on these mothers could be considerable, especially since homeschool families tend to be larger than average. They are called on not only to provide academic instruction to their children but also to manage myriad household duties, such as cooking, cleaning, and ferrying their child to activities and doctor's appointments. The weight of such burdens could leave women feeling overwhelmed, but many found their labors empowering and rewarding.[25]

The growth of educational technology facilitated the work of these women. Some research has suggested homeschoolers tend to be early adopters of computer technologies. This was evidenced in the first issue of *Wired* magazine in 1993, which included an article marveling at the array of computer hardware and software used by homeschoolers Bill and Mary Pride. Over the next two decades, homeschoolers embraced the internet and World Wide Web as essential means of facilitating their teaching at home. The increasingly widespread availability of broadband internet technologies provided easy access to emerging homeschooling support networks and curricular materials. One scholar posits that these technologies have become "a form of social glue binding a growing and increasingly diverse population of homeschool families together."[26] Linked together by the web, homeschoolers forged communities and shared information via websites, message boards, and even chat rooms.

For homeschooling, technology has been nothing short of a "game-changer," according to one recent account. Surveying this evolving landscape, Mary Rice Hasson, a Fellow at the Ethics and Public Policy Center in Washington, DC, notes that "students can communicate with educators, tutors, and peers using secure chat rooms, Skype, and instant messaging, providing opportunities for both academic instruction and peer discussions. New resources and curriculum materials use audio and video technology podcasts, webcasts, digital microscopes, video streaming of documentaries and educational videos—as well as hands-on resources, helping parents to incorporate the latest methods of instruction into learning environments most suited to their children's needs." Furthermore, with the pervasive use of smartphones and social media, homeschooled students can have robust social networks, engaging peers in a way that is not contingent on physical interactions at a traditional school.[27]

No one appreciates the connections between homeschooling and technology better than the growing number of tech-savvy entrepreneurs who are choosing to educate their children at home. A 2015 *Wired* article chronicles the rise of the "techie homeschooler," an innovative parent who has come to reject traditional models of education as outdated and ineffective. Applying the lessons they learned in places like Silicon Valley, such parents are creating new educational models on their own, in their homes. "There is a way of thinking within the tech and startup community where you look at the world and go, 'Is the way we do things now really the best way to do it,'" one parent told the magazine. "If you look at schools with this mentality, really the only possible conclusion is 'Heck, I could do this better myself out of my garage!'"[28]

As the experiences of "techie homeschoolers" shows, there remain many secular reasons for homeschooling. Another example is the parent who takes a child out of school after the child has been bullied. Intimidating behavior always has been an unfortunate dimension of school life, but the advent of social media seems to have exacerbated the problem by providing more venues for threatening conduct. Homeschooling has provided a welcome refuge for many children menaced by their peers at school. The director of a statewide homeschool organization in Washington said in 2014 that about one-third of the new families who came to homeschooling in that state did so as the result of a bullying incident.[29]

Other parents have turned to homeschooling because of frustration with the bureaucracy and red tape that seem endemic to the public schools. In her 2002 book *Real-Life Homeschooling*, Rhonda Barfield profiles a couple named Ann and Glen who had decided to homeschool their daughter before she started third grade. Their problem with their local school system centered on what Barfield describes as the "bureaucratic indifference" of administrators who seemed not to care very much about the welfare of the students they were paid to serve. The family was particularly appalled that repeated redistricting had resulted in some of their daughter's classmates enrolling in different schools in three successive years—an incredible disruption that was sure to negatively affect their academic development. "Children are not ping-pong balls, to be batted about at will," the frustrated father told Barfield. "Our efforts to put some common sense into administrative decisions affecting the education of children became time consuming and frustratingly unsuccessful. It was time to go."[30]

Some parents of children identified with autism spectrum disorders (ASD) also have turned to homeschooling after experiencing frustrations with school authorities. In a 2011 study of the experiences of such mothers and fathers, Karen Hurlbutt found that they often turned to homeschooling when school authorities proved unwilling or unable to provide effective programming for children with ASD. One dissatisfied parent described how her daughter was directed to a school where she would spend 80 percent of her school day working with paraprofessionals who had no training in working with ASD students. Another parent said that she had grown exhausted attempting to "fight with the school with every issue" relating to her child's schooling. The parents surveyed by Hurlbutt devised diverse, unique, and individualized approaches for teaching their children, and the work could be exhausting. However, they generally seemed to agree that the youngsters were "better off at home," as one mother put it.[31]

Aided by the proliferation of technology and a growing dissatisfaction with the doleful effects of "high-stakes testing" on children's experience in public schools, homeschooling only gained in popularity in the 2000s. No alternative to public schooling has grown at a greater rate in recent decades. The National Center for Education Statistics (NCES) estimates there were about 1.5 million homeschooled students in the United States in 2007—a 74 percent increase over the 1999 tally (850,000 students).[32] Between 2007 and 2012, the NCES estimates, the number of homeschooled children nationally grew by nearly 20 percent, far outpacing the growth of enrollment in public schools during that period (around 1 percent). The NCES's latest report suggests growth slowed after 2012 and the number of homeschooled children is now about 1.7 million.[33] This represents just 3.3 percent of the school-age population but is comparable to the percentage of school-aged children enrolled in more widely-scrutinized "school choice" options, such as charter schools, and also similar to the number of children attending Catholic schools today.[34]

With these increased numbers has come broader public acceptance of homeschooling as a legitimate alternative form of education. In 1985, when the journal *Phi Delta Kappan* conducted a survey asking if homeschooling was good for the nation, only 16 percent of the respondents answered in the affirmative. That number rose to 41 percent when the same question was asked in 2001—a clear sign of homeschooling's growing repute across American society.[35] Undoubtedly it would be even higher today.

The foregoing vignettes illustrate how families have turned to homeschooling for a variety of interrelated factors. The most common reasons for homeschooling that parents report in recent surveys are "concern about the environment of other schools, such as safety, drugs, or negative peer pressure" (80 percent), "desire to provide moral instruction" (67 percent) or "religious instruction" (51 percent), and "dissatisfaction with academic instruction at other schools" (61 percent).[36] "Other schools" presumably would include not only public schools but also private schools, which is the alternative to public schools that first comes to mind for most people, so there is an implicit message to operators of religious and other private schools as well. Many parents express a desire to maintain a closer bond with their children than they think possible if peer relationships begin to divert the children's attention.[37]

The experiences of one poster child of homeschooling, University of Florida (and later National Football League) quarterback Tim Tebow, show how secular and sacred motivations could neatly align for homeschoolers. Tebow's parents were dedicated Christian missionaries who began homeschooling their five children in 1982. "At the time, some people thought they were nuts," he later wrote. "Some wondered if homeschooling was even legal!" Tim, the youngest, showed enormous promise as a football player but faced a serious obstacle to playing in college: as a homeschooled child, he had no high school team on which he could showcase his talents. In response to his plight, Florida enacted a measure commonly known as the "Tim Tebow law," which permits homeschooled students to play for teams fielded by schools in their school districts. Although he never enrolled there as a student, Tebow starred for Allen

Nease High School and earned a scholarship to the University of Florida. His career at the latter included two national championships and, in 2007, the Heisman Trophy, awarded annually to the nation's top collegiate football player. The Heisman was seen as a watershed for homeschoolers—a kind of validation that they were "real" students whose talents extended beyond mastery of the Christian scriptures.[38]

Many aspiring athletes have followed Tebow's lead into the realm of homeschooling. They tend, though, to be involved in individual sports like gymnastics, swimming, and figure skating that are commonly practiced away from school, rather than in team endeavors like football that are typically tied to a school. Homeschooling provides many logistical advantages to students interested in these other sports. The inflexible schedules imposed by traditional schools limit opportunities for practice for youngsters interested in training intensively in individual sports. Homeschooling allows young athletes to train for longer periods and at times when facilities are uncrowded. A *Washington Post* story about homeschooled gymnasts in Maryland describes a group of young women who trained from 8 a.m. to 2:30 p.m. every weekday (for a total of roughly thirty hours per week). Once their daily practice was completed, they headed home for short periods of homeschooling with their mothers. Their parents justified this arrangement by explaining that, "without classmates, these driven children will finish their lessons in a few hours," in the words of the article.[39]

Homeschooling authority Mitchell Stevens of Stanford University has lauded such arrangements, arguing that they allow parents to "organize learning around the passions and skills of their children." Other observers, however, have taken a less sanguine view of parents who apparently subordinate their children's schooling to a pursuit of athletic glory. Political scientist Rob Reich (also of Stanford) insists that "there is valid moral criticism of parents who endanger their children's academic and employment futures in their quest for athletic stardom. How much of this is the child's decision and how much is it the parents'? These children are becoming hyper-specialized at a very early age."[40]

African American families have turned to homeschooling in increasing numbers as well, though still at a rate far below that for Caucasian families.[41] Scholars Ama Mazama and Garvey Musumunu have pointed to a variety of interrelated factors behind this trend. The "zero tolerance" discipline policies adopted by many school districts starting in the 1980s have had "the effect of criminalizing African Americans at an early age," they write. Eurocentric curricula have made it difficult for many African

American children to develop pride in their culture and confidence in their intellectual abilities. Moreover, urban schools throughout the country have been plagued by overcrowding, insufficient state funding, and a dearth of qualified teachers. (And many have been shuttered altogether, forcing children to attend schools outside their neighborhoods.)[42] Many other African American parents cite racial bullying and a culture of low expectations for black students as reasons to homeschool.[43] For some African American families concerned about these shortcomings, homeschooling has been an attractive—and empowering—alternative.

Other parents choose to educate their children at home in order to avoid the vaccination requirement that state laws impose for attendance at a public or private school. Though the overwhelming scientific consensus is that vaccines are safe and effective, some parents are disturbed by claims that vaccines can weaken children's immune systems or can be linked to such serious maladies as autism, and others are religiously opposed to all medical care, even preventive care. Homeschooling has appealed to many of these wary parents as a means of safeguarding their children against these supposed threats. "If you want to vaccinate your children, go ahead," one homeschooler in Mississippi explained. "But don't force me to vaccinate my children. These children are entrusted to us."[44]

Public health advocates have called this stance dangerous to children's health. The federal Center for Disease Control reports that unvaccinated children are thirty-five times more likely to contract measles and twenty-two times more likely to fall victim to whooping cough than their vaccinated peers. In a 2008 measles outbreak in the Chicago area, twenty-five of the thirty victims were homeschooled. A recent article on vaccine-preventable diseases in the journal *Pediatrics* relates that there were two reported cases of tetanus in Oklahoma in a single year, and both children were being homeschooled—one had never received a vaccination and one had not received the ten-year booster shot.[45] California tightened its law mandating vaccinations for children enrolling in schools after a measles outbreak in 2015 hit over 150 people, much of it connected to visiting Disneyland, but the state continued to exclude homeschoolers from its immunization requirement.

For homeschooling's critics, such illnesses underscore the potential of homeschooling to put children at risk of undetected harm. So, too, when severe maltreatment is discovered in a family whose children do not attend school, ostensibly because they were being homeschooled.[46] The case of the Turpin family in California is an extreme example; in January 2018,

thirteen offspring were found emaciated after many years of imprison-
ment, some of them chained to beds. School attendance is, among other
things, a safeguard against abuse and neglect; teachers and other school
employees often are the first outsiders to detect physical abuse, neglect,
sexual abuse, and emotional maltreatment of children in their homes.
Teachers are trained to look for (and report) indicators of these abuses,
which can be found in students' physical appearance, academic work, and
behavior. In addition, schools generally require that children receive a
physical examination by a doctor each year, and that along with the vaccination requirement should ensure that all children attending regular school
do not suffer prolonged, serious maltreatment. Homeschooled children
might never see anyone outside their family; parents who are inflicting
abuse naturally seek to avoid detection, and the number who succeed in
doing that are simply unknown. A 2014 study of child torture victims found
that 47 percent of the school-age victims had been taken out of school by
parents, under the guise of homeschooling, and another 29 percent had
never been enrolled in school.[47] The sample size was very small, so this
study is merely suggestive, but it is consistent with what one would expect
intuitively—that is, that parents who inflict horrible and prolonged abuse
on their children will try to keep the children at home rather than send
them to regular school.

The organizations Homeschooling's Invisible Children and the Center
for Home Education Policy compile records of cases of child maltreatment and death at the hands of parents claiming to be homeschooling.[48]
Among them is the case of a teen with cognitive impairments in Kansas
City who was handcuffed to a pole in his father's basement. Some such
cases end in death, and watchdog organizations believe fatality rates are
higher among homeschoolers than in the general population.[49] In Michigan, a teenager who had been removed from public school died in a house
fire while chained to her bed by a dog collar. (A state court later found
that the girl, Calista Springer, had been "tortured . . . over the course
of several years" at home by her father.) A North Carolina woman who
claimed she was homeschooling her sons evaded school authorities in
three different counties until she allegedly beat one of the boys to death.[50]
In 2014, an Illinois court upheld a finding of child maltreatment with respect to a mother who belonged to, and involved her children in, a religious group called Light of the World Ministries, whose spiritual leader
provides "light therapy" to women and girls that entails their being naked
and having the leader's finger inserted in their genitals.[51] Presumably all

the children confined to the many religious-cult compounds in this country are reported to school officials, if at all, as being homeschooled.

Critics assert that the emphasis many homeschoolers place on strict physical discipline creates an environment where physical abuse is more likely. Some books popular among homeschoolers, such as Michael and Debi Pearl's *To Train Up a Child*, advocate harsh disciplinary techniques meant to instill complete obedience. The Pearls' methods include hitting children, withholding food from them, and subjecting them to cold-water baths, a regimen that can begin with children only a few months old. Homeschool advocacy groups have bought and distributed thousands of copies of the book.[52] Individuals who have endured such treatment have become increasingly vocal in recent years. Journalist Kathryn Joyce has noted "the emergence of a coalition of young former fundamentalists who are coming out publicly, telling their stories, and challenging the Christian homeschooling movement." They often speak out on websites such as that of Homeschooling's Invisible Children and Homeschoolers Anonymous. The latter has a self-proclaimed mission to provide a platform for those who have been homeschooled to share "the good, the bad, and the ugly" of their experiences.[53]

Another reason for the concern that child abuse rates might be higher among homeschoolers is that evangelical Christian leaders urge followers to adopt children from abroad as a way of expanding the Christian community.[54] As a result, some people might undertake a foreign adoption not because of an inherent drive to adopt but to fulfill a religious duty, and the burdens such an adoption often entails might be more than they can handle. The missionary aspect of the choice might also make these followers less wary of adopting children who have special needs because of adverse experience in infancy.[55] This, too, is speculative, but it could explain a perceived peculiarity concerning homeschooled children who were adopted: whereas in the US population as a whole, rates of maltreatment are lower for adopted children than for children being raised by biological parents, among homeschoolers, according to Homeschooling's Invisible Children, a "disproportionate number of cases of severe abuse and neglect involved children who are adopted."[56]

Conversely, homeschool advocates might note that colds and flus predictably spread like wildfire at certain times every year in regular schools, whereas their children avoid much germ spreading, and that regular schools present danger of physical and psychological abuse by fellow students and even teachers.

In addition to concerns about maltreatment and inadequate socialization, critics of homeschooling worry that homeschooling is likely to be less effective than regular schooling in fostering in children core critical-thinking skills. Champions of homeschooling point to reports that students taught via home instruction have scored above average on some standardized tests or have progressed further than children of the same age attending regular schools. One study suggested a particular benefit for students with Attention Deficit Hyperactivity Disorder (ADHD): they are more academically engaged and progress better if homeschooled than if attending a public school, because of a better student-teacher ratio and greater flexibility in scheduling instruction. Homeschool advocates also point to the purported attractiveness of homeschoolers to college recruiters. Their argument is simple: If homeschooling didn't work, how could its products succeed at such prestigious schools as MIT, Harvard, and Stanford?[57] For example, Alex Newman, coauthor of the book *Crimes of the Educators: How Utopians Are Using Government Schools to Destroy America's Children*, voices the typical refrain that if homeschooled children were not getting a good enough education, they wouldn't be beating public-school students like they are now: "The undeniable fact is that homeschooled children outperform victims of NEA-controlled government schools on every objective metric by huge margins."[58]

Such arguments based on comparison studies, though, betray their proponents' own lack of scientific sophistication. There are readily apparent methodological flaws in the studies cited, as many critics have noted—above all, severe selection bias. Studies comparing test scores look at a small subset of homeschooling parents, those who have voluntarily chosen to administer standardized tests—in their homes, proctoring the exams themselves—and to reveal the results to the state or to the researchers. Homeschooled children take standardized tests and have the results reported to anyone *only if* their parents choose this, and not many do.[59] As noted above, few states require evidence of academic progress, and those that do give parents options other than tests for demonstrating progress, or if they require homeschooled children to take tests they do not require reporting of the results to school officials. Homeschooling parents are unlikely to subject their children to standardized tests unless they think the children will do well, and they are unlikely to reveal test scores to a school district, or respond to a survey, unless they believe their children's performance will make them in particular, and homeschooling in general, look successful. Intuitively, one would expect that the parents of greatest concern to the state—that is, those providing inadequate or no instruction—are highly unlikely to administer tests or to report the results of any tests they do administer or arrange for children. So researchers get test results only for a small and highly unrepresentative subset of all home-schooled children, whereas all public-school children must take the tests and have the results reported.

Thus, as the International Center for Home Education Research has concluded, "claims that the 'average homeschooler' outperforms public school students [are] simply not substantiated by the data."[60] Add to this the fact that most of the studies homeschooling proponents cite were commis-sioned by HSLDA or some other advocacy organizations and performed by researchers those organizations carefully chose. Thus, they contain de-sign flaws and draw unwarranted positive conclusions about homeschool-ing.[61] To their credit, most of the researchers state in their reports that their samples of homeschooled children are not representative, but professional advocates like HSLDA and the general population of homeschoolers sim-ply ignore or overlook these disclaimers and point to the studies as "proof" that homeschooling is superior.[62]

The most reliable indicator of anything regarding homeschool achieve-ment might be college-entrance exams, which can be used to compare the subset of homeschooled youths *who seek to attend college* with youths who attended regular school and seek to attend college. There is reason to suppose a smaller portion of homeschooled young people do seek to attend college—namely, that some religious conservative groups discour-age college attendance, at least for girls but possibly for boys as well. In any event, a comparison of those two subgroups shows that homeschooled children *on average* get somewhat lower SAT and ACT scores on the math component and somewhat higher scores on the verbal component.[63] And among those who do attend college, homeschool graduates on average do as well as regular-school graduates in terms of GPA and graduation rates.[64]

However, average scores for different types of schooling are simply ir-relevant to education policy. An average can mask a vast range in quality of education and in academic development, and the state should be con-cerned about any children who are not receiving a minimally adequate education within any category of schooling, regardless of whether there are also children receiving a good education within the same category and whose superior performance raises the average. If average test scores are indicative of the quality of all schools, then any study showing equivalent results as between public schools and homeschools should make home-school advocates say (illogically) that "public schooling is highly effective." Comparing averages for the best subset of homeschoolers (those reflected in the studies) with the worst public schools is disingenuous.

In any event, even some studies of aggregate scores raise concerns about homeschooling. One well-regarded study published in 2011, the Cardus Education Survey, compared the educational experiences of two groups of children whose mothers regularly attend church—those who are home-schooled versus those who attend a regular school, public or private. It found that homeschoolers had lower SAT scores and were less likely to attend college. When they did attend college, homeschooled youth were more likely to enroll at "open admission" (i.e., unselective) institutions and less likely to attend prestigious universities. Other parts of the Cardus report also seem to have troubling implications for homeschooling. A section dealing with cultural engagement found that homeschoolers were more likely than their peers attending regular schools to "feel helpless in dealing with life's problems."[65]

Anecdotal assessments also paint a mixed picture of homeschooling's academic effectiveness. Rachel Coleman praised her parents for having provided an "excellent education" for her at home. They were proficient and responsible educators who went far above their home state's virtually nonexistent requirements, creating detailed curriculum plans, amassing annual portfolios of her work, and administering regular assessments. As a result, she was able to attend college on a scholarship. But Coleman eventually learned that, thanks to a lack of state oversight in her home state of Indiana, not all homeschooled children receive the same robust education. A family friend was trapped in an "abusive and neglectful homeschool situation," she recalled, and school officials knew nothing about it.[66]

Josh Powell is, at least on the surface, a homeschooling success story: he learned to read when he was four years old and eventually gained admission to Georgetown University. But Powell's homeschooling path to college was anything but smooth. As his course materials became more advanced, his parents became less adept at teaching him. When he turned to his mother for assistance with a difficult problem in pre-algebra, she told him, "Pray to God. He'll help you." By the time he reached age sixteen, he had never written an essay, and he was unaware that South Africa was a country. "There were all these things that are part of this common collective of knowledge that 99 percent of people have that I didn't have," he later told the *Washington Post*. Concerned that he was not receiving an adequate education at home, Powell asked his parents if he could enroll in a public school, but they refused. His father wanted him to continue to learn in a manner consistent with the family's religious faith.[67]

Powell eventually passed a high school equivalency test and enrolled in classes at a community college. They were a revelation for him. "With the addition of lectures, the structure, the support, the tutoring—things just finally clicked," he said. "I remember my first semester sitting in my developmental math class. No one wanted to be there except for me. I was thinking, 'Oh, my God, I have a chance to learn!'" On the strength of his community-college record and other conventional credentials (including his scores on the SAT, which he took at age twenty), Powell gained admission to Georgetown.[68]

Observers have tended to view the "homeschool movement" that shaped Powell's early education as a kind of monolith, with a variety of individuals and groups uniting to promote a common agenda and safeguard shared values. The truth has been more complex. As happens with almost every movement, fissures have developed over strategies, ideologies, and resources. There are clear tensions in particular between the "ideologues" and the "pedagogues."[69]

Rumblings against HSLDA were given a wide public airing in 2000, when the online magazine *Salon* published a lengthy account about divisions within the homeschooling movement. The piece centered on claims that HSLDA had developed a "pervasive political focus" and was "actively pursuing the goals of the religious right," in the words of writer Helen Cordes. She quotes *Home Education Magazine* cofounder Mark Hegener as saying HSLDA is "part of a socially conservative constituency network using home schooling as a way to further its political goals."[70] A far more serious critique was voiced from within the movement by Raymond Moore, one of the founding fathers of homeschooling. Moore publicly called Michael Farris arrogant and claimed HSLDA was doing a disservice to the homeschool movement by engaging in high-pressure, partisan politicking.[71]

Such internecine squabbles will probably do little to slow down the homeschooling movement. Its proponents, driven by a range of ideological and personal motivations, remain adamant about its effectiveness and its importance as an alternative to standard modes of education for children. And while the percentage of youngsters being educated at home by their parents is still comparatively small, homeschooling continues to hold an enormous symbolic value for those who are more broadly concerned about a host of purported dangers: intrusion of state power into the realm of family life, shortcomings of public school systems (including their alleged hostility toward Christianity), and the pervasive immorality of American popular culture. Whatever its deficiencies, homeschooling is here to stay, at least in part because many view it as a quintessential American bulwark against such public perils.

Notes

1. Sam Allis, "Teaching Kids at Home," *Time*, October 22, 1990, 84–85.

2. William Celis, "Growing Number of Parents Are Opting to Teach at Home," *New York Times*, November 22, 1990.

3. Allis, "Teaching Kids at Home," *Time*, 84–85; Kevin Roderick, "More Families Turning to Home School," *Los Angeles Times*, September 28, 1981.

4. Reed and Reed, *Lifetime Learning Companion*, 18–19.

5. Roy A. Weaver, Anton Negri, and Barbara Wallace, "Home Tutorials v. the Public Schools in Los Angeles," *Phi Delta Kappan* (December 1980): 251–54.

6. Van Galen, "Explaining Home Education," 161–77.

7. Gaither, *Homeschool*, 142.

8. Both parents are quoted in Jean M. Krause, "Homeschooling: Constructing or Deconstructing Democracy?" (unpublished master of arts thesis, California State University, Long Beach, 2012), 1–2.

9. Kunzman and Gaither, "Homeschooling," 23.

10. Harding and Harding, *The Brainy Bunch*, 1–3.

11. Quoted in Nicholas Ducote, "Home Education Ideologies and Literature: A Review," Homeschoolers Anonymous, April 23, 2013, https://homeschoolersanon ymous.org/2013/04/23/home-education-ideologies-and-literature-review-part-1/.

12. Kunzman, "Homeschooling and Religious Fundamentalism"; Kunzman and Gaither, "Homeschooling," 23.

13. Jenny Westbrook, "About," West Brooke Curriculum, http://www.west brookecurriculum.com/about.html.

14. Knowles, Marlow, and Muchmore, "From Pedagogy to Ideology."

15. Gaither, *Homeschool*, 145; Scott Somerville, "The Politics of Survival: Home Schoolers and the Law," accessed February 3, 2014, http://www.hslda.org/docs /nche/000010/politicsofsurvival.asp.

16. Paul E. Peterson, ed., *Choice and Competition in American Education* (Lanham, MD: Rowman & Littlefield, 2006), 251.

17. See Jessica Huseman, "The Frightening Power of the Home-Schooling Lobby," *Slate*, August 27, 2015. There is some evidence of HSLDA softening its position in recent years. See Leslie Corbly, "Few Regulations For Oklahoma Homeschoolers," KGOU.org, November 30, 2015 (quoting a staff attorney for HSLDA as stating, "It is a fundamental right and responsibility of the parent to educate the

child and the state's responsibility is to obviously ensure that if that is not taking place that there are agencies that step in to ensure that education is taking place").

18. See Motoko Rich, "Home Schooling: More Pupils, Less Regulation," *New York Times*, December 29, 2015; and Ryan Quinn, "Home-School Rules Eased," *Charleston Gazette-Mail* (WV), March 30, 2016.

19. See Laurence H. Winer and Nina J. Crimm, *God, Schools, and Government Funding: First Amendment Conundrums* (New York: Routledge, 2015), 56–60. See also Virginia House Bill 389 (2016) (proposing a new tax-credit program to reimburse parents for homeschool expenses).

20. Minn. Stat. Ann. § 290.0674; Minnesota Dept. of Revenue, "Qualifying Home School Expenses for K-12 Education Subtraction and Credit," http://www.revenue.state.mn.us/individuals/individ_income/factsheets/fact_sheets_fs8a.pdf.

21. Celis, "Growing Number of Parents Are Opting to Teach at Home," *New York Times*.

22. Allis, "Teaching Kids at Home," *Time*, 84–85.

23. Klicka, *Home School Heroes*, 277.

24. Marcia Clemmit, "Home Schooling," in "Home Schooling: Do Parents Give Their Children a Good Education?," *CQ Researcher*, March 7, 2014, 219, 231.

25. Lois, *Home Is Where the School Is*.

26. Andrade, "Exploratory Study of the Role of Technology," 31.

27. Hasson, "Changing Conversation around Homeschooling," 1–3.

28. Jason Tanz, "The Techies Who Are Hacking Education by Homeschooling Their Kids," *Wired*, February 4, 2015, https://www.wired.com/2015/02/silicon-valley-home-schooling/.

29. "Bullies Spur Parents to Home School," Connecticut Homeschool Network, January 21, 2014, http://cthomeschoolnetwork.org/bullies-spur-parents-to-home-school-kids/.

30. Barfield, *Real Life Homeschooling*, 1–5.

31. Karen Hurlbutt, "Experiences of Parents Who Homeschool Their Children with Autism Spectrum Disorders," *Focus on Autism and Other Developmental Disabilities*, 26 (2011): 239–49.

32. J. Redford, D. Battle, and S. Bielick, *Homeschooling in the United States: 2012* (NCES 2016-096REV) (Washington, DC: National Center for Education Statistics, Institute of Education Sciences, U.S. Department of Education, 2017), 6.

33. Sarah Grady, Meghan McQuiggan, and Mahi Megra, *Parent and Family Involvement in Education: Results from the National Household Education Surveys Program of 2016: First Look* (Washington, DC: National Center for Education Statistics, 2017).

34. Kunzman and Gaither, "Homeschooling," 4–59; Murphy, *Homeschooling in America*, 10–11.

35. Kunzman, *Write These Laws on Your Children*, 4.

36. Grady, McQuiggan, and Megra, *Parent and Family Involvement*, 19.

37. See Kunzman and Gaither, "Homeschooling," supra, at 9–10.

38. Tebow, *Know Who You Are*, 1; Butterworth, "Passion of the Tebow," 17–33.

39. Lenny Bernstein, "Home Schooling for Child Athletes Raises Questions Large and Small," *Washington Post*, August 9, 2011.

40. Sal Ruibal, "Elite Take Home-School Route," *USA Today*, June 7, 2005.

41. Grady, McQuiggan, and Megra, *Parent and Family Involvement*, 18 (showing a 3.8 percent rate among respondents who characterize themselves as white, 1.9 percent among respondents who characterize themselves as black).

42. Mazama and Musumunu, *African Americans and Homeschooling*, 6–10. See also McDowell, Sanchez, and Jones, "Participation and Perception."

43. See Jessica Huseman, "The Rise of Homeschooling among Black Families," *Atlantic Monthly*, February 17, 2015; Ama Mazama and Garvey Lundy, "African American Homeschooling as Racial Protectionism," *Journal of Black Studies* 43, no. 7 (2012): 723–48.

44. Chris Joyner, "Parents Home-school to Avoid Vaccinations; Safety Concerns Surface on Both Sides of Debate," *USA Today*, October 22, 2008.

45. Joyner, "Parents Home-school to Avoid Vaccinations," *USA Today*; Matthew Richard Johnson, Kristy K. Bradley, Susan Mendus, Laurence J. Burnsed, Rachel M. Clinton, and Tejpratap Tiwari, "Vaccine-Preventable Disease among Homeschooled Children: Two Cases of Tetanus in Oklahoma," *Pediatrics* 132, no. 6 (2013): 1686–89.

46. See, e.g., Mark Miller, "12 Found Living In Deplorable Conditions in Steubenville," *The Intelligencer / Wheeling News-Register* (WV), December 30, 2015; Maria F. Durand, "Home-School Abuse Charged," ABC.com, August 24, 2015 (homeschooling father charged with abuse for torturing and threatening to kill his children when they did not win spelling bees); Kim Dacey, "Children Found in Deplorable Conditions . . . Naked, Locked in Bedroom," WBALTV.com (MD), March 25, 2015 (five- and seven-year-old children were deprived of contact with anyone outside of their family and did not know their names or how to use utensils for eating); Melissa Pamer, "6 Children, 60 Animals Found in 'Deplorable Conditions' in Lucerne Valley; Parents in Custody," KTLA.com (NV), August 29, 2014; Lynn Harris, "Godly Discipline Turned Deadly: A Controversial Child 'Training' Practice Comes under Fire—This Time from Christians Themselves," *Salon*, February 22, 2010 (discussing murder charges against homeschooling parents in California who, claiming to follow the popular No Greater Joy Ministries' teachings about child discipline, frequently inflicted severe beatings on their children and ultimately killed one daughter when they punished her for mispronouncing a word by holding her down for nine hours and beating her dozens of times on the back of her body, causing massive tissue damage); Jane Grossjan, "Lack of Supervision Noted in Deaths of Home-Schooled," *New York Times*, January 12, 2008 (a homeschooling mother abused four daughters for a long period and ultimately murdered them); Toms v. Hanover Dept. Soc. Services, 614 S.E.2d 656 (Va. Ct. App.

2005) (upholding the termination of parental rights as to eight children who had lived, with little food or clothing, for many years in a 16′ × 16′ room without plumbing or electricity, and who could communicate only with grunts and gestures).

47. Knox et al., "Child Torture as a Form of Child Abuse," 37–49.

48. See Homeschooling's Invisible Children, "Shining a Light on Abuse and Neglect in Homeschooling Environments," https://hsinvisiblechildren.org/blog/ (listing cases of physical abuse); and Homeschooling's Invisible Children, "Medical Neglect," https://hsinvisiblechildren.org/themes-in-abuse/medical-neglect/ (listing cases of severe medical neglect among homeschoolers), See also Jessica McMaster, "'Nobody Wants to Stop It:' When Abusive Parents Use Homeschooling to Sneak under the Radar," Kshb.com, February 29, 2016; Libby Anne, "When Abusive Parents Homeschool," Patheos.com, May 2, 2013, http://www.patheos.com/blogs/love joyfeminism/2013/05/when-abusive-parents-homeschool.html#sthash.aWLVScec .dpuf; and https://www.facebook.com/homeschoolgrad/.

49. Heather Hollingsworth, "David and Pamela Martin Charged with Child Abuse for Allegedly Handcuffing Teen to Pole," *Huffington Post*, February 13, 2013; Homeschooling's Invisible Children, "Some Preliminary Data on Homeschool Child Fatalities," 2016, http://hsinvisiblechildren.org/commentary/some-pre liminary-data-on-homeschool-child-fatalities/. Homeschool advocates dispute this. One source of disagreement is over whether to consider as homeschoolers those who simply did not send their child to school or those who asserted homeschooling as the reason for not getting their child to school but did not actually attempt home-based instruction. What is relevant from a policy perspective is whether a state's homeschooling laws, as a practical matter, facilitate abuse by enabling parents to completely isolate their children, and that counsels in favor of including these two groups that homeschool advocates wish to exclude.

50. People v. Springer, 2012 Mich. App. LEXIS 1740; *The Dispatch* (Lexington, NC), February 18, 1997.

51. See In re L.H., I.H., and C.H., 2014 IL App (1st) 133252-U, 2014 WL 3697067.

52. Pearl and Pearl, *To Train Up a Child*.

53. Kathryn Joyce, "The Homeschool Apostates," *American Prospect*, February 9, 2014, accessed January 29, 2014, http://prospect.org/article/homeschool -apostates; *Daily Mail* (UK), April 15, 2013.

54. See Kathryn Joyce, *The Child Catchers: Rescue, Trafficking, and the New Gospel of Adoption* (New York: PublicAffairs, 2013).

55. See Kathryn Joyce, "Orphan Fever: The Evangelical Movement's Adoption Obsession," *Mother Jones*, May/June 2013.

56. See Homeschooling's Invisible Children, "Adoption," http://hsinvisiblechil dren.org/themes-in-abuse/adoption/.

57. Steven Duvall, Joseph Delquadri, and Lawrence Ward, "A Preliminary Investigation of the Effectiveness of Homeschool Instructional Environments for

Students with Attention-Deficit/Hyperactivity Disorder," *School Psychology Review* 33, no. 1 (2004): 140–58; Lawrence Rudner, "Scholastic Achievement and Demographic Characteristics of Home School Students in 1998," *Educational Policy Analysis Archives* 7, no. 8 (1999): 1–33; Brian Ray, "Academic Achievement and Demographic Traits of Homeschool Students: A Nationwide Study," *Academic Leadership: The Online Journal* 8, no. 1, Article 7 (2010).

58. Paul Bremmer, "NEA 'Attack' on Homeschoolers Blasted as 'Outrageous,'" WND, June 29, 2015, https://www.wnd.com/2015/06/authors-nea-attack-on-home schoolers-outrageous/.

59. See Amy Schechter Vahid and Frank Vahid, *Homeschooling: A Path Rediscovered for Socialization, Education, and Family* (self-pub., September 16, 2007), 57 (noting it is quite uncommon for homeschoolers to take any standardized tests).

60. *USA Today*, June 2, 2009; International Center for Home Education Research, "About ICHER," accessed January 28, 2014, http://icher.org/icher.html. One proponent of homeschooling purported to refute the concern that some homeschoolers will impose sexist views upon, and thwart the life prospects of, daughters, by studying a small number of teens who were actually attending a public high school, after their parents had chosen to discontinue public schooling. Even after noting the enormous selection-bias problem with that sample, the report of the study presumed to ascribe significance for homeschooling in general in a comparison of course choice and of math performance between girls and boys in the sample. See Dick M. Carpenter II, "Mom Likes You Best: Do Homeschool Parents Discriminate Against Their Daughters?," *University of St. Thomas Journal of Law & Public Policy* 7, (2012): 24–50.

61. See Kunzman and Gaither, "Homeschooling," 5.

62. Kunzman and Gaither, 17.

63. Kunzman and Gaither.

64. Kunzman and Gaither, 29–31.

65. Ray Pennings and Kathryn Wiens, *Cardus Education Survey: Phase I Report (2011)* (Hamilton, Ontario: Cardus, August 16, 2011), https://www.cardus.ca /research/education/reports/cardus-education-survey-phase-i-report-2011/.

66. Rachel Coleman, "Good Homeschooling Is Not Something That Happens Automatically," Coalition for Responsible Homeschooling, December 16, 2013, http://www.responsiblehomeschooling.org/rachel-coleman/.

67. Susan Svrluga, "Student's Home-schooling Highlights Debate over Va. Religious Exemption Law," *Washington Post*, July 28, 2013; Clemmit, "Home Schooling," *CQ Researcher*, 219.

68. Svrluga, "Student's Home-schooling Highlights Debate."

69. Rob Reich, "Why Homeschooling Should Be Regulated," in *Homeschooling in Full View: A Reader*, ed. Bruce Cooper (Greenwich, CT: Information Age Publishing, 2005), 109–20 (citing "a kind of internecine warfare among the two

most prominent advocacy groups, the Christian-based HSLDA and the more secular and inclusive [though now defunct] National Home Education Network").

70. Helen Cordes, "Battling for the Heart and Soul of Homeschoolers," *Salon*, October 2, 2000, accessed January 20, 2014, http://www.salon.com/2000/10/02/home schooling_battle/.

71. Raymond S. Moore, "The Ravage of Home Education through Exclusion By Religion," 1994, https://a2zhomeschooling.com/thoughts_opinions_home_school /ravage_home_education_p1/.

CHAPTER FOUR

Common Themes and Disparate Concerns

The foregoing history reveals that home-based education in some form has always been a feature of life in America, but a feature that has changed dramatically in its nature and public reception. Once a norm, taken for granted but limited to basic literacy for purposes of religious devotion, homeschooling became anomalous and anathema after the creation of public school systems in the mid-nineteenth century. Then, in the latter part of the twentieth century, attitudes shifted once again, and it became an accepted—though still boldly chosen—full-fledged alternative to regular schooling, expected to entail instruction in multiple subjects and to prepare children for a wide range of possible careers in a modern society and an employment market that expects fairly advanced learning. Parents choose homeschooling for a great variety of reasons, but a significant feature of homeschooling in the United States today is that nearly all parents who do it judge it to be superior in one or more ways to the schooling that the state offers to all children free of tuition, and even superior to any available private school options.

The history also reveals that state laws in the United States have in recent decades become exceedingly permissive with respect to homeschooling, to the point where the practice is unsupervised and unregulated in the great majority of states. America has, one might even say, stopped requiring that children receive an education. Compulsory schooling laws are still on the books but, in nearly all states, are mere rhetoric with little or no practical effect, not actually holding parents at all accountable for the choices they make regarding their children's education. States have relaxed their oversight although they are quite clearly not constitutionally required to do so—in fact, they have done so even in the face of consistent Supreme Court declarations that states rightfully retain the power to substantially supervise and regulate all forms of education and even to mandate that all children attend a regular school.

At this point in the book, we switch gears to the normative, philosophical analysis of homeschooling and of the laws now governing it, with the historical background in mind. We now ask what stance the state *ought* to take toward some parents' desire to keep children at home rather than sending them out to school. Is the current legal regime morally appropriate? Are parents morally entitled to this power over their children's intellectual formation, even if not constitutionally entitled to it? Should the state go even further and financially support any parent's choice to homeschool? Or, conversely, do children have a right to attend a regular school, or at least to have the state exercise greater control over home-based instruction?

Our approach to answering these questions is more abstractly analytical than the preceding historical study, at times highly conceptual or theoretical, and at certain points making much of what might seem like small distinctions—for example, the distinction between having a *right* to decide certain things about children's lives and being *permitted* to exercise authority as to such things. The line of reasoning pursued will likely be unfamiliar, even jarring, to most readers. The aim is to induce people of good will on all sides of the issue to think about the "ought" question in a new and more rigorous way than is common in everyday discourse. Doing so might help opposing factions find points of agreement; regardless, it should be an interesting intellectual exercise for all.

Because normative views about the regulation of homeschooling tend to be polarized, we begin our analysis by ruling out the extreme views that have dominated public discourse about the practice—that is, the view of the most outspoken homeschool advocates that homeschooling is inherently superior to all other schooling and presents no reason for state concern, and, on the other side, the view of public-school teachers' unions and some other critics that homeschooling is inherently deficient and a threat to important values and so should be eliminated. By explaining why both extremes are untenable, we hope to clear a path for open-minded and nuanced thinking about this topic. We then lay the foundation for our analysis by identifying a series of questions one must answer in order to arrive at a position regarding homeschooling that can be explained and justified to other reasonable persons.

I. Ruling Out Extreme Views about Homeschooling

The first difficulty facing anyone who would take either extreme view is the plain fact of tremendous variety among homeschools today. Not only do parents' aims for their children's education vary, but there is also great variation with respect to parents' own educational level and talent for teaching, employment of instructors other than the parents (e.g., online correspondence programs, music lessons, homeschool co-ops), connection to a parent network or homeschooling organization that provides guidance, interaction with regular schools (e.g., participation in team sports), opportunities for nonschool educational experiences given location and financial resources (e.g., museums, travel), arranged interactions with peers outside the family, and types of curricular materials used (if any). This variety makes utterly implausible any blanket empirical assertion about homeschooling, such as that it is always good or that it is inherently bad for children.

Consider first blanket condemnation. Anyone taking this position is most likely operating from a liberal standpoint that accepts, more or less, the state's aims for children's education, as reflected in the curricular aims of public schools, and that assumes public education generally (even if not in all schools) fulfills those aims. The position is likely to rest on a supposition that homeschooling is inherently deficient in terms of those aims.

An initial reason to reject this position is that it would not follow logically from a premise that homeschooling is inherently deficient *in some respect* that homeschooling is inherently bad *on the whole* for children. (Certainly common schooling could be deemed inherently deficient in some respects.) It could be that any inherent deficiency of homeschooling is not important enough to make all homeschooling fall to some level properly characterized as "bad." And it could be that homeschooling is also inherently superior to other forms of schooling in other ways (e.g., potential for individualized curriculum, real-world context for learning, less exposure to disease, flexibility of schedule, no time wasted on transport), and that these outweigh the perceived deficiency. Much more would need to be said than simply that something is always missing with homeschooling. One would need to have some standard of "bad" and demonstrate that the alleged deficiency is so great as to make homeschooling fall below that standard even after taking into account any compensating benefits homeschooling can offer. We are not aware of anyone having done this.

In addition, it is difficult to imagine what could be *inherently* deficient about homeschooling, given the capaciousness of that concept. If we can describe an approach to education that fits within our understanding of what homeschooling is and that also fulfills all the liberal aims for children's education, then liberals cannot say homeschooling is inherently problematic. So imagine this scenario:

Someone who is, by liberal standards, one of the best teachers in America's public schools is also a parent. She decides to quit her job in order to homeschool her four children. She uses at home exactly the same materials the public school uses. In some ways, the experience she can give her children is clearly superior even to what she was able to give the children in her classroom when she worked in the public school. She is able to tailor her teaching to her children's individual strengths and weaknesses. Learning experiences occur more organically, as household events (repairs, parties) and projects (cooking, furniture building) raise questions that require study in one or more curricular areas. With fewer pupils and freedom from standardized testing, she is able to spend substantial time on the arts. Without having to worry about upsetting any pupils' parents, she can add a robust critical-thinking component, using "philosophy for children" books and online lesson plans that liberal philosophers have created,[1] and she has her four children debate and reason with each other, puzzling over answers to intellectually stimulating questions, after reading provocative essays that argue for positions unfamiliar to them. She has the children do progressively lengthy papers, both creative and analytical, and with only four pupils she is able to give them extensive feedback on all aspects of the writing. A few days each week she joins other homeschoolers, carefully selected to represent a variety of religious and cultural backgrounds, and they take their children for field trips to museums and various workplaces (e.g., factories, university science labs, government offices, and firehouses). They also hold events for socializing and for discussions of current events.[2] Twice per week her children go to the home of another homeschooling parent who has professional training in an area of study in which this mother is not so strong. On other days that parent's children come to this mother for instruction. She registers her children in various community recreation programs with non-homeschooled children. When her children reach middle-school age, the mother has them go the local public middle school to participate in after-school activities with the public-school children, such as sports teams, theater productions, and special-interest clubs. She imposes no restrictions on their socializing, except ones necessary to keep them safe and out of trouble (e.g., not allowing them to spend time unsupervised with children known to have serious behavioral disorders). She encourages friendships with peers in the neighborhood who attend public schools or private religious schools, allows the children progressively more unsupervised time with peers as they get older, and enrolls her children in the neighborhood summer swim team. They regularly attend local government meetings and occasionally attend sessions of the state legislature, and the mother discusses with the children the pros and cons of policy measures these bodies are considering.[3] They read the *Washington Post* every day and frequently write letters to their Congressional representatives urging support or opposition to pending legislation. The mother and her spouse take advantage of the flexibility homeschooling allows to travel with the children outside peak vacation times to big cities where they visit museums and see operas and plays, to national parks where they enroll in hands-on nature programs, and to other countries where they learn about other cultures and practice other languages.

What could a liberal say is missing from these children's experience that public schools generally provide? Is not the education just described patently *superior* to what children receive in the vast majority of public schools, in terms of liberal aims such as fostering critical and creative thinking and a love of learning, preparing them to have an "open future," developing respect for and an inclination to engage with persons of different worldviews, and teaching them how to participate constructively in the political process? And is it not less likely than public schooling to lead to unhealthy peer interactions that diminish self-esteem or result in life-limiting behaviors?[4]

One could, we believe, tell a similar story to satisfy a skeptic operating from any other worldview—that is, a story depicting a homeschool that incorporates all that they think is important in children's schooling. There might be a hypothetical worldview in which there is great value simply in spending thirty-five hours per week for nine months per year with the same twenty or thirty other students, in a building with some still greater number of children, repeatedly for thirteen years. But that worldview seems to be one that belongs to no actual person. One might say that schooling should prepare children for adult life in mainstream society and that many occupations involve participation in an institutional life of the sort large schools embody. To the extent that a large swath of potential careers is closed off to a person, there might seem to be some loss of well-being or narrowing of life prospects, even if there are countless other occupations available that do not require working in a large institution. There might even be empirical evidence that adults who were homeschooled are less likely to work in large companies or organizations than are those who attended regular schools. We are not aware of any such evidence, but even if that is true, it might be because of homeschool graduates' distaste for institutional life rather than discomfort or incapacity, and it might also be because those who attend regular school become so accustomed to and dependent on an institutional culture that they are fearful of being more independent and entrepreneurial. It seems unlikely that any type of education could prepare young people for every possible type of career, and it is not obvious that an education in regular schools leads to an optimal range of opportunities.

In short, it is difficult to identify any way in which homeschooling is *inherently* different from regular schooling, and if there is an inherent difference it is not clear that it counts against homeschooling rather than in favor of it. Now it might be that few actual homeschools fit the liberal ideal described above. But undoubtedly some are quite similar to that description; some homeschooling parents are in fact former public-school teachers who attempt to bring home the best of the regular-school experience while leaving behind the less attractive features of schools governed by bureaucracies and political bandwagons. Even homeschools that fall short of that liberal ideal might still be quite good by liberal standards. Moreover, the quality question must be a comparative one, the relevant comparison being with alternatives reasonably available for any given child. Public schools in many areas of the country meet no one's standards of a good school, and public schools that actually live up to the ideal of a liberal education might in fact be rare.[5] Recall the charges of anti-intellectualism and dumbing down the curriculum that have been leveled against public schools for at least half a century and that are no less legitimate today. Good private schools might be too far away from, too expensive for, or too unwelcoming to some families. A homeschool might fall substantially short of the liberal ideal described above and yet still be the best choice, even from a liberal perspective, for a particular child in a particular community.

So much for blanket condemnation of homeschools. What about blanket endorsement? Many advocates for unregulated homeschooling sometimes express this bald proposition: "Homeschools are better than public schools." When pressed, though, most concede that not *every* homeschool is a good one. There is ample anecdotal evidence of actual homeschools that are bad by almost everyone's standards.[6] Even someone who rejects liberal educational aims, whose own parenting is directed at something quite different, should regard some actual homeschools as bad—perhaps precisely because they *do* conform to liberal aims, or because there is no instruction of any valuable sort taking place, or because the homeschooling is really just a cover for abuse or neglect. Recall the divide between "ideologues" and "pedagogues" among homeschoolers, and the substantial variety within each group. Though they might agree on much, their approaches to instruction are quite varied and, as between some subgroups, radically divergent, even contradictory.[7] At a very basic level, some homeschoolers believe schooling should be child-directed, and, on the other hand, some believe schooling should be authoritarian.[8] The former philosophy tends to rest on a view of children as naturally good and capable, likely to thrive if adults do not get in the way.[9] The latter philosophy tends to rest on a view of children as improperly willful and naturally inclined to misbehavior and laziness, likely to thrive only if adults impose tight constraints.[10] How could parents adhering to and applying one of these outlooks possibly say that homeschools operated under the other outlook are good homeschools? Would evangelical Christian homeschoolers say, "Well, my children are inherently sinful and need severe control, but the children of those liberals are not that way, so a child-directed approach is right for them"? Conversely, could liberal pedagogues regard as benign the homeschooling received by Elizabeth Esther, author of *Girl at the End of the World*, who writes,

> Everything from politics and religion to your tone of voice, the clothing you wear, even how you open and shut doors—everything is based on doing it in a manner that was pleasing to God. I had never really lived in the real world. I didn't understand how Americans thought. All my language was religious language. I didn't know how to interact with people without trying to convert them. I had a lot of really discouraging experiences where I realized that you could leave fundamentalism, but at the end of the day fundamentalism was still inside of me.

What about the experience of girls under the oppressive hand of the Quiverfull movement, which forcefully teaches them to be silent and submissive and to have no life plan other than making as many babies as possible for the cause (and then homeschooling them to do the same)?[11] Or the use of packaged curricula like those produced by Bob Jones University and A Beka Book, noted in chapter 2, which command students to accept a "scientific" worldview derived from the Bible, without question and without learning any scientific methods that might enable them to confirm or refute claims such as that before the Flood there was no rain and humans' average life span was 912 years. Conservative Christian homeschoolers and liberal pedagogues also tend to differ dramatically in their views on the preparation of girls for adulthood, as many in the former group are "decidedly hostile to some basic tenets of liberal feminism."[12]

In fact, we should expect *all* homeschooling parents to take a dim view of the schooling being provided to a large percentage of homeschooled children—that is, the schooling provided by those who apply a quite contrary educational philosophy. A person could, with logical consistency, accept several pedagogical approaches as legitimate; many homeschooling parents struggle to choose one from among the many on offer. But some approaches are clearly antithetical to each other, based on contradictory and nonindividualized assumptions about children's nature or what values children should acquire or something else. No rational person could say "they are all good" or even "nearly all are good." Every homeschooler has explicitly or implicitly rejected as objectively bad certain approaches to instruction that a large number of other homeschoolers have adopted.

As with blanket condemnation, we might try to construct a hypothetical worldview from which every homeschool is necessarily good. That view would have to rest, it seems, on a belief that *whatever* any parents do with their children is ipso facto good for the children. But it seems highly unlikely that any actual person really holds that view, because it is inherently irrational. One would have to hold no standard of goodness other than "what parents do is good"; if one had any other standard, one could readily find homeschooling parents who do not meet the standard. And every conscientious parent has some standard they aim to meet. Notably "what parents do" is not even the same as "what parents want" or "what parents believe best for their children," because parents sometimes act contrary to their own desires and values. Just consider that a significant percentage of the population suffers from a serious mental illness, and that persons who have mental illness and are also parents and are not receiving adequate treatment might be especially likely to keep their children at home with them, under the guise of homeschooling, rather than send them off to school. Recognizing this, would any reasonable homeschooling advocate maintain that every parent, or even nearly every parent, who keeps their children out of regular schools is necessarily providing their children with a good education? We believe it impossible to rationally do so.

What most homeschooling parents more likely believe is that their own values are objectively good, and not just for their own children. From this it follows that they should view as severely deficient a great number of other homeschools. Many homeschooling parents extoll the benefits of being able to tailor their child's schooling to the child's unique characteristics, but that is quite different from asserting that the values one aims to promote for one's child apply to no one other than one's child. The values are typically thought to be universal—for example, that every child should express his or her authentic nature, or that every child should learn to defer to authority. A view that value X is objectively good, rather than merely subjectively important or attractive, implies the belief that everyone should aim to promote that value in similar settings. And so any homeschooling parent, adhering to any conception of the good, must regard *some* forms of homeschooling, practiced by a substantial percentage of other homeschooling parents, as bad, precisely because they are directly contrary to that parent's deeply held values, values the parent believes to be objectively good and essential to children's education.

For example, conservative Christians presumably would deem bad a homeschool in which children learn that atheism is true, that conservative Christians are knuckle-scraping know-nothings, that creationism is a manifestation of insanity, and that it is the state's proper role to stop the spread of Christianity. Or they might deem bad a homeschool in which overindulgent parents who have never imposed any limitations on their child are entirely unable to get the child to do any learning exercises they think he or she should do; the child refuses, manipulates, watches cartoons all day, and so forth. The staunchest defenders of unregulated homeschooling—religious conservatives—rationally should conclude that *a large percentage* of homeschooling is objectively bad, because it instills what they regard as objectively bad values (e.g., moral relativism), bad attitudes (e.g., willfulness), bad habits (e.g., questioning authority), and misinformation (e.g., that religion is myth, and the Bible fiction).

Regardless of ideological outlook, then, everyone should agree that homeschooling can be good, even great, or can at least be the best choice for some parents given their circumstances. But also everyone should agree that for many children staying home with parents instead of going to a school is bad, in the sense of depriving the children of something very important, whether it be education or proper values or physical safety or something else, something they could get instead by attending some regular school, public or private. In fact, there are some children whom every sane person, regardless of educational philosophy, would say are being harmed by homeschooling, because their parents are simply unable or disinclined to educate their children in any recognizable way or are keeping the children out of school in order to avoid detection of severe maltreatment.

Furthermore, just as parents vary greatly in their capacity and inclination, children are also quite varied in terms of their relationships with parents and their comfort in different environments or receptivity to different forms of instruction. It might be that some children really need the larger social environment, relatively regimented schedule, or experience of learning along with same-age peers that characterize regular schools. Or some children might be suited to a mix of instructional approaches (e.g., reading vs. lecture vs. hands-on) that are quite different from what their parents are inclined toward or able to provide.[13] It would contradict the mantra of homeschoolers—that children do best when their education responds to their individual needs—to stipulate that homeschooling is right for every child. They might contend that parents always make the right choice for their children, as between homeschooling and regular schooling, but that is an extraordinarily bold and unverifiable claim, one that would require the person asserting it to himself or herself judge what is best for each and every child and then observe that every parent decides in conformity with that judgment. Chapter 3 noted organizations today peopled by adults who were homeschooled and firmly believe they would have been better off if they had attended a regular school. There are undeniably also many adults who attended regular school and wish in retrospect that they had been homeschooled for at least part of their upbringing.

II. From Practice to Policy

Some people focus on the fact that homeschooling can be bad and jump to the conclusion that it should be banned altogether—that the law should compel attendance at regular school for all children. Others focus on the fact that it can be very good for children compared to the alternatives— even from the state's secular perspective—and contend that the state should empower parents to choose it, without restriction. State policy regarding homeschooling should reflect the full reality, that homeschooling can be very good or very bad (like other aspects of parenting and like other types of schools), and should reflect a sincere attempt to rationally answer certain difficult questions, such as, Is it possible to prevent the bad while facilitating the good? If some bad homeschooling is inevitable, in any legal regime that permits it, what is the threshold degree of bad homeschooling beyond which the state should exert more oversight or even eliminate homeschooling as an option for anyone? To whom does the state owe duties in connection with children's education, and what is the substance of those duties? If it is appropriate for the state to pass judgment on homeschools, on what bases should it make such judgments? The chapters that follow aim to answer at least some such important questions.

Notes

1. See https://www.teachingchildrenphilosophy.org/ (the website for the Teaching Children Philosophy online program); http://www.montclair.edu/cehs/academics/centers-and-institutes/iapc/ (the website for the Institute for the Advancement of Philosophy for Children); and https://depts.washington.edu/nwcenter/ (the website for the University of Washington's Center for Philosophy for Children).

2. Stevens, *Kingdom of Children*, 26 (discussing the proliferation of support groups for homeschoolers from the outset of the contemporary movement).

3. Cf. Nathaniel Klemp and Stephen Macedo, "The Christian Right, Public Reason, and American Democracy," in *Evangelicals and Democracy in America*, ed. Steven Brint and Jean Reith Schroedel, vol. 2 (New York: Russell Sage Foundation, 2010), 209–46. Klemp and Macedo found that the Christian Right in the United States is not only extraordinarily politically engaged but also adept at and inclined to invoke "public reason" rather than religious belief in advocating in political circles for their policy aims.

4. Though we are aware of no comparative statistics on teen pregnancy and substance abuse among homeschoolers relative to youth attending public school, studies have shown that markers of optimal decision-making about intimate relationships are much better among churchgoing evangelical Protestants (who make up a large percentage of homeschoolers) than among the US population as a whole. See, e.g., W. Bradford Wilcox, "How Focused on the Family? Evangelical Protestants, the Family, and Sexuality," in *Evangelicals and Democracy in America*, ed. Steven Brint and Jean Reith Schroedel, vol. 1 (New York: Russell Sage Foundation, 2010), 265–68 (finding substantially lower rates of nonmarital cohabitation, out-of-wedlock births, and divorce among churchgoing evangelicals).

5. On the intellectually deadening effect of normal public schools, see, e.g., Laura Eberhart Goodman, "What Do I Expect from My Children's Elementary School? Certainly Not This," *Washington Post*, January 5, 2016.

6. See, e.g., David Barrett, "Islamist Indoctrination of London Schoolgirl in Family Home Was as Bad as Sex Abuse, Judge Rules," *Telegraph*, August 21, 2015 (describing the training of a girl to become a jihadi bride); R. L. Stollar, "When Homeschool Leaders Looked Away: The Old Schoolhouse Cover-Up," Homeschoolers Anonymous, October 8, 2014, http://homeschoolersanonymous.org/2014/10/08/when-homeschool-leaders-looked-away-the-old-schoolhouse-cover-up/ (discussing the concealment of sexual abuse among homeschoolers); Stevens, *Kingdom of Children*, 58 (discussing a parent who planned to base their entire K–12 curriculum for a child on three verses from the Bible); Kristin Rawls, "Barely Literate? How Christian Fundamentalist Homeschooling Hurts Kids," Alternet, March 14, 2012, http://www.alternet.org/story/154541/barely_literate_how_christian_fundamentalist_homeschooling_hurts_kids. There is also a large literature on US religious cults, whose indoctrination of the young would be treated legally as homeschooling.

7. See Stevens, *Kingdom of Children*, 45 (noting the contradiction between arguments that different groups make for homeschooling).

8. Stevens, 60, 88.

9. See Stevens, 25 (stating that "inclusive homeschoolers" differ from Christian homeschoolers in viewing children as inherently good rather than sinful).

10. Stevens, 109. But see Gaither, *Homeschool*, 113–14 (stating that despite any conservative Christians' rhetoric about inherent sinfulness, "at the deepest level they tend to think of their children as precious gifts of God, full of potential, not as vipers," and many "have embraced the romantic cult of the child").

11. See Katherine Steward, "The Dark Side of Home Schooling: Creating Soldiers for the Culture War," *Guardian*, May 8, 2013.

12. Stevens, *Kingdom of Children*, 104.

13. There is much controversy now over the "learning style" theory that predominated in educational circles for decades, but the detractors do not contend that all children benefit equally from exactly the same learning environment or the same mix of instructional approaches. See, e.g., B. A. Rogowsky, B. M. Calhoun, and P. Tallal, "Matching Learning Style to Instructional Method: Effects on Comprehension," *Journal of Educational Psychology* 107, no. 1 (February 2015): 64–78.

CHAPTER FIVE

The State's Role and Individuals' Rights

A n important initial point in our analysis is that complete state detachment from children's education is not possible even as a conceptual matter, so those who think it is an option are confused. Following explanation of this point, we construct a framework for reasoning about what proper form the state's inevitable role in children's development should take. We view the state not as an entity with its own interests but rather as an agent for society—that is, for *us* members of American society, collectively and sometimes individually (as when its institutions—police, courts, etc.—guard our individual rights as against majority will). So when we speak of state regulation or oversight of schooling we mean, in effect, collective societal efforts to ensure that children in our society receive an adequate education. Each of us is therefore implicated in what the state does—that is, what laws it creates that serve or disserve children's developmental interests—because it is our agent.

I. Dispelling the Illusion of State Nonintervention

Almost anyone who has thought about state policy toward homeschooling has thought about complete state detachment—that is, the state playing no role in whether or how homeschooling is done—as a potential option. In fact, many people purport to advocate this position. The refrain of HSLDA and of litigants in the challenges to homeschool regulations described in chapter 3 was that the state has no business involving itself in child-rearing, at least not when fit parents are acting on principle, unless those parents request state assistance. Parents should have complete control over children's cognitive development, to carry out however parents see fit. The legal regime thought to follow from this position is one devoid of any laws regarding homeschooling.

This position rests, however, on a fundamental misunderstanding of what it means, conceptually, for parents to have complete control and freedom. It rests on a false view of parent-child relationships as arising entirely separately from the state and untouched by law unless and until the state decides to "intervene." It is difficult to shake this false view because it is so deeply entrenched, but we hope readers will digest the following explanation of how parent-child relationships come into existence in modern societies and of what, accordingly, people pushing an antiregulation platform are really demanding.

People in the United States, the United Kingdom, or any other developed country who become parents live in a society governed by laws. They do not live in a state of nature. The alternative today to a society governed by laws is lawlessness and therefore chaos, which no sane person truly wants. This is especially evident in connection with the creation of parent-child relationships. If the state were not involved in that process, custody of newborn children would be a free-for-all. And so in the United States and other modern states there are laws—that is, authoritative commands by the state—dictating who a newborn child's legal parents will be. Moreover, that legal status would be meaningless, giving persons designated as parents no protection against interference—or, indeed, seizure of the child—by other private parties or state officials, unless the state acted further to bestow various legal rights, privileges, and powers on those persons whom it has made legal parents. And so it does. The state makes people *legal* parents and gives them the legal tools they need to carry on a custodial, caregiving relationship. Thus, when people in a parental role demand the ability to do what they want with children, whether it be controlling physical development, cognitive development, or something else, they are not in fact demanding to be "left alone"; they are demanding that the state give them more of something, and something extraordinary—namely, greater legal power over the life of another person, the child. They assert a positive right to the state's intervention in the child's life, an intervention that subjects the child to even greater parental dominion. Ironically (given that most people who express the demand to be "left alone" are conservatives and traditionalists), our colonial forebears appear to have understood this better than most people today.

Of course, many people believe there are moral rules or "natural laws" that should govern the state's decisions about parentage. They would say, "Okay, yes, the state has maternity and paternity laws conferring legal status on biological parents, but the state *must* have those laws, to respect and recognize our God-given rights." We address those contentions below. But regardless of the reason *why* one thinks the state *ought* to confer legal-parent status and legal powers, the fact remains that the state, as a practical matter, *must* assign children to legal parents; the state must create *legal* parent-child relationships. Absent a legal rule conferring legal-parent status on them, biological parents could expect no help from the police, the courts, or any other state actor should the doctor who delivers a baby whisk the child away to the doctor's home or to the hands of someone who offered a lot of money. The birth parents would have no legal basis for complaint and would stand in no better legal position than the doctor with respect to having custody of the child. Any shouts they make about God-given rights or natural law would have no practical effect. Everyone who gives the matter a moment's thought will therefore acknowledge that it is a good thing the state decides who will be a child's legal parents. Even if the state did not do so directly by substantive rule, it would have to do so indirectly by commanding what other entity (e.g., a nongovernmental organization or certain private citizens) is to make such decisions, or else there would be no legal recourse against someone who thumbs their nose at any other entity purporting to have such authority. Again, the alternative is bloody chaos. Lawlessness with respect to parentage is not something any rational person could want.

In connection with this inevitable state decision as to who will be a child's legal parents, the child must have some moral right as to how the decision is made. A fundamental precept of modern Western legal systems is that every human being after birth is a distinct legal person. No such human being, regardless of relative mental or other capacity, is mere property of some other being who is a legal person. Further, every distinct legal person stands in a direct legal relationship to the state, with rights against the state and rights against all other private parties—including parents—that the state protects. The pro-life movement takes this principle very seriously and extends it further, to unborn children, insisting that they are persons distinct from the parent carrying them and persons who possess rights even before birth, rights the state should enforce by legally prohibiting abortion, by intervening in the lives of pregnant persons to the substantial degree of forbidding them from undergoing a medical procedure. Likewise, every sane person would concede that children after birth have a right against being killed by their parents, a right the state should enforce by legally prohibiting such killing and punishing those who do it. Were the state to authorize legal parents to kill children, it would be obvious that the state was violating children's rights. The same is true with authorization of less severe harms. And if the state made parentage decisions as to newborns in complete disregard for their interest in being raised by their birth parents—for example, by assigning them to just-released convicts in the hope that this would make the convicts less likely to commit more crimes—everyone, we think, would see this as a violation of the children's rights, even if everyone also viewed it as violating a right of the birth parents. Thus, children themselves have moral rights that constrain how the state chooses legal parents for them, whether it is their first parents at the time of birth or substitute parents in cases of adoption.

In addition to choosing parents, the state must decide what content the legal-parent role will have. There must be laws dictating what powers, rights, and duties legal parents have. Again, no one would, upon reflection, want it to be otherwise. If the state anointed people as parents but then said nothing further, anyone so anointed would be in the same predicament as a biological parent in a world with no legal rules about parentage—that is, without any legal recourse against other private parties or state actors who interfere with their relationship with the child or inject themselves into the child's life uninvited. If I physically seize my neighbor's child while he is out playing in the yard, in order to give him the education I think is best, and if the state has not imbued my neighbor's status as legal parent with any legal rights, not even a legal right to physical custody, then there is nothing my neighbor can effectively do to regain custody of the child other than attempt forcible physical recapture. He cannot expect the police to help, because the police enforce laws, and if there is no law that says my neighbor shall have exclusive custody of the child, then my neighbor is out of luck. So too with efforts by outsiders to influence the child's life in ways short of physical seizure; it is only because the state bestows a legal power of exclusion on legal parents that custodial parents can prevent such private influences if they wish to do so. Unless the law infuses the legal-parent role with legal power over the child's life, the legal-parent status is meaningless in practice. No sane person wants that.

Thus, the reality is that everyone actually wants the state to involve itself intensively in all children's lives. Everyone wants the state to enact laws dictating with whom a child will have family relationships, and laws empowering the persons whom the state has made a child's legal parents to exert substantial control over the child's life. What people really disagree about is *which* legal powers, rights, and duties the state should give persons in the state-created legal-parent role, or in other words *how much* legal power and practical control over children's lives the state should give parents. Those who assert that the state should "leave parents alone" do not really mean that. Quite the opposite. What they mean is that the state ought to go to the extreme of conferring on parents absolute legal power and extensive rights and privileges with respect to children's lives—that is, powers to dictate whether a child receives various benefits the state offers, rights to others' not interfering in their interactions with their child, and a legal privilege to treat the child physically and psychologically in ways that otherwise would be prohibited (e.g., undressing, restraining, perhaps even hitting). Likewise, when courts appoint guardians for incompetent adults, it would make no sense for guardians to say the state should "leave them alone" to do whatever they want with their wards; what anyone who wants complete control would actually need to request is that the state confer on them plenary legal powers over their wards, because otherwise they would have no effective legal authority. This is a severe state intrusion into private life.

Moreover, those who ask the state to give them monopoly control over the mind of a child need to give the state *reason* to do that. It is an extraordinary thing for the state to do, to place nonautonomous persons into family relationships they have not themselves chosen, and then to give the other persons in the relationships tremendous power over their lives and exemptions from the prohibitions that ordinarily constrain how one treats other persons. In certain times and places, governments have also done this with respect to competent adults—for example, arranged marriages and given husbands extraordinary powers over wives. But today in Western society we strongly reject the state's doing that with adults. We understand that the state must, out of practical necessity, do it to some extent with nonautonomous persons, but we should not lose sight of the fact that it remains a profound thing for the state to do to any private individual. The state must have legitimate and compelling justification for doing it, one that fully respects the personhood of the child or incompetent adult, and the state's action in conferring on other persons power over the life of the child or incompetent adult may not outstrip that justification and may not exceed what that justification supports. To do so would be a gross abuse of state power.

Because the state is necessarily intensely involved in children's lives, then, and necessarily establishes what legal powers, rights, privileges, and duties legal parents will possess, it does not make sense to think about the legal regime relating to homeschooling as posing a choice between regulation and nonregulation or between intervention and nonintervention. The state must enact legal rules that govern parental choices and behaviors relating to children's education. Abstaining is not an option. For the law to say absolutely nothing about children's education would *not* mean parents have complete *legal* authority to do as they wish; to the contrary, it would mean that parents have no legal powers, rights, or privileges relating to their children's education whatsoever, so they would have no *legal* basis for waiving their children's statutory right to a public education nor for preventing other private individuals from trying to control the children's minds. What those claiming to be antiregulation are actually demanding is not government noninvolvement but rather government involvement of a particular nature—namely, aimed at empowering parents to an extent that, at least with respect to children's intellectual formation, is extreme. They wish the state to empower parents to keep children at home regardless of what anyone else (including the children) might prefer, to entitle parents to receive the state's assistance if anyone outside the family attempts to interfere (e.g., a local teacher or minister who thinks she is better able to instruct the child), and to empower parents to shield children's daily experience and development from any outside observation. That is a monumental thing to demand from the state. Opponents of school-district oversight of homeschooling might be right that it is a justified demand; we consider that below. The point here is simply to recognize the truth about what they are demanding—extraordinary state action in their favor.

By analogy, consider how we would characterize a legal regime that treated husbands in relation to their wives the way some homeschool advocates want the legal system to treat parents. Imagine a state enacting a statutory right for all adults to attend a state university but then also legally empowering husbands to waive that right as to their wives, so that a wife could not attend university if her husband objected, and also conferring on husbands a legal privilege to forcibly keep their wives at home, to prevent their wives from interacting with persons outside the family, and to in other ways completely control their wives' intellectual lives, all without regard to their wives' wishes or interests. This would be an exception to general prohibitions on restraining other persons, but legislators might justify it by asserting that it is consistent with natural law. Some non-Western societies in the world today actually have a legal regime resembling this, citing religious authority to support it. The point here is not that children are exactly like adults or that this hypothetical law of marriage would be in every way just like the child-rearing law some homeschoolers want. The point is that in either case the state would be involving itself dramatically in the family relationship by passing the laws that give one person in the relationship such legally effective control over the life of the other person. That would be true regardless of what reasons any legislators had for conferring such power, whether because of supposed natural law or anything else. We see it more readily with the hypothetical marriage law because it is strikingly different from the way things actually are today, whereas laws giving parents plenary power over children's lives are so familiar to us as to seem natural, as if they dropped from the sky rather than emanating from the state. That is an illusion.

Given the inevitability of heavy state involvement in children's lives, then, the correct way to think about the regulation question is not *whether* the state will intervene in or establish rules for child-rearing but rather *how* it will do so. Will the state enact laws that bestow on parents the power to deny their children regular schooling and instead keep them at home, or will the state choose not to confer that power and instead either insist that all children attend a regular school or conduct individualized determinations as to every child's schooling? If the state does grant parents the legal power to ensure children stay at home instead of going to school, will it further empower them to control completely the content and nature of instruction children receive and to entirely exclude education officials who otherwise would oversee a child's schooling and ensure adequate progress? Or will it give parents a more limited power (as was true in this country's early history) so as to allow for meaningful oversight, so that no children are completely at the mercy of the persons whom the state has placed in the legal-parent role, so that no one has a complete monopoly over children's minds?

Such questions all effectively ask about the *degree* of power the state should infuse into the legal-parent role. As noted above, it would be senseless to have a legal status of parenthood but attach no power to it. Conversely, it would be indefensible to attach truly unlimited power to the status, such that parents could do absolutely whatever they wanted to a child, thereby obviating all child-maltreatment laws, civil and criminal. The best answer must lie in between these extremes of no power and absolute power. Moreover, neither extreme seems plausible even as a starting point or presumption or default, at least with respect to young children. Clearly, for children's sake, the state should give parents *some* legally protected control over children's lives and *some* legal power to prevent outsiders from interacting with the children. That is the point of the state's assigning legal-parent status. But conversely and just as clearly, children need parental power to be limited. Given legal permission, more adults would harm more children.

If there is any plausible *starting point* or presumptive position for analysis, it might be what Ira Lupu calls a "separation of powers" over children, a division of authority between parents and the state, each with the ability to challenge actions of the other, so that no party has a monopoly over the lives of such dependent persons.[1] What makes sense for governing a nation might also make sense for governing the life of a nonautonomous person—that is, a system of checks and balances. If Lupu is right, the questions laid out above might also be phrased in terms of asking how the law should best divide authority over a child's life as between state agencies and the persons on whom the state confers legal-parent status. In answering the question, one should keep always in mind the important point that intervention versus nonintervention is not a sensible way to think about it, nor is conceiving of it in terms of the degree of intervention. What we seek to understand better is not *whether* or *to what degree* the state should intervene in children's lives in connection with their education but rather *how* it should do so—how it should divide legal authority over children's cognitive development as among state agencies, parents, and other private parties.

II. Beginning Right

Having clarified that the proper question is how, not whether, the state should involve itself in child-rearing, we need some normative starting points from which to begin reasoning toward an answer to that question, some premises from which we can conclude what state policy and law concerning children's education should be. There are many possibilities. Many people are inclined to begin with what they view as natural law or moral rights. We saw in the early chapters' historical account that early Americans were likely to speak of a parent's natural *duty* to ensure children received what their society collectively deemed necessary, whereas many modern Americans are wont to claim that parents have a natural *right* to direct their children's lives however they (the parents) wish. Others would assert that *children* have certain moral rights, such as a right to a good education and a right to a broad social experience. Recall Horace Mann's insistence that children's natural right to a good education imposes a duty on society to ensure they all receive one, by compelling parents to enroll the children in school. Many today ascribe moral rights to both children and parents and recommend some sort of balancing of them, to the extent that they appear to conflict. Some political theorists begin with state policy, viewing education law primarily as a means of effectuating state interests such as the creation of a future citizenry possessing virtues like tolerance and a good work ethic. There have even been some who attribute a right to citizens collectively to have a say in the future of our society as represented by today's children.[2]

People operating from any of these standpoints might invoke a variety of normative frameworks. Some might say natural law gives children a right to an open future, others that natural law subordinates the interests of children to the community, still others that natural law dictates near-complete authority for parents. Many liberal philosophers ascribe highest moral value to individual autonomy and reason from this value to a conclusion that children have a moral right to become autonomous.[3] Many legal scholars assert that parents have a right to operate "autonomously" (a misuse of that term, as explained below) relative to the state.[4] Other people might insist that education policy aim to maximize aggregate well-being, thus allowing for some sacrifice of the interests of parents, children, or other private individuals if this would produce greater compensating welfare gains for others.

That philosophers continue to debate what is the true or best normative framework suggests an insolubility to the "where to begin" question, or at least too great a difficulty to expect a satisfactory resolution in a book that is about homeschooling rather than metaethics. What we offer instead is a "coherentist" analysis of the question as to how the state should involve itself in child-rearing. This type of analysis posits certain widely held values and examines the implications of them, identifying specific normative and policy positions that these values should rule out for those who hold them. The analysis therefore speaks to anyone who holds those values, regardless of the foundational moral framework from which they derive those values.

One very basic value nearly everyone holds is that it is important to be rationally consistent rather than arbitrary in one's beliefs and assertions. This includes endorsing general principles that cohere with one's more specific moral convictions. Some people find it more difficult than others to be rationally consistent, and some manifest in their speech little concern for being rationally consistent. But ask them pointedly, "Do you think you should avoid contradicting yourself?" Presumably everyone who is sincere would say yes. Most people find it embarrassing if someone shows that their views contradict each other, that one position they take rests on premises that are logically incompatible with the premises underlying another position they hold. For anyone inclined to say, "I don't care if I am consistent, I believe X and I'm sticking to it," the normative component of this book will have little appeal. Those of us who do believe we have a moral obligation to be rationally consistent, to avoid holding contradictory beliefs on matters of importance, and to give our fellow citizens justifications for our policy positions will always have work to do. Probably we all have some specific views that would, upon careful examination, turn out to be inconsistent with some of the general principles we endorse. Honesty and civic duty require us to be open to revising our specific views if they prove inconsistent with general principles we believe true, though we must also be open to revising our more general moral beliefs if we cannot square them with specific positions we are confident are correct. What we should not accept in ourselves is an inclination to simply put aside our general principles whenever we do not like their implications in some specific case. A morality of convenience is no morality at all. Those who bemoan the decline of values inculcation in today's youth should be especially concerned to model for young people important virtues such as honesty, intellectual integrity, respect for other persons, and humility regarding one's own ability to perceive truth.

A. Where to Find General Principles Relevant to Children's Schooling?

Some might suppose the best way to advance normative theory relating to children's education is to consult what philosophers have said about it or about family life more generally and then try to figure out who offers the best view. (We do not want to overstate here the public's esteem for intellectuals.) However, education, the fostering of children's cognitive development, is a social practice quite unlike the activities that have traditionally been the focus of political theorizing about the relationship between individuals and the state. Political philosophers have traditionally concerned themselves with legal prohibition or regulation of autonomous adults' self-determining behavior—for example, public speech, religious worship, and sexual conduct—and control over property and the products of labor. But the education of children and child-rearing more generally are matters of neither self-determination nor property rights. Rather, like adult guardianship, they involve behavior and choices of presumptively competent persons aimed at influencing the experience of other persons who are currently nonautonomous.

Nevertheless, political philosophers in recent decades have paid substantial attention to children's education principally because it has been a primary site of conflict between cultural minorities and the state in many Western societies. The topics of multiculturalism and toleration of minority ideological communities in a liberal democracy have been prominent in political theory at least since the 1980s, and philosophers writing on that topic inevitably address schooling of children within such communities. Education of the young is the cultural practice over which a nonliberal subculture and the state are most likely to come into conflict. Many subcultures adhere to nonliberal views, such as absolute ideological conformity and the subordinate role of women, and deem transmission of such views essential to preserving their way of life.

Yet the modern state promotes the values of liberty and equality, and an egalitarian outlook not only is hostile to subordination of particular groups within a community but also makes it troubling to simply leave some children to the fate that subcultural leaders wish for them. Most Americans regard with alarm, for example, reclusive cults like the Yearning For Zion Ranch community in Texas that appear highly oppressive of women and children and impose practices like child marriage and polygamy. We are fairly comfortable saying that autonomous adults should be free to conduct their own lives in accordance with nonliberal values if they wish, and that we should tolerate nonliberal cultural practices within minority groups that subordinate some adults to others (e.g., prohibitions on women working, husbands having all decision-making authority in families) so long as all are free to exit if they wish. It is a huge leap, though, from this live-and-let-live attitude as to relations among adults to the position that we should enable adults in nonliberal minority communities to subordinate and deny important goods to persons who are not autonomous and/or cannot exit, such as children. Philosophers have struggled to determine what position to take regarding adults' child-rearing preferences that conflict with the state's views of children's welfare. This question did not much arise in the homogeneous environment of most communities in early America. If it did, an answer in favor of state power would surely have come quickly and decisively. But today, the question arises often, and a sense of individual entitlement pervades our culture.

The great bulk of political theorizing that has been done about children's education has suffered from one of three *basic flaws*, all of which are reflected in some popular views regarding children's education, and all of which reflect a failure fully to recognize the separate personhood of children:

i. *Treating child-rearing as an aspect of parents' self-determination.* "Parentalists" analyze parents' preferences for the education of children, as well as other aspects of child-rearing such as medical care, the same way they would analyze adults' preferences regarding their own education, medical care, pursuit of careers, control of property, and so forth, as if "what I want for myself" and "what I want for my child" were one and the same thing.[5] Implicit in parentalist thinking is an erasure of children's separate identity; these theorists in effect treat children like mere appendages or possessions of parents, though they are unlikely to explicitly characterize children as such. They speak of child-rearing as a matter of "parental autonomy," but that term is actually an oxymoron; "parental" refers to an adult's governance of a child, which is inherently an act of "other-determination," whereas "autonomy" means "self-rule." Control of one's child's life is no more a matter of autonomy than is control of one's spouse's life. (Some speak instead of "family autonomy," but this is also simply code for "parental power," at least in families where children are not equal participants in decision-making.) Based on such misconstruction of child-rearing as an aspect of parents' self-determination, homeschool advocates and some political theorists speak as if the only interests competing with parents' preferences are just collective societal interests that the state is responsible for protecting in its "police power" role (i.e., as agent for society as a whole). Parentalists generally argue that the state should confer on parents legal rights that trump such societal interests, unless a particular form of child-rearing threatens imminent harm to outsiders (e.g., training children to be terrorists).[6] But their position rests on a basic mistake—that is, not respecting the separate personhood of children.

ii. *Treating children as a collective resource.* "Liberal statists" and proponents of "democratic education," on the other hand, give primacy to current adult citizens' desires to create or perpetuate a certain kind of society by making of today's children a certain kind of future citizen.[7] This view resonates with the reactions to influxes of new immigrants in the nineteenth and twentieth centuries, which predicated an argument for common schools partly on an assumption that assimilation and acculturation are necessary to preserve the type of society earlier immigrants had created. As with parentalism, within this statist outlook children are instruments for satisfying adults' preferences. Liberal statists differ from parentalists in insisting that a much broader category of adults has a right to use children to promote their aims. Both treat children in a way they would never treat adults, whether competent or noncompetent. This way of approaching the regulation question, found most often among antihomeschool extremists, thus also rests on a basic mistake. In law and policy publications, one also finds liberal statists opposing private alternatives to public schooling in general on the grounds that they weaken public schools, as if children whose parents wish to give them an alternative should be held hostage for the benefit of the public system.[8] This, too, is unjustified instrumental treatment of children.

iii. *Abandoning analytical rigor in favor of compromise.* Some participants in the theoretical debate try to resolve (or avoid thinking very hard about) the conflict between parentalists and liberal statists by positing that because there are these two competing (and, it is implicitly presumed, legitimate) views about the aims of children's education, the proper legal outcome is to accommodate both to some degree, to balance interests and stake out a middle ground. Thus, whereas parentalists might prefer plenary empowerment of parents to govern children's cognitive formation and liberal statists might prefer universal public schooling with a heavy dose of civic-virtue inculcation, compromisers are likely to suggest a legal regime that empowers parents to choose their children's school but imposes sufficient regulation and oversight to ensure the basic capacities and virtues necessary to good citizenship.[9] That is what we always do in a democracy, some might think—we compromise. But that is not true; sometimes one set of persons has a right, and others' interests are overridden or simply irrelevant. So compromisers need an argument as to why balancing is appropriate in a particular context; it cannot simply be assumed.

Representatives of any of these three flawed approaches might, when pressed, acknowledge that children are distinct persons with interests of their own in how their lives go, but then typically assert, with little support or analysis, that either (a) children's interests are entirely consistent with the preferences of the adults whom the theorists favor, or (b) children's interests might necessitate some side constraints on efforts to satisfy the favored adults' preferences. Certainly children's interests coincide to some extent with those of parents and of democratic society, but few scholars focus attention on identifying when interests coincide and when they conflict. And even theorists and legal scholars who take seriously the idea that the state owes an obligation to individual children to protect their developmental interests, or at least to not confer on other persons power over children to an extent detrimental to their developmental interests, are likely to recommend a compromise between those interests and the demands of parents or adult majorities when they conflict.[10] To many theorists and people in general, compromise seems simply the reasonable thing to do whenever faced with competing interests in any matter governed by law.

But, as just indicated, it is emphatically not the case that compromise is appropriate whenever there are competing interests at stake in connection with some policy question. In some realms of life, individuals have a right that simply trumps competing interests. For example, an exceptionally gifted violinist might decide to never play again, thus depriving music lovers of much enjoyment, but she has a right to make that choice, to not play if she does not want to, regardless of what reasons she has for quitting. Yet few scholars have made a serious effort to think about whether children have rights in connection with their upbringing, and if so what the content and weight of those rights might be—in particular, whether they should simply trump competing interests and desires of adults rather than being balanced with them.

Underlying all three of these flawed approaches to theorizing about children's education is an implicit assumption that the schooling of children is unique and therefore that sui generis reasoning is appropriate. There are two problems with this way of thinking. The first is that "sui generis reasoning" is also an oxymoron. You are not *reasoning* if you make no appeal to general principles, applicable to a broader set of cases than just the one at hand; you are, rather, simply making assertions. Stated otherwise, to the extent child-rearing is unlike any other activity, is unique, nothing follows from that. If you want to make an *argument* based on the nature of child-rearing, you have to identify some feature of it that brings it within some *principle*, some rule-like statement that can constitute the major premise in the argument, and in coherentist reasoning that is going to require showing the principle is recognized in other contexts having that same feature.

The second problem with this way of thinking is that, in fact, schooling of children does bear substantial resemblance to certain other social practices and so can be usefully subsumed within at least three broader categories of social practice where certain principles are well established:

(1) developmental services for nonautonomous persons more broadly (including adults with mental disabilities); (2) child-rearing more broadly (including physical and emotional care); and (3) efforts of some individuals to control the lives of other individuals (autonomous or nonautonomous). Reference to settled convictions about practices within these three categories other than children's schooling can suggest more general principles that presumptively should also govern legal rulemaking about the style and content of children's education. In the analysis to follow, we therefore occasionally draw analogies to habilitation of adults with mental disabilities, to other aspects of child-rearing, and to other instances of some persons desiring to dictate the life course of others.

B. Foundational Assumptions

However, our analysis of homeschooling does not rest principally on reasoning from analogy. Rather, it proceeds from a set of six foundational normative and empirical assumptions. These are for the most part incontrovertible or uncontroversial, and they help to clarify the framework within which we present the less familiar points that make up the core of the argument.

I. CHILDREN ARE DISTINCT PERSONS   First, children are distinct persons, not appendages or property of their biological or legal parents nor things owned by society collectively. This is a modern view of children; in colonial America, many people did think of children (and wives) as property of the male head of the household, albeit a special sort of property whose care the community took great interest in and whom fathers possessed as a matter of state-bestowed privilege, or as a community resource. Though a view of children as property seems still to operate at a subconscious level for many adults and to explain many of our public policies, the prevailing "official" view today is that children are neither chattel nor mere appendages of parents, nor societal resources like minerals and trees, but rather persons in their own right. This does not rest on an atomistic view of persons as disconnected psychologically from others; each of us can have strong relationships with others, even be greatly emotionally dependent on others, yet still be a person distinct from all others. Thus, the legal system in many ways does treat children, despite their dependency and close psycho-emotional ties to parents and others, as distinct persons. One cannot reject this proposition and expect to participate meaningfully in public discourse about state policy toward child-rearing. As noted above, the premise that even unborn children are distinct persons with rights underlies the anti-abortion position that many homeschoolers hold.

2. RIGHTS TO CONTROL OTHER PEOPLE'S LIVES ARE ANATHEMA   There is a profound moral difference between self-determination and what one might call "other-determination"—that is, between having control over central aspects of *one's own* life, such as what education one will receive oneself, and having control over central aspects of *another* person's life, such as what education your spouse or neighbor or child will receive. Failure to recognize this is a core failing of many philosophical attempts to justify the notion of parental-control rights.

Rights in Western legal culture arose as protections of self-determination, because the post-Enlightenment notion that an individual person has intrinsic value and self-ownership, rather than being a mere instrument of church or state policy, gave rise to a belief that a person should have a kind of sovereignty over himself and the products of his labor, and therefore protection of his person and property against incursions by state or private actors. More recently, justification for rights has expanded to include personal integrity and respect for personhood per se. The moral foundation for our ideas about rights has never included an assumption of entitlement on anyone's part to sovereignty over the life of another "person." The great seventeenth-century political philosopher Thomas Hobbes, for example, wrote, "The right of nature which writers commonly call *jur natural*, is the liberty each man hath to use his own power as he will himself for the *preservation of his own nature*; that is to say, of *his own life*."[11] John Locke, the political theorist who had perhaps the greatest influence on the American founders, likewise wrote of a natural right to *self*-preservation and a right to retain the products of one's labor, whereas parental governance of children was a *duty* rather than a "prerogative" or right.[12]

Thus, to the extent that men have in modern Western history exercised legal dominion as a matter of "right" over other human beings—namely, enslaved persons, wives, and children—their doing so has depended on a cultural assumption that those other human beings were not distinct persons. Enslaved persons were legally property, children were viewed by some as property, and women legally lost their separate personhood upon marrying, becoming under the law of "coverture" mere appendages or possessions of their husbands. Only by denying personhood could slaveholders' control and disposition of enslaved persons be characterized as elements of self-determination, and so today a white business owner who whipped a black worker would not be viewed as engaging in an act of self-determination or autonomy. Husbands in the early nineteenth century could be said to exercise self-determination when they beat a disobedient wife only because coverture law erased her separate personhood upon marriage.

Today, there is incomplete societal and legal realization of children's separate personhood insofar as many people still think of parental control over children as a matter of the parents' self-determination, a simple extension of their control over their own lives, and the legal system still treats it as such in some ways. As noted above, many speak of "parental autonomy" to obscure the fact that parenting is actually a practice of "other-determination." Others speak in baldly proprietary terms: "Those children belong to me, and it's my right to educate them the way I want." But if one accepts that children are persons, one should see how the notion of parental "rights" is problematic, regardless of how extensive one believes parents' *authority* over children should be. So there is an important distinction between entitlement and authority; one may possess authority as to some aspect of life as a matter of privilege, without having any right to that authority on the basis of which one could object to its being more limited than one would like. Likewise with government officials; properly speaking, they wield authority as a matter of privilege, not entitlement.

Consider again the analogous case of a guardian for an incompetent adult; the guardian's authority to decide important matters is not held as a matter of "right" and certainly not as a matter of the guardian's "autonomy." The guardian-ward relationship is structurally similar to, and can closely resemble in practice, the parent-child relationship, but we characterize the guardian as a fiduciary holding certain powers and authority as a matter of legal *privilege*, a privilege courts stand ready to withdraw if the guardian breaches fiduciary duties owed to the ward. And we accept that the state is entirely free to define those duties in accordance with the incompetent adult's prior expressed wishes or best interests *as the state sees them* (an important point we return to below). So there is no inconsistency between acknowledging that children must have other people making decisions and caring for them, acknowledging that parents are presumptively in the best position to make decisions as to many aspects of children's lives, and at the same time rejecting the notion of parents' rights. If parental authority over education is important to children's welfare, then we should say that *children* have a right to their parents' holding such authority.

Many philosophers have nevertheless argued that parents have a moral right to control their children's lives, an entitlement entailing duties that the state and other private parties owe to parents. They cite the profound and unique value parents derive from raising their children with a great deal of freedom and according to their own conception of the good. Or they rest their argument on the sacrifices parents make for the sake of children (birth parents in enduring pregnancy and childbirth, legal parents in devoting time, attention, and resources to caring), or on the moral duties parents believe they have regarding child-rearing. In advancing these arguments, these philosophers have simply failed to confront the inconsistency between them and the general principles we apply in every other relationship context. Husbands might also derive profound and unique value from controlling their wives, and guardians for elderly parents from controlling their wards, yet in those contexts we absolutely reject the notion of an other-determining *right*. Many spouses and guardians sacrifice a great deal in order to provide necessary care, and most believe they have moral duties to advance the welfare of their spouse or ward, but no one argues that the sacrifices or duties give rise to an entitlement to control the other's life. Philosophers who defend the anomalous notion of parents' rights might say, "But the parent-child relationship is unique; there is no other relationship like it." Again, nothing follows morally from uniqueness. Every type of relationship is unique; that is what makes it a type. If uniqueness gave rise to other-determining rights, then people in every type of relationship would have rights to control the other person in the relationship, but that notion we soundly reject.[13] So although it is true that being a parent and having substantial power over children's lives in that role satisfy substantial interests and strong desires that many people have and that cannot otherwise be satisfied, it simply does not follow that anyone has a right to be a parent and hold such power. There are many aims in life that people have that would satisfy substantial interests and strong desires (to hold political office, to marry, to be a professional actor), yet to which they have no right.

The failure fully to respect children's personhood is also reflected in the way some political theorists today talk of the state's "right" or the "right" of adult citizens to shape children's education for the sake of collective ends. Nineteenth-century proponents of common schooling also suggested a societal right to assume control over children's education, for the purpose of assimilation. Many in the general public today suppose that if one rejects parents' rights, then one must agree with these political theorists and assimilationists and believe that the state has a right to dictate children's lives or, worse, "owns all children." But that is an invalid inference. The notion of the state having a right to control children's education is also nonsense. We would never speak similarly of the state or citizenry collectively having a right to decide what education adults receive at university, or say, "I have a right to participate in decisions about what today's college students will study." Not the state, nor society collectively, nor any individuals—not even parents—can properly be said to have a "right" to control a child's life. Yes, someone must, as a practical matter, exercise authority over the lives of young children, but it is neither necessary nor appropriate to characterize that authority as held by anyone as a matter of right. *No one is entitled to it.* Talk of a right to control another person's life is simply nonsense talk. In every other situation of dependency, we characterize the caretaking role as a fiduciary one, held as a matter of legal privilege, and there is no reason not to do so also in connection with child-rearing.[14]

The distinction between possessing a right and enjoying a privilege might seem merely semantic but makes an important practical difference. If guardians for incompetent adults had a *right* to be in that position and a *right* to be unfettered in their treatment of their wards, they could object in their own behalf to the state's removing them or imposing restrictions on them, simply on the basis that they do not like what the state is doing, and then the state would bear the burden of justifying the removal or restriction. The heaviness of that burden would depend on how strong the right is supposed to be. But because our legal system and collective morality treat guardianship for incompetent adults as a legal privilege rather than a right, guardians have no basis at all for complaining *in their own behalf* about removal or restriction. To oppose the state's action they must show it is contrary either to an advance directive by the ward or to the interests of the ward and is thus a violation of *the ward's* rights. Likewise, the state is not viewed as having an entitlement to govern the lives of incompetent adults for the state's own sake, to serve collective aims. It exerts authority over the lives of such adults also as a matter of privilege and pursuant to an assumed duty rather than right, and if it exerts that authority in such a manner as to harm an incompetent adult, it cannot defend itself by invoking any right it possesses, because it has none. There is no rational justification for treating children differently from incompetent adult wards (who could, incidentally, be persons with mental disabilities who just turned eighteen and are in the care of their parents) in this respect.

The distinction between a right and a privilege is recognized in numerous other contexts as well where people exercise authority for the sake of another person. Lawyers representing a client do not assert their own rights in court, even though the lawyers must sometimes exercise independent judgment, because they have no rights in that context; rather, they must speak in terms of the rights of their client. A trustee exerts control over trust property and can lodge complaints against anyone who harms that property, but any such complaint must invoke the rights of the trust settlor or beneficiaries, not any rights of the trustee, who possesses none as such. And neither a lawyer nor a trustee is *entitled* to remain in that position of representing clients or beneficiaries; their service is merely a legal privilege, terminable without recourse at the behest of the client, grantor, beneficiaries, or a court acting as agent for the client or beneficiaries. Elected officials provide another example. They are not entitled to hold a government office; their doing so is a matter of privilege conferred by the people they represent. There are, in fact, many kinds of fiduciary roles that people occupy as a matter of privilege, roles of profound importance for the individuals served and for society as a whole, and the role of parent is one of them.

Now, to say it is inappropriate to speak of parents or the state having a "right" to control how children's lives go is not the same as asserting that parental interests and societal interests can play no role whatsoever in policy formation or in legislation about central aspects of children's lives, such as their education. What it means is rather that questions as to which policies and laws are morally appropriate cannot sensibly or defensibly be answered by invoking parental or state *rights*. It might be appropriate in some contexts for the law governing child-rearing to be designed to protect or promote societal interests or the interests of persons as parents, but that will not be because either is *entitled* to use children's lives to serve their own ends. It will be because this indirectly benefits children as well—for example, by making parents more satisfied in the caregiving role, or by improving the quality of discourse in the public square in which today's children might someday wish to participate—or at least has no adverse effect on individual children. In other words, children's rights might be somewhat indeterminate in some situations, leaving room for more than one outcome, and then interests of others might permissibly influence the choice.

We are not positing at this point the appropriateness of any particular policy that serves parental or societal interests, but rather only making the conceptual point that ruling out talk of parental *rights* and state *rights* per se, with the connotation of moral entitlement those concepts entail, does not amount to categorically ruling out consideration of parental or societal interests. It simply changes the conversation, so that someone urging protection of parental desires or promotion of social causes through education policy should have to explain how doing so is consistent with proper respect for the separate personhood of children, which they might do by demonstrating that what they recommend is consistent with children's interests. But simply assuming that all affected interests must be balanced against each other, such that significant interests children have in connection with their own development might be sacrificed to benefit parents or society generally, is indefensible.

3. CHILDREN HAVE THE GREATEST INTERESTS AT STAKE IN THEIR SCHOOLING
Ordinarily our legal system and moral culture ascribe rights to persons as to matters central to their lives or impacting their most important or basic interests.[15] Thus, even pro-lifers concede that a woman's control over her own body is a matter of right for her, such that the state must bear a heavy burden of justification to deny her control of her body. They do not claim to have an entitlement themselves to dictate what pregnant persons do with their bodies, because they understand that controlling someone else's body and life course is not a matter of one's own fundamental interest or a central aspect of one's own life, even though one might attach immense subjective importance to it. The abortion debate is rather about whether the state should recognize a right of the unborn child to live, a right that might trump the right of a pregnant person in some circumstances. Pro-lifers say yes, pro-choicers no.

With this background understanding of what is a fitting basis for having a right, we proceed with the third starting assumption that, on the whole, a child has greater interests at stake in connection with his or her schooling than does any other person or entity. In fact, a child's education is a central aspect of his or her life and a matter of fundamental interest for the child. It would be difficult to find anyone who disagrees with this assumption. Though they often assert their own "rights," even the most anti-statist of homeschoolers would likely agree that their child has greater interests at stake in connection with his or her schooling than they (the parents) do, just as they themselves had greater interests at stake in the education they received as children than did their own parents. In asserting "parental rights," they primarily do so, one would assume, in order to serve what they believe to be their children's interests, and it would seem that they simply do not perceive the conceptual confusion such talk reflects. If they did, they would speak instead of their children's rights. They would contend that their children have a right to the best possible schooling and a right against the state's forcing them to leave home to attend a school, and that what they (the parents) want does constitute the best possible schooling for them, despite any contrary views of state education officials. Some homeschoolers in fact defend their view of what the law should be by invoking rights of their children.

In addition to assuming that children have more at stake in connection with their schooling than parents do, we also assume that a child's interests in his or her own education are greater than the interests that society as a whole has with respect to that particular child's education. Of course, both parents and society have interests that a child's schooling can affect; this is true also when children become adults and face choices about college. Parents' interests might be mostly vicarious; they presumably love their children and want their children's lives to go well, so they are happier if they perceive their children receiving what they regard as good schooling. But parents also have self-regarding interests at stake; they live and regularly interact with their children during the child-rearing years and want to feel a sense of shared purpose and values. Child-rearing is akin to a career in being something most parents have undertaken intentionally to fulfill a subjectively important ambition, and parents might need their offspring's help and financial support in old age.[16] But neither their vicarious nor self-regarding interests come close in importance to the interest the child has in his or her own cognitive and social development. With societal interests, one might think that even if the interest of any one citizen or taxpayer is small compared to that of a child, there are so many people who make up society that their combined interests in the school system outweigh that of the child. But whereas the school system as a whole might greatly impact societal interests, the schooling of one individual child has little or no discernible impact. That is likely the reason why there is little public concern that there is virtually no public oversight of homeschooling in the United States, and that as a result there are some children out there now who are not receiving schooling anyone would deem even minimally acceptable. What happens to one or even ten thousand children does not sufficiently affect a society containing hundreds of millions of people such that the rest care.

4. THE STATE MUST ULTIMATELY DETERMINE CHILDREN'S INTERESTS   Our fourth starting assumption is that the state must decide what the basic interests of nonautonomous persons are. This is a difficult premise for many people to accept. After all, legislators and bureaucrats do not know these persons the way their caretakers or other family members do. How could the state be in the best position to say what interests a child or an adult with mental disabilities or some other nonautonomous person has?

The first step in defending this assumption is to recall the point explained at length above that the state must establish the legal rules governing children's lives and that parents cannot claim a right—that is, a moral entitlement—to have the legal rules simply defer to them just because they are parents, end of story. In fact, most people who assert parental rights as a basis for parental decision-making authority defend that position by arguing that parental authority best serves children's interests. But how can they expect the state, which ultimately must decide who has legal authority over children's lives, as explained above, to agree with them unless the state itself has made some conclusions of its own about what children's interests are? For state actors (or you, the reader) to take the position that parental power best serves children's interests would require determining themselves (or yourself) what is generally in children's best interests and then who, among potential holders of authority, is most able and inclined to wield authority in such a way as to protect and promote those interests. You cannot logically say that parents are the best caretakers of children's interests without presuming yourself to know what children's interests are. It is astonishing how commonly people make the internally contradictory statement that "only parents know what is best for their children." How can one say that without presuming oneself to know what is best for all children? One must presume this omniscience for oneself, observe parental behavior, and then compare what one observes to what one supposedly "knows" about children's welfare. It is a quite arrogant statement to make, masquerading as deference.

A second step in defending this assumption is to note that although every human is unique, there are many commonalities among humans in terms of their characteristics, inclinations, and needs. That is why it makes sense to think of humans collectively as a species, a group of individual beings sufficiently like each other and sufficiently unlike beings outside the group to be treated as "a kind." One of the areas of human life as to which there are commonalities among all humans, or nearly all, is child development. Empirical studies have revealed generic needs that children have for their psychological, emotional, cognitive, and physical development at different stages of early life; these needs must be met in order for them to experience health, happiness, and opportunity for a flourishing life. Whether a particular child needs protein, for example, is not something that child's parent needs to figure out in the course of living with the child and observing his or her individual characteristics and inclinations; scientists who spend their careers studying nutrition and child development tell us that every child needs protein, and any parents who insist that their child does not need protein we should assume to be cognitively impaired and dangerous to the child. So, too, with loving nurturance; children who do not receive it uniformly manifest adverse psycho-emotional consequences and are at high risk for social pathology. We do not need each parent to figure out whether his or her child is the sort of child who needs emotional nurturing.

Another commonality among humans is what a person needs in order to have a wide variety of opportunities for the life he or she will lead as an adult. This is determined by social circumstances, such as job-market expectations and norms for socializing, which have changed considerably over the past two centuries and which establish certain conditions anyone must meet in order to participate (e.g., literacy, communication skills, math ability, understanding how things work in various parts of the social and physical world). It is nonsensical for parents to say that their child is unique to such an extent that their developmental needs are entirely unlike those of other children and that what their child needs in order to have broad opportunities in life is entirely personal to him or her, not the same as for any other child, thereby making the parents' greater familiarity with the child of utmost importance. Parents might deny the value of having broad opportunities or having certain particular opportunities, but that is quite different from claiming to have child-specific expertise about what will ensure broad opportunities. Yet many people confuse these two things—disagreement about values and knowledge about how to promote a particular value. Much homeschooling is motivated by the former, by rejection of mainstream values. And with respect to disparate values, a claim of superior knowledge—that is, that "parents know best"—is simply impertinent; it makes no sense. A parent who rejects the value of gender equality, for example, should not be understood to say, "Well, I know my Sally better than anyone, and I know she is the kind of person who does best when told she is inferior to males, that's just the sort of person she is." What the parent is instead effectively saying is "I have different values, which I think should be imposed on *every* child by their parents, and I insist that I am entitled to act on my values rather than the values of the secular state in controlling the life of the child as to whom the state has made me a legal parent." Knowledge and expertise are simply not part of the equation.

Because there are many commonalities among children that are relevant to children's schooling, regardless of what values the schooling is supposed to reflect, the adults who are in the best position to determine what children's interests are in connection with education might actually not be adults who have experience with only one child or a few children. The best persons to make those judgments about *common* interests or needs might be adults who have observed a lot of children, have studied the large literature presenting and pulling together studies of large groups of children, or have experience teaching a large number of children. In other words, child development could be something as to which there is such a thing as expertise that is based on observation of many cases and rigorous review of scientifically valid studies. The behavior of most homeschooling parents in fact suggests this is so. Most, whether "ideologues" or "pedagogues," seek expertise from others to help them educate their children. Recall the discussion in chapter 2 of the booming business in homeschooling curriculum publication and how-to guides for homeschoolers. There are many quite profitable publishers of homeschooling manuals, guidebooks for parents, and packaged curricula. Parents attribute expertise to these publishers and pay to consume the expertise. Their doing so belies any claim that every parent is inherently an expert as to the education of his or her own children.

This is not to suggest that a child's particular attributes are irrelevant to proper decision-making about his or her schooling. Children certainly vary to some degree in how they learn best (e.g., some absorb spoken or written instruction well, others learn best by hands-on experience). They also vary in terms of comfort in different social circumstances, as some thrive in a highly structured environment whereas others do best in a more freewheeling setting. Many children struggle with disabilities of various kinds. Parents are in a good position to know a child's individual traits, inclinations, strengths, and weaknesses. But even these are shared with many other children, so there can also be expertise regarding them—for example, how to present a lesson to a child with an unusually short attention span or dyslexia—expertise more likely to be held by professional educators than by parents per se. The ideal decision-making framework would seem to be one in which parents communicate their child's particular characteristics to education professionals who know what research has shown is most effective with children possessing such characteristics— that is, in which there is a dialogue and a sharing of knowledge between parents and well-trained educators.

We do not mean to overstate professional expertise in the realm of education. Many things about children's learning are still a mystery to researchers, and competence among education professionals varies, as in any occupation. But it certainly would not follow from lack of professional knowledge that parents know what is best. If education researchers have not yet figured out how best to teach a child with a particular characteristic, as a general matter or as to specific subjects or skills, then they can communicate that; they can tell parents, "I understand that you believe this will be best for your child because of this fact about them, but actually extant research does not support that belief. We just don't know." Or parents might be justified in their belief by their own trial and error with their child, even if the experts cannot explain what parents have observed, and state actors should respect that experience, but this scenario is likely fairly rare, and when it arises the state can ask parents to demonstrate the success of their methods.

In short, there is little purchase to a claim that "parents know best" when it comes to the schooling a person receives in the eighteen years between birth and adulthood. There is generally little "expertise" as to education that inheres simply in occupying the parental role and living with a child, and in any event for the state to conclude that parents are good decision makers the state would first have to decide itself what children's interests are. The state must be the ultimate decision maker as to the aims of schooling, because it must decide what the law governing children's education will be, and in carrying out that function it can and does call on the expertise of professional educators.

Yes, let us be quite clear about this: the state often does a poor job of setting education policy, and this is a problem for children. No one in their right mind would suggest the state is omniscient, perfectly rational, and singularly devoted to doing what is best for children. To oppose state regulation of schooling by ascribing that view to proponents of state oversight is to create a strawman. State decision-making is susceptible to political and ideological battles that might have nothing to do with children's interests. State education officials have been known to jump on bandwagons just because they want to appear progressive or traditionalist, without thinking through the likely consequences of the latest policy fad. They sometimes react defensively to attacks on public schools, driven more by concern for their reputation than anything else. Education agencies are vulnerable to capture by interest groups. And sometimes school boards and superintendents are driven more by a desire to avoid controversy than by sound reasoning about educational objectives. There are many reasons to be wary of state decision-making in the realm of education as in other realms. But, as explained above, there is no feasible alternative to the state's making the ultimate decision about what children's basic interests are, as a general matter, and moreover the state is able to hire many professionally trained child-development and education experts to inform its decision-making (even if the expertise is incomplete), decision-making that usually occurs after deliberation and debate in a public setting where parents and other concerned citizens can participate. Education policy today certainly rests on a far more professional and sophisticated basis than in our nation's early years. The ideal regime today would seem to be one in which the state makes the ultimate decisions, because it must establish the legal rules, but parents and other private individuals have ample opportunity to challenge a state agency's decision and to have an entity independent of the education agency, such as a court, review the agency's specific policy decisions for compliance with established general objectives.

Notably, we are generally quite accepting of ultimate state authority to determine the interests of nonautonomous adults. If any of us should one day become incompetent, a court will appoint a guardian for us, based on its judgment of what is in our best interests (which could be what we have chosen ourselves in an advance directive, if we are among the minority of people who have done that, but need not be). The law will impose various legal duties on that guardian, all based on assumptions the state makes about what is in the interests of incompetent adults generally, or in the interests of adults who are incompetent for particular reasons or who have particular traits. The state develops these assumptions using its expertise—that is, the professional training of experts whom the state's department of social services has hired. Even though every elderly person with dementia, every middle-aged person with mental disabilities, and even every person in a persistent vegetative state is unique, we accept that the state is the appropriate locus of ultimate authority to determine what those persons' interests are and to what extent it should delegate practical decisions to guardians or other fiduciaries. The contrary inclination many people have to reject ultimate state authority to decide what children's interests are does not rest on any empirical belief that children are factually different from nonautonomous adults in terms of uniqueness—that is, a belief that each child is unique in more salient ways than is each incompetent adult. Its source is, rather, ideological or visceral opposition to conceding anything to the state in connection with child-rearing, because child-rearing is a locus of ideological and cultural warfare in modern Western societies in a way that care of nonautonomous adults has never been.

What is likely to be the last defense of such opposition, in the face of the points made above that the state has to establish the legal rules allocating authority over child-rearing and that the state would need a reason to agree with those who claim that plenary parental authority is best for children, is natural law. Some might retreat to the position that the state should enact laws giving complete control to parents and none to state agencies (unless parents choose to delegate their authority to state agencies) because natural law says that is the way things ought to be. We saw such contentions on display in the homeschooling litigation described in chapter 3. Note that the argument has to be something different from simply "nature has given parents the strongest inclination to do what is best for their children and greatest insight into how to do that," because that is an empirical hypothesis the state would need to verify before it could accept it and verifying it would entail the state's making its own determination of what is best for children and then comparing it to what parents are observed to do and decide. So that kind of appeal to nature just brings us back around to the state's having ultimate authority on what is best for children. Rather, the argument would have to be that some authority superior to the state has proclaimed that parents are the ultimate authority on what is best for their children, and the state must simply accept that as true and act accordingly. The state cannot verify or refute that proclamation because it does not have the knowledge, wisdom, or normative standing of this superior authority. This type of argument leads us to our fifth starting assumption.

5. THE STATE CANNOT ACT ON THE BASIS OF RELIGIOUS BELIEFS   Natural law has meant many things to different people over the course of Western society's history and does so still today. To most contemporary natural-law

scholars, it means simply a set of true moral precepts prior to and above law and policy, to which we ought to try to conform our laws and policies. We fallible humans try to discern what these precepts are by examining the requisites for human flourishing and by reasoning about how to obtain them in a manner consistent with fundamental moral principles, such as respect for human life and the Golden Rule. One of the most prominent of these scholars, John Finnis, emphasizes that natural law need not be thought of as emanating from a divinity, and that natural-law reasoning is something quite different from dogmatism or conventionalism (i.e., an appeal to "how we've always done things").[17] Natural-law thinking thus bears resemblance to moral realism, the position that there are objective and eternal moral truths that should guide our actions.

We see nothing objectionable about state actors appealing to natural law in the sense just described. In fact, such an appeal is much like the form of reasoning we undertake in this book. We begin with fundamental normative principles and assumptions about basic goods, and we reason on the basis of those toward specific conclusions of law and policy. We assume these principles and assumptions should guide state decision makers when they choose among potential policies relating to children's schooling. The main difference with our approach is that we bracket the metaethical question about the source and truth status of the moral principles with which we begin, because that question is superfluous to our analysis. We adopt particular general principles because they are widely held in modern Western society. Probably most people who hold them believe they are objectively true moral principles. But others might reject or be agnostic regarding the notion of moral truth while still endorsing these principles for other reasons—for example, because they coincide with ethical intuitions. It does not matter for our purposes why one accepts X or Y as a basic moral principle. We will explore the implications of accepting those principles for those who do so, and we assume most people do.

An approach to natural law of the sort Finnis describes—that is, one that begins only with the most basic moral principles and assumptions about human flourishing and that entails commitment to honest and open-minded deliberation with others in the moral community about the practical implications of those principles and assumptions—does not present the dangers that arise from some other appeals to extralegal normative authority, dangers that have motivated classical liberal theorists and the US Supreme Court to insist on substantial separation between religion and the state. What most people "on the street" would likely mean by natural law, however, is a set of divine commands, many quite specific, that are not subject to debate. For a great number of people in our society, "Natural law gives me a right" and "I have a God-given right" are synonymous. This is essentially a religious outlook, and it generally also entails the view that the state should recognize in its laws what some people believe nature/God has commanded. Such a view was pervasive and controlling in much of colonial America, though what early Americans understood to be the content of natural law relating to child-rearing (parental duty to conform to community expectations for child-rearing) is significantly different from what many contemporary Americans claim.

Today the particular content of the religious perspective from which natural-law claims emanate varies considerably from one individual or group to another. A significant percentage of homeschoolers believe the Bible communicates literal truth in its every word. This makes their assertions about God-given parental entitlement odd, as the Bible speaks only of parental duties and says nothing about opposition to state-imposed requirements for secular education, but they appear to not recognize the incongruity between their political positions and the Bible. Other Americans look to the Bible not for detailed prescriptions but for deeper themes, which should include humility and a trustee conception of parenthood. Still other Americans believe that other, quite different religious texts and traditions supply truth and guidance. A great danger inherent in the state's adopting or endorsing a religious view per se is destructive divisiveness; because modern Western societies are ideologically diverse, there is intense disagreement about theological questions and about specific normative rules believed to emanate from God. Even if the government were competent to determine the truth on theological matters when confronted with competing assertions among the population (and we generally suppose that it is not), the cost to our society of its declaring that "truth" and making it the basis for state policies would be too great. One cost would be violent struggle to control the state so that it espouses one view of religious truth rather than another; even if government officials *were* theologically or morally omniscient, many people would not believe the state is omniscient and many others would fight for control of the state regardless. Another cost would be the danger that particular religious prescriptions the state might adopt would entail discrimination and even violence against persons with a different religious view, and anyone in the religious majority now should worry that one day they will not be.

In short, Americans have rejected theocracy in favor of a secular state that limits itself to making decisions on the basis of temporal considerations, empirical assumptions verifiable at least in theory by observable evidence, basic widely held moral and political principles, and an assumption of human equality. Thus, in making any sort of decision about the well-being of nonautonomous persons, the state may not base the decision on an assumption as to the truth of any religious beliefs per se. Rather, it must reason on the basis of temporal interests, empirical evidence, and basic moral and political principles like "equal respect for all persons." Thus, if some parents insist on feeding their children only lettuce and nothing else because they believe God has commanded them to do so and will give their children physical and spiritual health only if they follow this command, the state may not accept their beliefs as true and may not empower the parents to deny their children all other foods on that basis. The state must act on the basis of secular science's conclusions as to children's dietary needs and a normative assumption that it is wrong for the state to empower one person to inflict on another, innocent person suffering and death from starvation. Likewise, if the state appoints a sibling to serve as guardian for an adult with Down syndrome, and it turns out the sibling adheres to a religion teaching that persons with mental disabilities are possessed by the devil and must be confined at home, the state may not assume the sibling's belief to be true, nor may it defer for any other reason to the sibling's preference that her ward not participate in educational and work programs outside the home. The state must reach its own conclusions about what best serves the welfare of such an adult, from the state's nonreligious perspective, and act on the basis of those conclusions.

The same is true with respect to children's education. Though many parents want to homeschool their children for religious reasons, they cannot reasonably expect the state to adopt their religious beliefs as true nor to accept that their god supplants the state's authority and responsibility. With respect to adults' control *over their own lives*, it is generally unproblematic, even obligatory, for the state to leave people free to act in accordance with their religious beliefs. This is a matter of respect for individuals' basic right of *self*-determination, of sovereignty over his or her *own* person and life. But when adults' actions affect other persons, or when adults demand legal power to dictate the course of other persons' lives, then regardless of the relationship those adults have with those other persons the state cannot simply defer to whatever religious authority those adults might invoke in defense of their actions or in support of their demand for power. Even if the state ultimately decides to leave those adults free to act in accordance with their religious beliefs when dealing with other persons, it may do so only after judging for itself, based on nonreligious considerations, that this freedom will not result in what it (the state) regards as harm to others, and is consistent with equal respect for all persons. Thus, the US Supreme Court held that members of the Westboro Baptist Church should be free to stage anti-gay demonstrations near funerals (as long as not too near) not because the court deferred to the religious authority of that church or assumed that church's beliefs to be true, but rather because it found that the offense the demonstrations occasion to family and friends of decedents does not rise to the level of "harm" in a legal sense. But if demonstrations at funerals or abortion clinics or political conventions do rise to the level of inflicting physical harm or psychological damage on other people or substantially interfering with others' exercise of their rights, then the state may and should curtail them. It cannot allow the harm on the grounds that the demonstrators' beliefs are true. And if the state does confer other-determining legal power on someone, it cannot rightly be because of that person's religious beliefs but rather must be because that is conducive to the other person's well-being.

Accordingly, if homeschooling parents insist that the state give them complete power over their children's schooling because God has bestowed this entitlement on them, the state simply may not accept this religious claim as true, any more than it could accept as true a parent's claim to a God-given right to limit a child's diet to lettuce or a pro-choice advocate's claim that God commanded her to burn down the headquarters of the National Right to Life organization. To the extent that invoking natural law amounts to an insistence that the state abjure its responsibility to protect and promote the developmental interests of children out of deference to divine authority, then the state must ignore that invocation. If instead it means that conferring on parents plenary legal power over children's schooling would be most conducive to flourishing lives for children—as the state understands "flourishing"—and is consistent with fundamental moral principles (as opposed to specific, question-begging moral conclusions like "parents are entitled to this"), then that is something with which the state could potentially come to agree. But it should do so only after examining the matter itself and deliberating rationally and objectively on the basis of generally applicable assumptions about basic goods, widely held fundamental moral principles, and reliable empirical evidence. The remainder of the book is intended to embody that sort of deliberation.

6. IN ESTABLISHING SCHOOL LAWS, THE STATE ACTS AS A FIDUCIARY FOR
CHILDREN   Our final starting assumption concerns the essential role of
the state in connection with legal regulation of children's lives. The state
has two basic types of interests relating to children's schooling, reflecting
the fact that the state potentially serves two roles in connection with any
policy making or lawmaking concerning nonautonomous persons. As a
general matter, the state most commonly acts in what legal theorists call
a "police power" role, as an agent for society collectively, promoting societal well-being, preventing disorder, adjudicating disputes between autonomous persons, and so forth. In that role, the state, as agent for society
collectively, has an interest in today's children receiving schooling that will
make them law-abiding and hardworking adults who apply themselves to
socially useful endeavors. We saw the creation of common schools justified principally in terms of the benefits to society it would produce as the
economy began to demand more advanced learning, and so as an exercise
of the state's police power.

But the state in Western society has for centuries also taken upon itself what legal theorists call a "parens patriae" role, acting as the ultimate
guardian over the welfare of individuals who are not autonomous and who
therefore are highly vulnerable to abuse and exploitation at the hands of
private parties. In that role, the state has an interest in ensuring each individual child an education conducive to his or her own immediate and long-
term well-being. For example, when the Pennsylvania Supreme Court in
Commonwealth v. Fisher (1905) justified removal of a child from parental
custody so that the child would not "end in maturer years in public punishment and disgrace," it was invoking the state's parens patriae duty to
protect children from deficient parenting; the state was "compelled to take
the place of the father."[18] Likewise, in its earlier 1839 decision in *Crouse*,
the same court had asked rhetorically, "May not the natural parents, when
unequal to the task of education, or unworthy of it, be superseded by the
parens patriae, or common guardian of the community?"[19] In the police-
power role, the state is a fiduciary for society collectively. In the parens
patriae role, the state is a fiduciary for the dependent individual.[20]

The state's dual role could lead to conflicting policy conclusions. For example, in deciding what course of action doctors should take with a person who has fallen into a persistent vegetative state, the state might best
fulfill its police-power role by favoring quick termination of life-sustaining
treatment because this will reduce medical costs that might benefit no one,
or because this will ease the suffering of family members while seemingly

depriving the patient of little (i.e., just the remote possibility of recovery). But the state might best fulfill its parens patriae role by maintaining life support, either because the person asked for this in an advance directive or because the state assumes that this is what most persons would choose if they were to execute an advance directive. In the context of education, there could be many such conflicts between roles. In its police-power role, the state might, at least in some localities, impose a curriculum aimed at producing a lot of docile future workers who will fill a pressing societal need (e.g., miners). In its parens patriae role, in contrast, the state would design a curriculum aimed at giving every child a flourishing life, so each child is able to pursue careers or other endeavors consistent with his or her talents and abilities as well as have an enjoyable time while in school. There can be overlap between these two aims, of course, given that children will have a better chance at finding jobs upon reaching adulthood if their education has been mindful of likely future labor-market needs. But the two approaches are likely to lead to significantly differing schooling experiences for children.

An important question that therefore arises in policy making about child-rearing, though few people recognize it, is how the state should resolve any such conflict when making choices about the lives of persons presumed unable to adequately choose for themselves. Most theorists who perceive a potential conflict of interests between a child and a society collectively, or between a child and his or her parents, simply assume, implicitly or explicitly, that the state should take all interests into account and, when conflict arises, balance them—that is, should act in a police-power capacity. This assumption is usually false.

First, even when the state acts in a police-power role, it is not the case that it must weigh the interests of every potentially affected person in making policy decisions. As noted earlier, sometimes rights trump others' interests, rendering the latter irrelevant. For example, though many people care greatly about abortion and would be happier if the state prohibited it, the state need not balance the happiness interest of those people against the rights of pregnant persons in order to arrive at a correct legal regime. Pro-lifers have a free-speech right to protest abortion, because every individual's interest in freedom of self-expression is thought strong and deserving protection, but they have no right to make their happiness per se part of the policy or legal analysis of the permissibility of abortion. In turn, the fact that distant pro-choice onlookers find the pro-lifers' demonstrations annoying should be irrelevant to the policy and legal question of whether the state should tolerate such demonstrations; the distant on-lookers' interests are not part of the legal equation and, at least within a deontological ethical framework, are also off the moral table.

Second, when the state does put on its parens patriae hat, it must take off its police-power hat. As a practical matter, it is impossible to serve in both roles simultaneously. Both roles are fiduciary roles, and what it means to serve as a fiduciary is to act with undivided loyalty as an agent for a group or for an individual person. A fiduciary for an individual must stand in the place of the person and make decisions in behalf of that person exclusively in the way the person presumably would do for himself or herself if able. In the absence of a contrary, autonomous choice by the principal, the law presumes a person would make decisions for himself or herself based only on self-interest. Thus, the law requires fiduciaries to have a single-minded focus on the welfare of their client and not serve as fiduciary also for others with conflicting interests. Trustees are required to act exclusively for the benefit of trust beneficiaries and are not allowed to make decisions for the trust with the aim of serving their own interests or the interests of other persons who are not beneficiaries. Similarly, lawyers making decisions in behalf of their clients, whether the clients are autonomous persons or nonautonomous, have strict duties of loyalty to their clients; they may not aim to serve the interests of others while purporting to represent their clients. Because a fiduciary must be singularly focused on promoting the interests of the client, the fiduciary cannot also serve as a fiduciary for another client that has conflicting interests. Thus, lawyers must do a "conflicts check" before taking on any new client. The state similarly cannot serve two principals at once, society as a whole and a nonautonomous individual, when there is any potential conflict of interest between the two, and there clearly can be such conflict between society as a whole and individual children in connection with schooling, as explained above.

The important question, then, is *when* the state must put on the parens patriae hat and, accordingly, take off its police-power hat. It does not follow from the fact that the state does sometimes act in a parens patriae role and the fact that children need the state to protect their interests that the state is always acting in a parens patriae role with respect to every decision it makes impacting minors. The state certainly may impose on minors' behavior limits that are intended to protect the interests of other people—for example, prohibitions on driving before a particular age, on committing acts of violence, and so forth. In deciding whether children may drive, the state properly acts in a police-power role, balancing whatever interests children might have that count in favor of their driving against the interests of the rest of society that count against their driving. So when should the state be viewed as acting in a fiduciary capacity for an individual child rather than as an agent for society collectively?

The most sensible answer is that the state must see its role as purely a parens patriae one, acting as an agent for a nonautonomous individual, when it presumes to make for a nonautonomous person decisions of a type that autonomous persons are generally entitled to make themselves and solely on the basis of their own interests—that is, self-determining decisions as to central aspects of one's own life that threaten no harm (wrongful injury) to others. In those situations, there is no warrant for the state's involvement in the decision at all, *except for* the nonautonomous person's need for an agent to act in their behalf.

For example, as a general matter autonomous persons are entitled to decide if they will receive or decline recommended medical treatment. The state cannot force a competent adult to undergo surgery for a heart problem. If the state makes a medical decision for an incompetent person, that person's lack of competence is the only legitimate reason for its doing so, and the state's power goes only as far as that justification for having it. Thus, the state must attempt to instantiate what the incompetent person would choose for himself or herself if competent, and may not take into consideration collective societal interests or the wishes of other individuals. In the absence of a prior competent direction from the person or clear evidence of the person's values, the state must act on the basis of what it supposes to be the person's best interests (though it may certainly solicit input from the person's family or friends in doing so). Thus, the United States Supreme Court, in *Cruzan v. Director, Missouri Dept. of Health*,[21] rejected a claim by parents of a woman in a persistent vegetative state that they had a right to decide whether their daughter would continue to receive life support, holding that only the patient herself had any rights in the matter and that those rights included effectuation of her values or supposed best interests. Similarly, if the state has custody of (e.g., has in foster care) a three-year-old with a heart defect, the state's decision as to whether the child will undergo surgery to correct the defect must be based exclusively on what is in the child's best interests as the state perceives them. That undergoing the surgery would give pediatric surgeons more practice and so improve medical care in the society is not a legitimate consideration; if the surgery has no chance of helping the child and would cause her great suffering, the state should not order it, period. In contrast, competent adults are *not* deemed entitled to decide for themselves whether they will strike another person, and so when the state decides the rules for children's striking others it need not don the parens patriae hat but rather may wear the police-power hat in deciding what limits to impose on children's conduct toward others and what penalties it will use to enforce those limits.

Schooling is like undergoing surgery and unlike hitting another person. We competent adults are absolutely entitled to decide what schooling, as among the opportunities practically available to us, we will receive, if any. And we are entitled to make that decision based solely on what we believe to be in our best interests, even if the state offers some form of schooling to us at its own expense. (And allocation of state funds among types of schooling or between schooling and other public purposes is a separate matter, one to which the state's police-power role applies.) Thus, when the state steps into the shoes of children to make schooling decisions for them—that is, to decide which forms of schooling parents may choose for them (assuming, as we do, that no single form alone is best for all)—it may do so only as a fiduciary for the children, singularly focused on what is in their best interests. Giving content to that much-contested concept of best interests is the task of the next chapter.

SUMMARY   The analysis of state policy regarding homeschooling will proceed from these assumptions:

1. Children are persons.
2. No one has a "right" to control the life of another person.
3. The child has the greatest interests at stake in connection with schooling.
4. The state must have the ultimate authority to determine what children's interests are.
5. The state may not act on the basis of religious beliefs.
6. In establishing laws about schooling, the state acts as a fiduciary for children.

Notes

1. Lupu, "Home Education, Religious Liberty."
2. For a description and critique of these various perspectives, see James G. Dwyer, "Changing the Conversation about Children's Education," in *NOMOS XLIII: Moral and Political Education*, ed. Stephen Macedo and Yael Tamir (New York: New York University Press, 2002).

3. See, e.g., Levinson, *Demands of Liberal Education*, and Brighouse, *School Choice and Social Justice*.

4. See, e.g., Chiu, "Culture Differential in Parental Autonomy," 1773, 1777; Stephen G. Gilles, "Parental (and Grandparental) Rights after *Troxel v. Granville*," *Supreme Court Economic Review* 9 (2001): 69, 74 (asserting that some third-party child-visitation statutes do not "meaningfully protect parental autonomy"); Goldstein, "Medical Care for the Child at Risk," 645, 646–47.

5. See, e.g., Galston, *Liberal Purposes*, 102 (characterizing child-rearing power as an aspect of parents' "expressive liberty").

6. See, e.g. Galston, *Liberal Purposes*, 252–56.

7. See, e.g., Gutmann, *Democratic Education*; Macedo, *Diversity and Distrust*.

8. See, e.g., Fineman and Shepherd, "Homeschooling," 57, 102–4.

9. See, e.g., Callan, *Creating Citizens*.

10. See, e.g., Reich, *Bridging Liberalism and Multiculturalism*, 158 ("Given the triad of interest holders, and the significance of their respective interests, a theory of educational authority that claimed only the interests of one party mattered could potentially establish a kind of parental despotism, state authoritarianism, or child despotism. Any defensible theory of educational authority, then, will strike some balance among the three parties."). This cursory explanation for balancing might be called "argument by characterization." One wonders whether Reich would similarly characterize my right to refuse surgery as a "despotism of the patient."

11. Thomas Hobbes, *Leviathan* (1651), chap. XIV (London: Penguin Books, 1968).

12. John Locke, *Second Treatise of Government*, ed. C. B. Macpherson (Hackett, 1980; orig. 1690), sec. 67, 37.

13. For a fuller critique of philosophical arguments for parents' rights, see James G. Dwyer, *The Generalizing Parental Rights* (forthcoming, 2019).

14. See Dwyer, *Religious Schools v. Children's Rights*, chap. 4.

15. Readers uncertain whether nonautonomous persons can possess rights can find an extended explanation of why the "interest-protecting" view of rights is superior to the "choice-protecting" view or "Will Theory" of rights in Dwyer, *Relationship Rights of Children*, 291–307.

16. Recent work by Brighouse and Swift emphasizes this parental interest. See, e.g., Harry Brighouse and Adam Swift, *Family Values: The Ethics of Parent-Child Relationships* (Princeton, NJ: Princeton University Press, 2014); and Harry Brighouse and Adam Swift, "Family Values and School: Shaping Values and Conferring Advantage," in *Education, Justice, and Democracy*, ed. Danielle Allen and Rob Reich (Chicago: University of Chicago Press, 2013), 199–220.

17. See Steven D. Smith, "Natural Law and Contemporary Moral Thought: A Guide from the Perplexed," in *The Natural Law Reader*, ed. Laing and Wilcox, 336–40.

18. Commonwealth v. Fisher, 213 Pa. 48, 53 (1905).

19. Ex parte Crouse, 4 Whart. 9 (1839).

20. Parents, too, might believe they serve a dual role—namely, as devoted, loving caregiver of a child and as servant of a divine authority or the public good. We do not need to examine such a duality closely; we can just assume some parents take certain positions regarding their children's schooling that might diverge from the state's aims.

21. Cruzan v. Director, Missouri Dept. of Health, 497 U.S. 261 (1990).

CHAPTER SIX

Getting Facts Straight

To reach a conclusion as to what stance the state should take toward homeschooling, given that there must be *some* law relating to the practice—either empowering parents to waive their children's state-law right to regular schooling and to keep the children at home during school hours, or requiring that all children attend a regular school—and that it is the state that makes laws, and bearing in mind that the state may dictate a child's schooling only in a parens patriae role, we take this approach: First, we identify basic goods whose acquisition by children can be impacted by the nature of their schooling. Second, we consider whether some children actually do not need or benefit from those goods, or have competing needs that might be more important. That analysis of basic goods is the work of this chapter. Then, in the succeeding, final chapter, we consider what moral principles come into play when parents have aims for their children's schooling that are opposed to the state's aims, and we apply those principles to reach conclusions about what general stance the state should adopt toward homeschooling—that is, whether to permit it without restriction, to permit it but only subject to certain regulations and oversight, or to prohibit it and require attendance at a regular school.

I. Schooling and Basic Human Goods

Schooling is most obviously about (a) cognitive and intellectual development, but it inevitably also entails (b) acquisition of knowledge, (c) development of habits in interpersonal relationships, and (d) identity formation. Moreover, schooling can have a significant indirect effect on (e) family relationships. And because of children's great vulnerability, a school can pose a danger of maltreatment or provide protection from it, and so where and how children are schooled can impact (f) their basic physical, psychological, and emotional security. These important aspects of a child's experience are largely determinative of a human's ability to enjoy a fulfilling life. We consider each in turn below, aiming to provide enough specific content to reveal where some parents or other individuals and the state might diverge in their attitude toward schooling.

We note at the outset, however, that different people have widely divergent views about the content of many of these basic goods. For example, what constitutes a properly developed mind means for some a mind trained to accept the dictates of an external authority without question and interpret all experience consistently with moral and empirical precepts emanating from that authority. For others, it is a mind trained to think independently, question authority, and repeatedly reexamine its own fundamental beliefs. How, then, can we say anything definitive about what the law governing children's education should promote in terms of cognitive development, knowledge, habits of interpersonal interaction, and so on?

Some might contend that because there is great disagreement about certain basic goods, the state should not presume to impose one view on everyone but rather should leave people free to make their own choices about that. That contention suffers from many defects. First, it overlooks that, with respect to children's education—at least, young children—the people doing the choosing are not the people whose cognitive development is at issue. Adults are choosing for children. Adults are not choosing for themselves, and children are generally not choosing for themselves. So it is inapt to respond to the fact of disagreement among adults as to the aims of children's education with the libertarian credo "Let people choose for themselves."

Second, if the state deferred to individual opinion on every policy matter as to which there is disagreement, the state would be quite thoroughly paralyzed. No one really believes the state should always refrain from taking a position as to all contested welfare questions. Considering other possible policy issues makes this obvious. Just in the realm of child-rearing, one finds divergent views on medical care, diet, discipline, drug and alcohol consumption, exposure to sex and violence, gun use, and driving. No one would seriously maintain that the state should simply empower all parents to decide everything as to which there is any disagreement, including whether children in their custody will receive vaccinations, whether a child with diabetes will receive medical treatment, whether children should eat every day, whether children should eat anything other than lettuce, whether burning a child with cigarettes is an appropriate form of discipline, whether five-year-olds should drink beer, and at what age children should begin to watch or participate in sex (and with whom), own a gun, and start driving. For each of these matters, the state must establish a legal rule dividing the permissible from the impermissible, despite the fact that there will always be some parents who disagree.

In creating such a rule, the state must make its own judgment. To render a judgment, the state needs to make value decisions and must have information. What information is relevant depends very much on the value decisions. Once the values are determined, the state can purchase pertinent expertise (in the form of permanent employees or temporary consultants), to the extent expert knowledge exists, that will guide pursuit of those values. Giving content to the basic goods, for purposes of lawmaking, therefore leads to the fundamental question of how the state is to determine the values children's schooling should serve.

In answering this question, we should always be clear about which hat the state is wearing—police power or parens patriae. As explained in the previous chapter, despite the widespread tendency among government officials, scholars, and the general public to speak about education as a means to serving collective ends, such as having a productive future labor force or a cohesive civic society, this is a realm in which the state must be acting in a parens patriae role. Whether one devotes a substantial portion of one's life to attending an educational institution is clearly a matter of self-determination for adults and something as to which competent persons are entitled to decide for themselves. Whether a particular eighteen-year-old attends college can affect societal interests, yet the state may not order the eighteen-year-old to do so. There might be many ways in which the state could strengthen civic society, increase patriotism, or make the economy more efficient by ordering adults to undergo certain training programs, yet the state is not permitted to do that. We adults decide for ourselves based on what we believe to be in our best interests whether we will undertake a course of study to develop new skills or acquire knowledge.

When the state presumes to make such decisions for nonautonomous persons, it is permitted to do so only because such persons need a proxy decision maker, and the authority to make proxy decisions extends no further than that justification. Thus, in acting as a proxy the state must aim to replicate individuals' self-determining choices—that is, based presumptively only on that individual's own interests. This is generally recognized with respect to nonautonomous adults; persons with mental disabilities receive rehabilitation services aimed at promoting their interests, not aimed at serving some societal need. Otherwise, we might see persons with mental disabilities being trained to remove toxic waste or perform other low-skill tasks that other persons refuse to perform without high compensation.

The question of what values should guide state decision-making about children's education therefore becomes a question of what the state should assume to be in children's best interests. Such a question frightens some people because they imagine an ominous Big Brother standardizing children, a blundering bureaucracy incapable of making and implementing sound decisions, or both. As noted above, however, we already entrust the state with the authority to draw lines between permissible and impermissible parenting in numerous other domains, based on judgments of children's well-being, as well as between permissible and impermissible ways of treating children who are not one's own and of treating other adults, both autonomous and nonautonomous (as in prescriptions and proscriptions pertinent to guardianship of incompetent adults). Despite undeniable flaws in the practices of various child-welfare-focused government agencies, as well as in the performance of private professionals who provide government-mandated services, we continue to entrust authority to such government agencies (which, after all, are staffed not by robots or aliens but by ordinary people who are mostly themselves parents) because there is no sensible other place to put it in this imperfect world. Regardless of what legal regime one might think should govern children's schooling, it is, as explained above, ultimately the state that must establish that legal regime, and the state needs reasons to favor one regime rather than another. And those reasons must be child-centered because the state must operate in a parens patriae role in this context.

Thus, if one believes the law should give parents plenary power over children's cognitive formation, one should have to convince the relevant state actors that doing so would be in children's best interests, which just leads us back to the question of what the state should accept as constituting children's interests in connection with schooling. So we might imagine ourselves in the position of legislators deliberating about legal issues relating to education, such as whether school attendance will be compulsory, what the permissible forms of schooling are, what content school courses should or should not have, and what limitations there should be on schools' treatment of children. We must decide these issues within the constraints enumerated in the previous chapter. In particular, we may not act on the basis of religious beliefs. Thus, as legislators we must consider what children need in this world rather than, for example, what will secure their eternal salvation. Fortunately, our fellow legislators are under the same constraint, so we should not have to worry about their voting to impose on our children *their* religious visions, which might be diametrically opposed to our own. In addition, in deliberating about these issues, we should recognize that children are generally embedded in families, living in the custody of the persons whom the state has made legal parents, and that parents in our society manifest a tremendous variety of worldviews, empirical beliefs, and dispositions toward children. This is the perspective we adopt in considering each basic good below.

The list we have presented is not exhaustive of human goods. We note, though, that those described below underwrite some other goods on which many education theorists focus, such as equal opportunity for careers, self-sufficiency, autonomy, and effective participation in civic life, so it would be redundant to list those additionally. With respect to autonomy, for example, philosopher Harry Brighouse has done excellent work explicating what it takes to acquire or achieve it. His prescription includes what we characterize below as critical thinking skills and disposition, knowledge about the natural and social world, knowledge of diverse ethical perspectives, social interaction, and freedom from psychological abuse (e.g., making a child terrified of questioning received views or of choosing a different way of life).[1] At the same time, we do not claim that the goods listed below are irreducible; there might be even more basic goods that the ones we list partially constitute or promote. Our aim is the practical one of identifying at a workable level of generality some things the state should consider presumptively valuable for all children.

A. Cognitive/Intellectual Development

The main reason why the state and the vast majority of parents consciously choose to create some sort of learning experience for children is that they believe children's minds develop (i.e., they are not fully formed at birth) and certain learning experiences will positively and substantially affect that development. Regardless of their particular views of what things are important and valuable in life—that is, their "conception of the good"— all thinking persons will acknowledge that a properly developed mind is a basic human good. And, as established above, in thinking about what the law should dictate regarding children's development, we should adopt the perspective of a legislator whose field of concern today must be limited to secular considerations. Those considerations have necessarily evolved over time.

We might usefully begin by thinking about essentials, what children need most in terms of intellectual formation, and then consider whether there are less crucial but still desirable aims the state should adopt in its role as proxy decision maker for children. Surely we would conclude that it is essential for all children to develop the capacity to think for themselves. Given the great importance that we adults ascribe to autonomy, independence of mind and will, and reflective and rational judgment in our own lives, we should deem this central to a flourishing human life. Homeschool advocates would not dispute this. Robert Kunzman, a leading authority on the sociology of homeschooling, has found that most conservative Christian homeschooling parents (at least those willing to speak to him) "consistently voiced the sentiment that they want their children to grow into adults who can think for themselves" and has speculated that homeschooled children achieve autonomy to at least the same degree as do public-school students.[2]

Thus, we should not empower any parent or state actors to deny any child an educational experience that trains and prepares them to examine views—empirical, moral, political, and so on—critically, to evaluate the validity of arguments, to reconsider premises, to recognize and weigh competing considerations and evidence, and to reach his or her own conclusion about what is true. Some individual parents might prefer that their own children not become critical and independent thinkers, because they fear this will lead to false beliefs about matters of faith and morality, and they hold a conviction that the ultimate value for their children is to have what the parents regard as true beliefs. Kunzman recounts the story of British poet Edmund Gosse, whose religiously conservative father educated him at home, and who described himself as "a bird fluttering in the network of my Father's will, and incapable of the smallest independent action."[3] Recall the Amish parents whose dispute with the state led to the Supreme Court's *Yoder* decision; their chief concern was that adolescents in the community might come to question their faith if exposed to persons outside the community. Legislators simply cannot adopt such a view themselves when deciding for children generally. This is so both because legislators cannot assume any religious beliefs to be true and because it would be logically impossible to say that *all* parents are correct about the ultimate importance of believing certain things, given the multiplicity of divergent views parents hold. Legislators should look at the adult population and recognize as a good thing that most adults are autonomous, able to think and decide for themselves what they believe, and then conclude that it is a good thing for children to develop in such a way that they, too, will at some point have that capacity.

A thought experiment can help demonstrate the correctness of this conclusion. Imagine that you will die tonight and be born again tomorrow, only this time your biological parents will hold ideological views diametrically opposed to the most important beliefs you now have. Then think about legislators empowering your new parents to prevent you from becoming capable of thinking for yourself about matters of faith, so that you will spend your life in unthinking acceptance of beliefs that today, in your real life, you find totally repugnant. Do you not think it would be better for you in the new hypothetical life you are going to have if the law instead requires that you receive an education aimed at enabling you to think independently of your parents, to rationally critique the beliefs of your parents and of other people, and to reach your own thoughtful conclusions about what is good and true in life?

The inclination of some readers at this point might be to insist, "But my views *are actually* true." That is what innumerable other people would also say, however, including people whose views you find despicable or tragically misguided. And you might hope that legislators will share your views, but in a democracy lawmakers change with some frequency, and the new batch next year might include many whom you think are tragically misguided. Catholics can recall the hostility with which legislators and public schools once regarded members of their faith, and evangelical Christians who view the public schools today as devoid of religion—or, worse, propagating "secular humanism"—should worry that a more theocratic government would openly pronounce Christianity false and the Bible purely myth. It is better for all of us and for today's children that we withhold from legislators the power to legislate matters of faith or to act based on their religious beliefs, and that we adopt a legal regime ensuring all children receive an autonomy-promoting education.

Parents inclined to favor conformity over independent thinking in choosing a form of schooling for their children should reflect on their own mental life and their own sense of entitlement regarding freedom of thought. Do they view themselves as blind conformists, not thinking for themselves? Do they not value their ability to reason critically and reject views and purported authorities that their reason determines to be false? Do they not believe they have a right against the state forcing beliefs on them, directly or indirectly (e.g., by empowering other individuals to control and brainwash them)? If they would answer as we expect they would, they should, as a matter of rational consistency, concede that independent thinking is valuable for their children also and that all children have a right against the state's directly or indirectly subjecting them to schooling that thwarts rather than fosters their native capacity for becoming independent thinkers. Many homeschoolers—not only pedagogues but also many ideologues—endorse the idea that children should be trained to think for themselves; one of their chief objections to public schools is that they appear to encourage conformity to a particular worldview.

Additionally, one might expect parents convinced of the truth of their moral beliefs to have some confidence that a child trained to think independently will also come to see the truth of those beliefs, which the parents will certainly have ample opportunity to teach the child regardless of what sort of school the child attends. And they should recognize that the child will then have a depth of understanding that comes only from examining beliefs closely rather than adhering to them because of parental compulsion. The danger the parents should worry about is not their children's being trained to think critically and independently but rather their children's lacking that ability and therefore being more vulnerable to false views to which they might be exposed later in life.

Prioritizing autonomy thus in part responds to the diversity of conceptions of the good in modern Western society, and it in part reflects a judgment implicit in our expectations for our own lives that autonomy is central to a flourishing human life. From today's perspective, we might judge life in most of early America to be deficient in this important respect—that is, deficient due to an expectation of conformity to a single conception of the good. And if we today value our own capacity for self-determination, for choosing among different value systems and worldviews, and if we insist on the freedom to disagree with others, the Golden Rule requires that we endorse the same capacity and freedom for others, including our children.

Moreover, as Randall Curren has articulated, independent critical thinking is a broadly applicable capacity, conducive to well-being in all aspects of one's life in modern society. It enables better decision-making about how to run a household and a business, how best to conduct personal relationships, how to harmonize potentially competing aims in one's life or one's family, and how to maximize one's health and job prospects.[4] Thus, acquiring it takes a child a long way toward a flourishing life and an "open future," toward being capable of pursuing a wide range of careers and other lifetime projects in the modern world. Critical thinking also depends on training in several disciplines; one must not only develop an ability to break down

arguments into component parts and assess the logical validity of infer-
ences, but also have an understanding of scientific concepts and methodologies in order to assess the truth or plausibility of empirical assumptions
and the reliability of studies upon which people make claims about public
policy, medicine, nutrition, product safety, and so forth.

In addition, there are other cognitive abilities prerequisite to developing
autonomy or of great importance regardless of any connection with autonomy. For example, there is general consensus that children should acquire the ability to read and write and to perform mathematical operations.
Illiteracy and innumeracy are demonstrably disabling in modern society.
Legislators might reasonably suppose that being able to read and understand newspapers, enjoy great literature, and learn from nonfiction texts in
any area of interest are essential to the kind of life they should presume any
person would wish to live.

Capacities for analytical reasoning and for understanding and critiquing scientific claims are also instrumental to political participation, for self-
protection as well as for the betterment of society collectively. Our lives are
inevitably greatly impacted by policy choices government actors make concerning the economy, the environment, and other important aspects of life,
and those policy choices typically rest on empirical assumptions as well as values, so effective participation in democratic self-government requires an ability to assess the validity of empirical claims, by examining evidence offered
and critiquing the way in which it was acquired and/or the ways in which it is
being used. A command of scientific principles and research methods is prerequisite to doing this. Without that command, people are easily swayed by
unsupported claims, bad research, and misuse of scientific studies.

As to any of the intellectual abilities just identified, it might be that not
all children are natively capable of acquiring them. For the children with
more substantial disabilities, different goals for schooling seem appropriate, the overarching aim being a life that is flourishing for them. But for
those who are born with the capacity to acquire these abilities, the state
should treat not only reading, writing, and arithmetic as basic goods that
schooling should foster, but also autonomy, analytical reasoning, and scientific principles and methodology.

B. Knowledge and Beliefs

In addition to certain intellectual capacities, children must for their own
good acquire a substantial body of knowledge. Knowledge in many subject areas underwrites the intellectual capacities and is prerequisite to

successful pursuit of higher education and employment and to effective operation in cultural and political spheres. Academic institutions in modern Western societies can be faulted for overemphasizing accumulation of content or memorization of facts. But all of us must call on a great store of knowledge just to maintain a home and interact effectively with the world beyond our homes, let alone have an "open future" in terms of careers suited to our talents and abilities and other meaningful pursuits. One acquires much of that knowledge just by living in a home and a community. But much of the knowledge one would need in order to attend and successfully complete a degree program at a good university or to secure a skilled-worker position is unlikely to be simply breathed in from the environment; schooling in some form is needed to impart some crucial knowledge. A child entirely shielded from national history, mainstream culture, and current affairs might also have difficulty forming relationships with anyone outside of her or his immediate family or outside a reclusive community. This is uncontroversial.

More controversial is the notion that children must be exposed to and understand certain scientific precepts, such as evolution, and ideological worldviews different from that of their parents. A common motivation for homeschooling is a desire to prevent children from being exposed to beliefs and ways of life that parents deem false or otherwise objectionable. To a large extent, this is more about values and behavioral norms; parents worry especially about children from other families conveying a positive attitude toward sinful or illegal things like sex and alcohol consumption. But, for many parents, there is also a desire to prevent their offspring from learning about empirical claims and moral beliefs inconsistent with the parents' religious views. This is increasingly difficult for parents to do if they rely on internet research in a home education program. Kunzman and Gaither note, "The internet has, especially since the mid-2000s, transformed the world of homeschooling by limiting the power of conservative Protestant groups to serve as information gatekeepers for the practice."[5]

As for empirical beliefs, liberals have manifested an odd preoccupation with evolution, insisting that all schools should teach it rather than creationism, even though they know a substantial percentage of parents teach their children that creationism is true and evolution is false. This focus on evolution seems to exaggerate the importance of one particular scientific precept and to foment unnecessary conflict. Biology courses generally presuppose the validity of evolutionary theory, but one can study many aspects of biology (i.e., how living things today are categorized, the body parts of members of different species and their functions, how living things reproduce, what causes diseases, etc.) without learning that theory. A child can have a substantially open future and grow up to have a very fulfilling life without studying evolution or other scientific ideas in tension with biblical literalism (e.g., carbon dating) during childhood. Moreover, even if one believes creationism to be a false view of history, one should concede that being taught it is rather harmless, as harmless as growing up believing that other biblical stories or folk myths are true, as children all over the world regularly do. Indeed, to the extent that creationism conflicts with observed reality, it can perplex children in a way that makes them think harder, thus developing their intellectual capacities. An "education" full of false views is undoubtedly bad for a child, and some particular supposedly scientific claims (e.g., that all physical illness is an illusion) are dangerous ones for children to hold, so we as legislators should not empower parents to exempt their children from whatever scientific study the parents wish. But children's struggling with some small number of beliefs that are discordant with experience can be quite salutary. Listening to older children puzzling about the severe practical obstacles Santa Claus must face in delivering presents to every child in the world on a single night, as all familiar with that myth do at some point, should be very gratifying for anyone who enjoys observing children's development of critical thinking ability. Many of us parents often "kid around" with our children by making demonstrably false statements to see if and how they can figure out that we are "pulling their leg," and when we see their "wheels spinning" we know they are sharpening their analytical capacities. Some textbooks used by homeschoolers who are adherents to creationism actually teach children critical thinking and scientific method through that lens, guiding them through critiques of the claims that scientists make in favor of evolution.[6] So the real deficiency in some homeschooling, in terms of scientific study, is not exclusion of evolution or inclusion of creationism but rather a more or less complete deprivation of instruction in scientific methods, which I have included in the category of intellectual abilities.

One area of knowledge we legislators should deem truly important for children's education to include is worldviews different from their own. This is not merely conducive to development of autonomy, as discussed in the previous subsection, but also arguably prerequisite to having a broad range of opportunities in life. A child in whom parents instill a unitary and comprehensive nonmainstream worldview while not allowing the child any glimpse at other ways of seeing the world and life in it, or, worse, instructing the child that the world outside is full of heretics doing the devil's work, would likely experience debilitating trauma upon attempting to traverse the world outside the family or the insular community of birth and be bewildered by confronting ideological difference and highly distrustful of the new people they encounter.

This basic idea is also mostly uncontroversial; one might be hard pressed to find any parents who wish to deny their child any knowledge of beliefs and ideologies that diverge from the parents' own, or who admit that they teach their child about other viewpoints in a nonobjective and distorted fashion. But people argue, heatedly, over how children are to acquire knowledge of other belief systems. If the aim is to prepare children to interact peaceably and effectively with people of diverse mindsets, some forms of "religious studies" curriculum are ruled out—for example, one that instills in children the idea that anyone who has beliefs different from their own is an agent of the devil. The opposite approach, teaching children that every conception of the good is equally valid, has problems of its own; it might foster a more positive disposition toward others that will be conducive to positive interactions, but it could have detrimental effects on children's relationship with their parents and their community, on children's sense of identity, and on children's feeling of security and meaning in life. If teachers present to children alternative worldviews in a way that allows children to understand the basic precepts by which others live and to accept that a person can be a decent human being and reasonable in endorsing those precepts, even if the precepts are different from one's own, this should be sufficient to generate the desired benefits.[7]

C. Social Interaction

Humans are social creatures. We flourish in interaction with others. Relationships with others have instrumental value, enabling us to engage in exchanges that benefit us. They are also the avenue through which we develop a sense of who we are and what is special about us, and through which we seek to improve ourselves by developing virtues, character traits, and skills. We also generally experience friendships, family relationships, and engagement with some larger community as intrinsically valuable, and many people seem naturally inclined to fill a great deal of their lives with social interactions.

Undoubtedly, there is a great variety of "relationship packages" a person might have during life that more or less equally provide the benefits that interpersonal relationships generate. There is no clear minimum number of relationships one must have. We can say with great confidence, however, that one type of relationship is crucial to healthy development—namely, a secure attachment to caregivers. We address that type of relationship in the subsection on family life below. But any developmental psychologist would say that children must also have for their healthy development horizontal relationships with peers, in addition to the parent-child attachment relationship. Through such horizontal relationships, children learn to interact as equals, to negotiate over competing preferences, to make choices for themselves, and to bond in a way that is distinctive to nonhierarchical and voluntary relationships.[8]

Much of this children can experience with just siblings and/or a few friends. One need not have as many real friends as the typical social-media user has Facebook friends or Twitter followers in order to learn how to cooperate with equals, to assert one's own preferences, and to love. There is no reason to think these experiences were unavailable to persons living in small, isolated communities in colonial New England or on the prairie in the nineteenth century.

To become prepared to live in the larger world today, which the state might suppose is in every child's interest, what might be more important than the number of personal relationships is the diversity of them and that some are voluntary. A child's relationships with siblings, all of them living together in the small community of the family and under the same parental authority, without the possibility of exit, are insufficient by themselves to prepare the child to interact with other citizens who can choose not to associate and with whom the only common authority is the state, let alone with fellow citizens who come from dramatically different ideological perspectives. Efforts any states have made to assimilate all newcomers and maintain a homogeneous population have largely failed; the challenges of civic life in today's highly diversified America are different from what they were in the colonial era. One need not interact closely during childhood with people carrying out every other way of life or belief system in order to be well prepared for adult life in mainstream society, but the experience of confronting substantial difference and having to get along with others in that situation should be repeated a significant number of times during the stage of life when children still have the security of parental care to retreat to. The "getting along with others" lesson of social interaction is a particular concern for many critics of homeschooling because they perceive that certain religious groups—groups that appear to predominate in the homeschooling population—foster in children attitudes of hostility and uncompromising adamancy in dealing with persons who hold a different conception of the good.[9] Most such critics worry only about the effect this can have on society generally (i.e., on them and their children), but there is also a deleterious effect on any children who acquire those attitudes; it impairs their ability to engage positively with a huge swath of their nation's population. That concern is somewhat alleviated by the recognition that homeschooling ideologues and conservative Christians are hardly a monolithic bunch; there is significant diversity of belief among them, and so children are likely to develop some skill at getting along with those who disagree even if their socializing is limited to other conservative Christians.[10]

Thus, for children, relationships with peers outside the family are important in part because of their mostly voluntary nature. Unlike siblings, schoolmates are more or less free to refuse a relationship, so children in regular schools learn that if they want to maintain a normal social existence they must cooperate, compromise, and conform to shared notions of fairness and civility. At a time when ideological division in America is intense and public civility appears severely lacking, the current generation of children also has a strong collective interest in acquiring social virtues that will enable them to coexist more peaceably and respectfully. Diversity in one's relationships would seem also conducive to better self-understanding and to shaping of one's self-identity in a way most consistent with one's inner nature, which might diverge from that of parents and of siblings. All of these interests tied to social experience increase as a child gets older, so a small social universe might be adequate in early childhood, but adolescents today need to interact with a much larger number and greater variety of people.

The networking that a large portion of homeschooling parents do can *in theory* provide this good of social interaction. To what extent it does so in practice depends very much on the extent and nature of the networking. If parents carefully limit the network to families who conform strictly to a narrow worldview, the child's interactions with peers from other families would be unlikely to provide opportunity for confronting meaningful difference in outlook. It is true that even within such a network, there is likely to be divergence of opinion on some matters, such as small doctrinal points, specific public policies that do not come too close to fundamental values, optimal household routine, or best curriculum publisher. The children would therefore get some experience with confronting difference, thinking about why they adhere to their particular opinion, and seeing that reasonable people can disagree and remain mutually respectful. But such a narrow network might not prepare children to go forth as adults into mainstream society and successfully navigate the challenges to living, studying, and working in a dramatically heterogeneous environment. In contrast, if parents actively seek out families who differ from their own in ideology and culture, it might well be possible for children to get a very robust experience of heterogeneity through a homeschooling network.

With respect to the need to develop an ability to cooperate, compromise, and conform to norms among peers in voluntary relationships, the ability of homeschool networking to satisfy that need would seem to depend on whether it allows children substantial time together to interact freely and without close adult supervision. If the networking consists solely of meeting once per week for an hour of special instruction, or of socializing that is closely monitored by parents, it cannot suffice for this purpose.

Another aspect of successful civic life is the ability to advocate for one's interests or positions. This can at times require the ability to cooperate and compromise with people who sharply disagree, but homeschooling advocates appear to have had great success in combatting regulation without calling on such abilities, though perhaps only because there is little or no pushback from anyone who wants more robust regulation. Many in the ideologue camp of homeschoolers make a deliberate effort to train children to take up this mantle one day. This entails a more robust civics education than one will find in most public schools—for example, the Generation Joshua program that HSLDA runs.[11] The adversarial approach many ideologue homeschoolers instill, however, is likely to perpetuate and exacerbate the ideological divisiveness and incivility now plaguing social discourse in America and to leave homeschooled persons with a lifelong sense of being embattled and under attack, which is not conducive to happiness or great academic achievement or extensive career possibilities. They admirably aim to instill strong character in children, but the character is that of a religious soldier rather than that of a citizen, a brother or sister to all fellow citizens. Civics training can amount to "ideological amplification" if it consists only of learning how to defend and advance unquestionable views of one's belief community.[12] Again, though, we should acknowledge when a perceived problem is not limited to homeschoolers or to religious conservatives; one can point to numerous liberal groups and individuals that display absolutist animosity toward anyone who disagrees with them. And religious conservatives accurately perceive that many liberals fail to treat them with respect or genuine concern as fellow citizens. Civility seems in short supply all around the political spectrum these days, and "common schools" do not appear to be doing much to replenish it.

Now, we have supposed here that it is in every child's interests to be prepared to function fluently in mainstream Western society, which is quite diverse along many dimensions. Some might object that there are numerous counterexamples of people living insular lives outside the mainstream who are flourishing in their own way. The Supreme Court's *Yoder* decision was predicated in large part on empirical assumptions about the positive nature of insular Amish life and the potential that Amish children have to enjoy flourishing Amish lives as adults. Most people think of isolated aboriginal groups in a similarly favorable way. Persons in such groups have lives resembling that of many premodern societies, before global transportation and migration became possible for billions of people. There was likely sufficient diversity of views and lifestyle choices even in more culturally homogeneous premodern societies to challenge children and thereby facilitate their cognitive development. Surely we cannot say it was impossible in such premodern societies to become autonomous and to enjoy a life in which one applied one's talents and abilities to such an extent that it could be deemed a flourishing life. So, what if parents living in an insular cultural community wish to homeschool and to confine their children's social interactions to that community?

There are a couple of responses to this line of thinking that bolster the conclusion that preparation for life in an ideologically and culturally diverse environment is important for all children today. First, that a flourishing life is *possible* in a certain environment does not mean that it will actually occur for all or even most in that environment, or that a flourishing life is *likely* for any or merely possible for all. There are many people who do *not* have flourishing lives in homogeneous communities and yet could have a flourishing life if they were able to exit and join a different sort of community. Many do leave such communities and write books about how miserable they were in those communities and how much happier they are outside them.[13] One fact the *Yoder* court chose to ignore was that even at that time, in the early 1970s, between one quarter and one third of young people raised in Amish communities left to enter mainstream society upon reaching adulthood, and had to do so without any academic learning beyond eighth grade (though at that time this was true of a great portion of non-Amish youth as well).

In the premodern world, exit was impossible or much less feasible. But today, adults in any minority cultural community can, as a practical matter, fairly easily transport themselves to the very different environment of mainstream society. It is an opportunity formally available to all. So in Amish communities, aboriginal communities, and other insular minority communities, there will inevitably be some percentage of young people who will find it difficult or impossible to have a flourishing life if they remain within their community of birth after reaching adulthood, but who could have a flourishing life if adequately prepared to enter mainstream society.

We must then ask whether that group of children should drive education policy. Does it matter what percentage of a community they represent? What if the vast majority of children could have flourishing lives without the kind of schooling experience that would enable them to leave and to thrive in mainstream society? Should the state force that kind of schooling experience on every child for the sake of the few who cannot have flourishing lives without it? The same sorts of questions arise when we consider other ways in which problems relating to education might exist for only a subset of all children if the state empowers parents or local communities to do whatever they want with children. Most pertinent to homeschooling might be the concern that some parents might be incapable or disinclined to provide their children with an education the state regards as adequate. Nearly all homeschool advocates admit that such parents exist, but many insist that the state should not inhibit the freedom of the many for the sake of (what they assert are only) a few. We therefore address this set of questions in a general way in the next chapter, in considering education regulation. We will ask whether, as a general matter, the state must act to ensure no child is left behind, so to speak, or should instead let the normal case drive policy and law.

A final concern relating to socialization is that it can take negative forms; some interactions with peers can pose a threat to other basic goods, such as positive self-conception (discussed next), autonomy (perhaps through the imposition of an anti-intellectualist attitude), and an "open future" (for example, if the result is teen pregnancy or substance abuse).

D. Identity Formation

Everyone during childhood forms some sense of who they are in relation and in comparison to other people. Adults refine and revise their identities over time, but one's core sense of self—including one's sense of inherent worth, one's strengths and shortcomings, and one's values—develops most intensely and fixedly during childhood and adolescence. Children define themselves first by identification with their caregivers, then by differentiation from their caregivers, and then by affinity with or divergence from others, including other family members, others in their local communities, and the rest of the world. In addition to examining their own experiences in this process, children absorb what others communicate to them about their talents, virtues or vices, appearance, and destiny.

What self-conception a person has largely determines the quality of his or her life. It influences one's core emotional state to see oneself as good, competent, and worthy of love rather than the opposite. It influences one's choices as to friendships and pastimes in childhood and how one approaches schoolwork or other challenges. Children need affirmation of their positive worth and qualities in order to lead flourishing, satisfying lives. A child made to believe he or she is stupid, unattractive, or wicked is likely to be chronically unhappy, have few positive friendships, and have little enthusiasm for play or schoolwork. All of this childhood experience in turn greatly affects a person's adult life. Chronic unhappiness is likely to persist. Poor socialization and poor school performance in turn constrict one's opportunities for college, reinforce the underlying negative self-image, and likely persist in college and beyond. Political philosopher John Rawls treats self-respect as a "primary good" for such reasons; a positive sense of self-worth is a psycho-emotional foundation for a flourishing life, an essential internal resource for successfully navigating life as a youth and as an adult.

Many homeschoolers emphasize personal identity as a concern motivating them to keep their children out of regular schools. They worry about negative influences other children and teachers might have on their children's identity formation. Some worry that children will develop an exaggerated sense of self-worth or come to view themselves as persons entitled to decide for themselves what constitutes a good life, and so become less obedient to parents and God's word. Others worry about teachers or peers turning their children into mindless conformists. Some worry their children's sense of self-worth will be undermined by peers' unkindness or obsession with wealth, fashion, and attractiveness. Another common fear is that children will adopt bad values modeled by peers—for example, coming to believe that taking drugs and having extramarital sex are okay because feeling good and fitting in are more important than being a moral, responsible person. Those who homeschool in substantial part for such reasons implicitly concede that a healthy personal identity is an important good and that a child's schooling has a large influence on identify formation.

Critics of homeschooling worry, contrariwise, about any parents having monopoly control over children's identity formation. Such a monopoly is not inherently problematic; much depends on how particular parents choose to exercise it. Critics worry, though, that some parents will use it to unduly restrict the experiences children have to draw from in seeking to understand themselves, and they worry that some parents will use the monopoly control to impose on children a negative or stultifying self-image. A parent might do this out of ideological conviction—for example, if he or she believes and communicates to a child that all children are naturally wicked and need severe constraint to avoid Satan's clutches. Some homeschoolers impress on their children what outsiders view as a severely limited view of acceptable life paths for women, one that coerces daughters into lives of subservience and domesticity, with threats of devastating spiritual consequences should they seek to pursue a college degree and a career outside the home. Other parents impose a negative self-image simply because they are emotionally and psychologically abusive, perhaps themselves suffering from low self-esteem, depression, or untreated mental illness. Of course, there are also non-homeschooling parents who do these things, but a child attending a regular school might be more likely, the argument goes, to receive countervailing positive messages about themselves.

E. Family Relationships

We place the good of family relationships in fifth position not because it is less important than the preceding goods. Arguably, it is more important than any other, and for that reason we begin the regulation discussion in the next chapter by viewing the child not as an isolated learner but as a person first and foremost situated within a family. In particular, a child's relationship with parents in infancy and in early childhood is crucial to psycho-emotional and cognitive development. That relationship serves a different, and arguably somewhat less important, role in adolescence and then in adulthood but can continue to influence a person's basic well-being to some extent throughout minority and beyond. Relationships with siblings can also play a significant role in a child's development, though there are plenty of adults who were an "only child" to attest that having siblings is not essential to positive development in the way that a secure attachment to one or more caregivers is. Children ordinarily also have relationships with grandparents, cousins, and other extended family members that are significant both for the inherent effects of interpersonal interactions and for their impact on other goods such as identity formation.

We address family relationships relatively late in this list simply because most people do not think of them as immediately relevant to education policy. But they are, because a child's schooling experience typically impacts family relationships. One impact is simply the amount of time children spend with family members. Recall the objections in the nineteenth century to laws compelling attendance at common schools, that these laws were tearing apart families. Many homeschoolers report that they have much closer relationships with their children, and that siblings have stronger bonds with each other, because of the additional time together and because there is less competition for the children's time and attention. A child who spends seven hours in a regular school for 180 days of the year is not only away from his or her parents for at least 1,260 hours each year but in addition is quite likely during those hours to form relationships with other children in the classroom and on the bus, relationships that will occupy some of the child's attention even when he or she is not in school. Another impact is on family harmony. In a regular school, and in a public school in particular, a child might over the years develop habits and ways of thinking that conflict with a parent's outlook and way of life, and that could create tension between child and parent that makes their relationship less close.

Could regular schooling have any positive effects on family relationships? Sending siblings together to school, where they share a milieu and typically support each other in the absence of parents, tends to strengthen sibling relationships. If cousins attend the same school or if other extended family members previously attended the same school, that could strengthen a child's bonds to kin. But what about the core parent-child relationship? Some homeschoolers speak proudly of their personal sacrifice of career and alone time in order to provide their children with a better education, but they would undoubtedly concede that the sacrifice is genuine and substantial and that some parents might be less capable of doing it. Hence the popular saying "it takes a village" and the qualification many homeschooling parents express that "it's not for everyone." Sending one's children off to school can give parents a break some really need from parental responsibility, or just free them to do other things that bring them happiness and personal fulfillment. Happy parents are better parents; when we are happy, we are able to give more love and attention to our children while with them. A child's being in regular schooling can elevate parents' enthusiasm for child-rearing and thereby make parent-child interactions more positive for the child. And, conversely, a growing body of evidence shows that parental stress has a negative impact on children and on parent-child relationships.

In contrast, a parent who chooses to homeschool but is overwhelmed by the constancy of parental duty this might entail, and possibly also preoccupied with the financial strain of forgoing employment, might spend more time with a child but bring little positive energy to the interactions. Researchers have documented the tremendous burden homeschooling can place on a parent, especially if she also bears responsibility for cleaning, cooking, and so on.[14] At the extreme, sheer exhaustion and depression can lead to maltreatment. This would seem more likely with those who assume the homeschool instructor role at a husband's or a pastor's urging rather than because of a self-originating desire to do this.

Because of this risk of "parent burnout," many homeschoolers find ways other than regular schooling to distribute the child-rearing responsibility, such as hiring babysitters, trading off with other parents, and enrolling children in educational or recreational camps. Those strategies really make the child's experience a sort of hybrid between homeschooling and something resembling regular schooling, insofar as they entail authority figures other than parents providing formal or informal instruction and guidance, possibly in a group that also includes children from other families. For many parents, then, there appears to be some trade-off between controlling the child's experience and maintaining a positive and healthy attitude toward the homeschooling situation and the child.

In sum, homeschooling has the potential to strengthen the core parent-child relationship, but it also has the potential to damage the parent-child relationship if it is too onerous for particular parents. A child, too, might experience the relationship as oppressive and a source of suffering if it is unrelenting, or might simply long for the social experience or learning opportunities of a regular school, and as a result might develop resentment toward the parent. Recall the experience of Josh Powell, who unsuccessfully pleaded with his parents to let him attend school.

F. Physical, Psychological, and Emotional Security

"Pure homeschooling," as we might call it, in which parents do not enlist persons outside the family for instruction or social experience, presents another danger for children—namely, the potential for undetected maltreatment. Chapter 3 described just a few of the instances in which ostensibly homeschooled children were essentially living in barbaric captivity. For any person or institution to have monopoly control over a nonautonomous person, such that they can completely deny that dependent person any contact with the outside world, is a very dangerous thing, given human nature. Thus, when courts appoint guardians for incompetent adults, they require the guardians to periodically report to the court and to permit service providers access to the ward, thus ensuring some monitoring.

In contrast, the law generally does not require legal parents to report periodically to any state authority; instead, it empowers parents to wield unsupervised control over children. Children can go years without any contact with the outside world. This might have been more likely early in the nation's history, when the population was much sparser, but parents can easily locate themselves in remote areas even today, particularly in the West. Even in large crowded cities, every year there are families discovered who have been living for years reclusively and in horrible conditions, the children manifesting severe retardation of physical and cognitive development. Public officials say explicitly that they expect compulsory schooling to provide some guard against this danger with older children, though this does not help children below the age of compulsory schooling, who are the most common victims of maltreatment, and it does not help older children whose parents claim or are assumed to be homeschooling, especially in the great majority of states that do not require any contact with school officials or independent evaluators. In addition to hiding abuse, parents might keep their children out of school in order to put them to work, a phenomenon documented in tobacco-farming states, among immigrant families in agricultural areas of the Southwest, and elsewhere in the United States. Hundreds of thousands of American children each year are working in violation of child labor laws, and homeschooling laws that abjure oversight facilitate this.

There are some legal checks on parents' power. First, the law threatens legal parents with after-the-fact criminal prosecution or disruption of their relationship with their children if it discovers maltreatment. That could influence the behavior of some parents otherwise inclined to abuse or neglect their children, if they interact regularly with outsiders, but parents who live in seclusion might feel confident that they can avoid detection, and homeschooling laws bolster that confidence. Many abusive parents simply cannot control their actions, especially if they are abusing substances or suffering from untreated mental illness. Second, in support of the first, the law designates certain professionals as mandatory reporters of maltreatment and authorizes anyone who happens to observe maltreatment to report it to the local child-protection agency. The problem is that abusive or neglectful parents generally attempt to keep their children away from all outsiders, not just state officials and not just schools. They are less likely to take their children to doctors, who are the most common mandatory reporters to detect maltreatment in pre-school-aged children. Even attendance at a private school would offer some safeguard, so long as the school is substantial enough to worry about legal action against it if it fails to report maltreatment. But when the state empowers parents to keep their children entirely outside of schools, to keep them at home 100 percent of the time if they wish, upon declaring that they are home-schooling (or even without declaring anything), and does not condition this on periodic home visits, the state incidentally leaves many children with no real safeguard against maltreatment.

On the other side, many who homeschool express worry about children's security in school. Typically, they target their dire descriptions at public schools, claiming that they are rife with bullying, weapons, drugs, and coerced sexual activity. There is no denying that bullying is widespread, that weapons and drugs show up at most public high schools and even at many public middle schools, and that there is substantial pressure in American high schools, from peers and occasionally from teachers, for young people to engage in sexual activity. From the standpoint of any nonabusive parents, therefore, sending their child to a public school rather than homeschooling the child *increases* the dangers to the child's security. How much it does so varies tremendously across public-school districts, from infinitesimally to considerably. Sending a child to a private school might also increase the dangers of harm from adults or from other students.

G. Equality

Our description of basic goods above does not limit the category of children for whom the listed items are basic and important. For example, we posited that intellectual development is a basic good for all children, not just male students or Asian American students or any other group smaller than all students. We consider below whether some of the goods in our list are actually less important or irrelevant for some children because of their individual family's cultural situation or beliefs. A great number of homeschoolers are motivated primarily by religion-based aversion to liberal values, so we address, directly below, the objection to our list that many homeschoolers would make—namely, that whereas the list might be correct as to other parents' children, they have a different list for their children, because of their faith or culture.

Notably, adherents to religious faiths that endorse highly gendered roles generally do not explicitly assert that females are inferior to and less deserving of a good life than males, but instead claim that different roles and expectations are consistent with equal personhood. Just as different people perform different roles in the commercial realm yet are considered equal persons, they might say, women and men can perform different roles in familial and social realms yet still be considered equal. We therefore address in the next section of this chapter the view that some goods might be inapt for one gender or another not because of a hierarchy of worthiness but because of "separate but equal" life paths.

An assumption of equality was thus implicit in the foregoing analysis of particular goods. Here we suggest that equal treatment by the state, in and of itself, is a basic good and worthy of separate mention. It might be also true with respect to membership in intermediate institutions, such as a church or a professional association, that equal standing with similarly situated other persons is an intrinsic good. But the state, in particular, should assume that there is intrinsic and substantial value for all in enjoying equal citizenship in a fairly robust sense. Unequal treatment can have a psychological impact of a sort that affects the self-worth underlying personal identity, especially when those responsible for the inequality intend to denigrate those treated less well. But it need not do so. Equality before the state and the law has an inherent value that is distinct; it represents full membership in a community, belongingness, and a standing to demand the benefits of membership. Similarly, exclusion from a club can entail denigration of personal characteristics but need not do so. One who is denied membership might always be denied a kind of dignity, but the denial could result from bad luck; it might not reflect or entail personal insult. This is clearly true of acquiring citizenship in most countries; an applicant for it might be denied on grounds that are not inherently denigrating. Yet one very important thing gained through naturalization is equality before the law. Indeed, one basis some states have asserted at times for denying some children access to public school systems is that those children are not citizens. They are not members, so they cannot enjoy that benefit. For those children to have equal standing before the law would clearly be an important good because they would have the dignity and the rights of membership. They would have the safety of being part of a very large group (all citizen children) whom legal actors are less likely to treat adversely.

Of particular relevance to homeschooling is whether the state affords the same legal protections for education-related interests to all children or instead discriminates on some basis. Many states' laws speak of a right of all children to an adequate education ensured by the state. The constitution of Washington State, for example, proclaims, "It is the paramount duty of the state to make ample provision for the education of all children residing within its borders, without distinction or preference on account of race, color, caste, or sex."[15] A state might nevertheless fail to treat children equally. It might do so for reasons that do not entail denigration of personal attributes, but the denial of equal treatment could still amount to treating some children like they are outsiders to the community—not belonging like other children to the society that the state serves, not possessing the same standing and rights. In doing so, we maintain, the state denies those children a basic good. We would clearly think this so if the state denied us the benefit of certain regulatory protections, even if the state did so on a random basis—for example, spinning a wheel to determine which neighborhoods would receive police protection and which would not. If we waive protections and rights offered to us, that is a different story. And so, certain children might not be denied a basic good if it is plausible to impute to them a hypothetical choice to waive some protections (perhaps by concluding it is in their best interests to be left out of some law's ambit). But if it is not plausible to impute such a waiver, the state's denying to some children any protections of its education code that other children receive would be denying them the basic good of equality before the law.

*   *   *

It is useful at this point to acknowledge what is not among the things the state treats as a basic good for children. The state need not declare these things unimportant or bad for children, but there are things some parents or outside observers might regard as basic goods that the state need not, and perhaps may not, say are basic goods that it aims to ensure for children.

One, related to the previous chapter's fundamental principle of state agnosticism concerning religious questions, is salvation. The state may not decide that some outcome for individuals in the afterlife is a basic good and aim to promote it. No one should feel sanguine about state officials deciding theological questions and imposing on everyone, by deploying the full power of the state, their fallible views of what would please their god or gods. We might like the officials who would be doing it today, but even they would be fallible, and we might not like the officials who would be doing it tomorrow.

Relatedly, the state should not endorse the view of some religious homeschoolers that unquestioning adherence to a particular religious faith is essential for a good life. A parental aim of fostering such unreflective religious conviction is not necessarily incompatible with the first on our list— that is, intellectual development. In theory, a child could be taught to think critically and creatively about every aspect of life other than religion, which should be sufficient to develop that cognitive skill. Every society, even the most liberal, has taboos that never receive critical attention in schools, yet children can still develop the capacity for critical thinking because there are plenty of other precepts to examine critically. But regardless of whether religious faith can be bracketed in this way, the secular state simply has no basis for sharing any parent's view that this is a good. Presumably the state would have to say this is a good for all children. Again, no one should be sanguine about state officials choosing a particular set of religious doctrines and declaring that all children should be made to adopt those doctrines without question.

A secularized version of these faith-related aims also fails to merit state endorsement. Some parents might say the state should treat singularity of ideological instruction and exposure as a basic good because children are unable to deal with conflicting messages about such a profound matter. Such claims are common in child-custody battles following the dissolution of the parents' relationship with each other. Custodial parents sometimes ask a court to order a noncustodial parent not to teach a child about a different religion or bring a child to the worship meetings of a different church, asserting that exposing the child to two, inconsistent religions will cause psychological problems. Courts uniformly reject that empirical claim about the effect on children because there is no research support for it. To the contrary, there is ample evidence that children benefit, in their intellectual growth and development of moral autonomy, from learning about competing conceptions of the good and being challenged to think about which make more sense or have appeal for other reasons.

Any trauma children experience from the fact of ideological diversity in the world is rather typically a result of adults' imposing great pressure on or instilling great fear in children—for example, telling children that other worldviews are espoused only by the devil's agents who want to capture the children. If the state effectively rewarded parents for such behavior by empowering those who would otherwise traumatize their children in this way to insulate the children from all competing worldviews, it would create a moral hazard; it would give parents an incentive to traumatize their children in order to obtain that power. Even if the state did this, the basic good it would thereby be endorsing would not be ideological insularity per se but rather freedom from parent-imposed trauma, a basic good that could support an entirely opposite state action—namely, the removal of children from parental custody.

Finally, some homeschooling parents might make the somewhat different, but still ideologically grounded, claim that it is a basic good for children to abide by specific moral precepts, such as adherence to divinely assigned roles (e.g., male as breadwinner, female as tender of home and children), accepting no teachings incompatible with the Bible, placing service to a divinity above any personal pursuits, rejecting the authority of the state, rejecting all religious authority, doing violence to infidels, suppressing all sexual desire, not suppressing any sexual desire, and so on. Some such precepts the state cannot aim to impose on children because of its religious agnosticism, as discussed above. But as to any such specific precepts, the state should also say that parents are free outside of schooling time to teach their beliefs to children, so the state need play no role in presenting such precepts to children, nor must children's schooling be oriented toward instructing children about them. I noted above that mandatory school time takes up 1,260 hours of a child's life each year (seven hours per day for 180 days). Even if we add an hour a day for bus time (so 1,440 hours per year), that is only a little over one-fourth of all the hours that children are awake in a year (5,475, if one assumes nine hours of sleep per day), leaving parents with over four thousand nonschool hours per year in which to inculcate whatever beliefs and values they want in their children, and much more than that in the preschool years. Thus, the state would need to assist with transmission of specific beliefs only if it were essential for children to accept them without question and without exposure to competing beliefs, but that sort of straitjacketing of children's minds we dismissed above. The secular state has no basis for concluding that any particular moral precepts must be imposed on children for their wellbeing. There are some moral precepts the state explicitly aims to instill in public schools as well as in fora where adults are the target audience, but they are generally precepts necessary to social order, such as nonviolence and civil respect for others, and so the state legitimately promotes them among adults and children principally in its police-power role, though these precepts would seem to be also consistent with the well-being of individual children.

II. Exceptional Children

Might some children actually not need or benefit from the goods we have enumerated? Or might some children have competing needs that might be more important? We consider these possibilities directly here, though some of the preceding discussion has already provided partial answers.

Why might a child not need cognitive and intellectual development, acquisition of mainstream knowledge and beliefs, capacity for productive interpersonal relationships, and other basic goods we have identified? One possibility is that they are genetically constituted differently—for example, with a severe learning disability. Naturally, at a specific level the aims for such a child must be different from the norm, but in the most general terms the goods described above are fitting also for children with developmental disabilities. Children with autism, Down syndrome, or other mental disabilities can develop cognitively and socially and acquire useful knowledge. The schooling question will therefore be similar for such a child: Is homeschooling equivalent or superior to what the child could have in a regular school, or at least adequate?

The more likely argument along these lines is that a child without genetically created disabilities does not need some of the basic goods we have identified because the parent has established very different aims for the child's life. Some parents might say, for example, that for their daughters, intellectual development presents a danger rather than a good. The ultimate aim for each of their daughters is to serve a man as wife and as mother to his children, by remaining home and doing household tasks. Promoting their daughters' intellectual development would be worse than a waste of time; it would tempt them to choose the selfish and sinful path of attending college and working outside the home, perhaps not ever submitting to marriage and motherhood or doing so only after a long period of having several nonmarital intimate relationships, and it might make them insufficiently obedient of their husbands. Some parents might make arguments of this kind also against acquisition of particular knowledge and development of interpersonal skills; what the state sees as good, the parents say is bad, because of their ideology.

For the reasons explained previously, such arguments ask the state to grant parents legal power on grounds that the state cannot consider. The state simply cannot accept parents' religiously based views about their rights or about their children's status any more than it could accept as true religious claims as to their having rights with respect to their spouse, their neighbor's children, their neighbors, women seeking abortions, strangers who have diametrically opposed moral views, or anyone else whom they wish they could control. The state can and must take the position that a child is a distinct person, and from the state's perspective there is no such difference between males and females with respect to the basic goods.

More plausible would be a contention that some children have countervailing, empirically verifiable, secular needs that should preclude the state from requiring promotion of certain goods on our list. This is different from simply claiming a right as a parent to establish entirely different needs and aims for a child's life. It points instead to more or less immutable facts about the child that the state can acknowledge and alleges that those facts create a different cost-benefit calculus for that child. As a concrete example, a parent might plausibly say that instilling habits of critical and creative thinking or understanding of some body of knowledge like evolutionary theory would likely generate turmoil in the family, jeopardizing the child's relationships with family members and the child's emotional and psychological well-being.

This argument appeals to concerns the state can share—namely, the child's interests in family harmony and in being able to receive positive nurturing and guidance from parents. It is not inconceivable that a child given a "liberal education" could come to view parents as ignorant and unworthy of respect, reject their lifestyle, refuse to attend religious services with them, and so forth. As noted, this is a kind of argument some parents make in custody disputes following divorce, an argument that courts generally reject. In this context of intrafamilial tension within intact families too, there is a concern that some parents might try to secure exemption from some schooling law by trying to show disruptive conflict with a child following the child's exposure to some competing belief or after the child manifests independent thought. If that seems unduly cynical, ask any divorce lawyer what she or he has seen parents do to children in order to gain legal advantage.

Were a trustee conception of parenthood the norm, as it was in the Anglo-American world a couple centuries ago, we might expect few parents would have such an expectation of ideological dominance over children that they would find a child's intellectual development and acquisition of knowledge so threatening. But that moral regime is also too far from current reality (in the United States at least) to presuppose in our analysis. We must assume a significant number of parents think they have a God-given right and responsibility to ensure their children never question what they are taught about anything of moral importance. Some such parents might be familiar to us, but we should imagine all possibilities—that is, also parents who adhere to ideologies unfamiliar and even bizarre to us. What if they are capable of having positive, nurturing relationships with their children (i.e., do not have mental illnesses in a way that prevents attachment and loving care), but only if the children remain unquestioning believers? How should the state react to that reality, which it has participated in creating?

We might restate the question thus: Supposing the state will continue to create some legal parent-child relationships in which the state-chosen parents would be extremely upset if their child thought critically about the parents' moral and religious instruction, acquired particular knowledge the parents believe is dangerously false, or became comfortable interacting with people holding different conceptions of the good, should the state accept that the good of nurturing family relationships outweighs other goods and on that basis exempt such families from certain legal schooling requirements? Without suggesting that the answer to this question is easy, we give a negative answer for three reasons.

First, the basis for exemption is so broad and difficult for the state to deny that the state would be deluged with demands for exemption, threatening to eviscerate a rule that all children should receive an education that promotes critical thinking and provides particular knowledge. Any parents who want to homeschool (or to send their child to a church school) and be exempt from state-imposed conditions can too easily claim that fulfilling the conditions would destroy family harmony, and the state would be hard-pressed to falsify any such claims. Second, there is the moral hazard: parents might create turmoil in the home just to demonstrate to the state why they must be exempt from regulation. Third, there is too little evidence of such family turmoil actually having occurred to real families that have experienced such a conflict between parental ideology and children's learning. Such conflicts do occur even in the current laissez-faire legal regime, either because parents have no practical choice other than to send their children to schools where the children learn to think independently and encounter contrary views, or because of split-custody situations in which parents are living apart and have quite divergent ideological outlooks. The state generally supposes, as homeschool advocates persistently claim, that all parents are loving until proven otherwise, and it is reasonable for the state to suppose loving parents will show care for their children despite becoming upset by what the children are learning outside their home.

Certainly more could be said about this particular potential conflict among basic goods, so our position here is provisional. Other types of conflicts could present themselves as well. But lest this become too great a detour from the main line of analysis, we proceed to the principal normative question of what legal regime should exist, carrying over the assumption that the state should assume all the items listed in part 1 of this chapter are basic goods for all children.

Notes

1. See, e.g., Brighouse, *School Choice and Social Justice*, chap. 4.

2. Robert Kunzman, "Education, Schooling, and Children's Rights: The Complexity of Homeschooling," *Educational Theory* 62, no. 1 (2012): supra at 83–85.

3. Kunzman, "Homeschooling and Religious Fundamentalism," 17.

4. See Randall Curren, "Judgment and the Aims of Education," *Social Philosophy & Policy* 31, no. 1 (2014): 36–59.

5. Kunzman and Gaither, "Homeschooling," 15.

6. See Kunzman, "Homeschooling and Religious Fundamentalism," supra at 24.

7. For further elaboration of this position, see Harry Brighouse, "Religious Belief, Religious Schooling, and the Demands of Reciprocity," in *Deliberative Democracy in Practice*, ed. David Kahane, Daniel Weinstock, Dominique Leydet, and Melissa Williams (Vancouver: University of British Columbia Press, 2010), 35–53.

8. See, e.g., Judy Dunn, *Children's Friendships: The Beginnings of Intimacy* (Oxford: Blackwell, 2006) (showing that relationships with peer equals who are free to exit the relationship—so, for children, nonsiblings—are crucial to moral development); and Jean Piaget, *The Moral Judgment of the Child* (New York: Academic Press, 1932/1965).

9. There is a real basis for this concern. See Kunzman, "Homeschooling and Religious Fundamentalism," supra, 18–19.

10. Kunzman, "Homeschooling and Religious Fundamentalism," 24.

11. Kunzman, "Homeschooling and Religious Fundamentalism," supra, 21.

12. Kunzman, "Homeschooling and Religious Fundamentalism," 26 (quoting Cass Sunstein).

13. In particular, there has been a rash of autobiographies by women who exited cultlike polygamous communities. See, e.g., Flora Jessop, *Church of Lies* (2009); Elissa Wall and Lisa Pulitzer, *Stolen Innocence: My Story of Growing Up in*

a Polygamous Sect, Becoming a Teenage Bride, and Breaking Free of Warren Jeffs (2009); Carolyn Jessop, *Escape* (2008); and Irene Spencer, *Shattered Dreams: My Life as a Polygamist's Wife* (2008).

14. See Kunzman and Gaither, "Homeschooling," 12.

15. RCWA Const. Art. 9, § 1.

CHAPTER SEVEN

The Regulation Question

Just as empirical views about homeschooling run the gamut from those who think it inherently bad to those who insist it is always good, views about what law should govern homeschooling span the possible range from absolute prohibition to absolute parental empowerment. We explained in chapter 4 why neither extreme empirical view is plausible. In this chapter we reason toward a conclusion about what legal regime is most appropriate. Is it one of the extreme policy positions, or something in between?

At the outset, we remind readers that thinking about the law of homeschooling in terms of "whether the state will regulate" is misleading, insofar as it suggests state abstention is a realistic possibility. We explained in chapter 5 that the proper question to ask is not *whether* the state will involve itself in children's schooling but *how* it will do so. The state must have some laws pertaining to children's education, either conferring on parents the legal power to waive their children's statutory right to attend public school and to keep the children at home, along with some degree of power to dictate the nature of home-based instruction, or legally guaranteeing all children attendance at a regular school. For the state to have no laws whatsoever relating to children's education would mean parents would have no legal basis for making decisions about children's education and no legal basis for excluding anyone else who wanted to try to educate their children, a situation no one actually wants.

I. Where to Begin?

There are several potential starting points for analysis of what legal regime should govern homeschooling. In the preceding chapter, we frequently asked what arguments parents desiring to homeschool could make for why the state should empower them to waive their child's statutory right to regular schooling and keep their child at home when others are attending school. In this chapter, we come at the legal aspect of homeschooling from a different direction, one that puts a burden of persuasion on the state rather than the parents. The starting point for this approach is not at parents' rights, however, as it is for most homeschool advocates and for political theorists we have termed "parentalists." We explained in chapter 5 why the concept of parental entitlement to control a child's life is anomalous, disrespectful of a child's personhood, and without rational support in any general moral principles. Our approach begins instead with children's rights, consistent with our starting assumptions that children are persons, capable of possessing rights, and have the greatest interests at stake in connection with their schooling and their upbringing more generally. Several rights of children are relevant and will be considered at some point in the analysis to follow. Which right one begins with is not so important, we think, so long as all pertinent ones receive consideration. It can be illuminating to highlight the unfamiliar, and so we begin in a place that might surprise readers, even though once expressed it seems to be a natural starting point. One children's right that protects what is arguably the most important good on the list of goods presented in chapter 6, yet generally goes unrecognized in debates over homeschooling, would impose on the state the burden of justifying its compelling children to leave their homes to be schooled.

We explained in chapter 5 that the state creates *legal* parent-child relationships and thereby effectively also creates *social* parent-child relationships. This parent-child relationship and the family life that grows from it are the center of a young child's world. When healthy, these relationships provide stability, security, love, and comfort. They are the starting point for identity formation, self-understanding, and interaction with the outside world. First and foremost, children need protection from unwarranted interference with their home and family life. Many homeschoolers emphasize this aspect of child well-being, and rightly so. Educational deprivation is a very bad thing, but even worse for a child is to lack a secure and nurturing home life with loving parents. Parents who comply with compulsory education laws by sending their children to regular school might also perceive a trade-off with family closeness, and probably many would complain about the impact on their children's family relationships were the state to greatly increase the amount of time children must spend in school each year (e.g., by imposing longer days, six-day school weeks, and attendance throughout the summer).

We therefore suggest, as a default legal rule and starting point for normative analysis of homeschooling, that a child has a right against the state's forcing him or her to leave home. Each of us adults has a constitutionally protected liberty to remain home, to not be forced to leave, and that right, though generally taken for granted, is extremely important and valuable for us. There is no reason to deny that right and that constitutional protection to children; indeed, they arguably have a stronger prima facie right to remain undisturbed in their homes than adults do, because important aspects of their personal development naturally occur within the home environment and because they are more vulnerable. This is so even if there are especially strong countervailing interests—that is, greater reason to override the right—in the case of children. Justifications for infringing a right are conceptually distinct from the nature and prima facie strength of the right. Children are more dependent on family relationships than we adults are, and home is where families can be together without interference. In the normal case, that is where children feel most secure. As with other rights young children possess, parents are appropriate persons to represent children and assert this right of children against the state.[1]

From this perspective, the state would carry a burden of justifying a law that orders children to leave their homes for any reason, and certainly so with a law requiring children to leave home for seven or more hours at a stretch, day after day, to be placed into the custody of adults who are not their parents. Like parentage rules based entirely on biology, we tend to think of compulsory school attendance as natural and in no need of defense, simply because it has become so familiar, but it too is actually an extraordinary thing for the state to do to people and requires strong justification. If we adults were inclined and practically able to stay home all the time, the state would need compelling reason to order us to leave for many hours each day to undergo training. Likewise, people would be shocked if a US state suddenly decided to mandate school attendance for three- and four-year-olds and would demand that the state defend this forced removal of children from their homes, because compulsory schooling at that age is unfamiliar to us.

So, suppose a state passed a compulsory education law requiring attendance at a state-licensed school, public or private, with requirements for licensure that effectively precluded homeschooling. And suppose some parents filed a petition in court, as agents for their children, requesting an injunction against enforcement of that law, asserting that it infringes *their children's* Fourteenth Amendment due process clause right against state interference in their liberty. Even when they accept that children possess rights of the same type as adults possess, courts sometimes treat those rights as weaker, in part because of children's lesser decision-making capacities. But let us suppose courts would treat the children's right asserted in this lawsuit as equally as strong as an adult's right not to be forced to leave home to spend many hours in some state-licensed training facility, because of children's great interest in protection of family relationships. This would likely cause the courts to apply a heightened form of scrutiny that puts a heavy burden of justification on the state, thus generating a normative framework quite consistent with the way homeschoolers generally view the question of state regulation—that is, by presuming that such state action is wrong and demanding to know on what legitimate basis the state dares impose such a law on private citizens.

Taking this approach to normative analysis of homeschooling illustrates why supposedly child-welfare-based justifications for parents' rights—that is, defenses of parental entitlement that rest on a claim that it is good for children that their parents have certain rights—are unsuccessful. If the ultimate justification for a right is the welfare of a child, then logically the right should belong to the child, not to someone else. Ascribing it to parents just muddles analysis. It misdirects attention to the parents' interests and desires. Then children's interests, paradoxically, get put on the other side of the equation, as a component of the state's interests, measured to determine whether they are great enough to override parental entitlement. It is simply nonsensical. If homeschooling advocates believe the state's empowerment of parents to choose homeschooling for children is appropriate because that is best for children, then they should argue that *children* have a right to this—that is, to the state's so empowering their caregivers.

Thus, we suppose parents first assert that their children have a right to remain in the home. To begin instead with an assertion that children have a right to be homeschooled per se, which presumably would have to rest on a factual claim that homeschooling is better for children than any available regular school alternative, would put parents in the position of first having to present evidence to support this factual claim. One cannot simply assert that one's children have a right to whatever one happens to prefer for them in any realm of their lives (e.g., to eat only lettuce) and expect a court to accept that assertion and recognize the supposed right. One must demonstrate why one's children have a right to something, which typically will entail showing, at a minimum, that it is good for them. In some circumstances, it might be easy for parents to show homeschooling is good for their children relative to the available alternatives—for example, where the only practically available regular schools are patently horrible. But in most of society, laying a factual foundation for the existence of such a right would be quite difficult for parents because a court would find that local regular schools provide an adequate, perhaps even good, education. A right presumptively to stay at home is a stronger place to begin, we believe, because it is a well-established, universal, incontrovertible right that all persons have, given the presumed value for everyone of being undisturbed in their home. This right should suffice to put the burden of justification for compulsory regular-school attendance on the state, a burden of demonstrating that the presumed value does not pertain in some particular home (e.g., because of abuse) or is generally outweighed by some other value served by forcing persons to leave home (e.g., their educational needs).

The analysis to follow therefore takes the form of suggesting possible justifications that the state might offer for requiring children to leave their homes for twelve hundred or more hours each year, and subjecting those justifications to careful scrutiny. In constitutional terms, the state would have to show that the law it seeks to impose is necessary to serve a compelling interest. The state must (a) identify a compelling interest such a law serves, and (b) show it could not serve that interest sufficiently well by some other means that entails a lesser infringement or no infringement of children's liberty interest, of children's right to stay home.

II. Interests That Could Justify Forcing Children to Leave Home

Identifying compelling interests that *might* justify requiring children to leave home for school is the easy part of the analysis. We listed in the previous chapter several basic goods for children, some of which they cannot acquire except by receiving education somewhere. Children's needs for cognitive development, knowledge, social interaction, and healthy identity formation are all interests to which critics of homeschooling point as justifications for legally mandating school attendance by all, and many would even say every child has a *right* to each of these things—a moral right, a natural right, and perhaps a constitutional right. A corollary to the right to stay home would be a right to leave home if either the home is a threatening place, as in cases of abuse, or leaving is necessary in order to experience important aspects of well-being such as intellectual stimulation and connection with other human beings.

Courts uniformly treat children's welfare, including those aspects tied to schooling, as a compelling state interest that can justify attaching all sorts of legal duties to the role of legal parent, and no one seriously disputes the importance of securing such basic goods for children.[2] Homeschool advocates do not deny that children's cognitive and intellectual development and acquisition of knowledge are of great importance; to the contrary, this is a fundamental premise of their advocacy, because their central claim is that homeschooling is a superior way of generating these goods.

Other interests that critics of homeschooling sometimes assert, though, might be insufficient to justify infringing children's liberty—for example, collective societal interests such as a stronger economy or a more tolerant citizenry. These interests might not suffice to justify forcing anyone to leave home for over a thousand hours of training per year. If they were sufficient reason for such compulsion as to anyone, we would suggest the state first force adults to do it, and only if that were not enough to serve the collective interest then perhaps the state could force children out of their homes. Children are more vulnerable and less able to participate in the public debates that produce such policies. If the state is going to treat anyone instrumentally for the sake of collective aims, one might suppose, it should be competent adults. Probably most readers will think the state should *not* treat *them* instrumentally in such a way, in which case they should say the same about children, absent some rational demonstration that it is more appropriate to treat children instrumentally to serve collective aims than it is to treat adults that way.

As explained in chapter 5, as to aspects of life we treat as matters of self-determination for adults, the state may presume to control them for children only pursuant to its parens patriae authority, stepping into the shoes of individual children and deciding in their behalf in a manner resembling as much as possible the self-determining decision-making of adults. That means laws requiring schooling of some kind for children are justifiable only on parens patriae child-welfare grounds. The state must be able to plausibly contend that any child would, if able, endorse a compulsory schooling law as in his or her individual best interests, and therefore as fully respectful of his or her personhood. Assuming the right not to be forced to leave home is a fairly strong one, the state would need to show that compulsory schooling outside the home is *necessary* to secure certain important goods for a child. Identifying children's interests is, as just noted, easy. And some we might view as giving rise to children's rights, such as a right to an adequate education and a right to socialize outside the family. The truly challenging part is showing that regular-school attendance is necessary to serve those interests or, conversely, that the state's empowering parents to deny their child a regular-school education necessarily thwarts those interests.

If it turns out that the state cannot justify compulsory attendance at a regular school as necessary to ensure basic goods for children, and so it must permit homeschooling, the further question will arise as to whether the state may or must oversee and impose requirements for homeschooling. It is less clear that there is any basic individual right pertaining to that latter question. Whereas all persons have a fundamental-liberty interest in remaining in their homes, it is less clear that one has a fundamental-liberty interest in other persons' (in this case, parents) not being restricted in how they treat one. For example, is there any plausibility to a claim that a person who is married has a right against the state's restricting his or her spouse's conduct toward him or her by means of domestic-violence prohibitions? That would be a very odd sort of right, not entailed by any of the usual bases for ascribing rights to people. The regulation question, should we conclude that states must permit homeschooling, would essentially be whether the state may or must constrain parents' freedom in how they conduct schooling within the home, or, in other words, whether the state may or must condition the empowerment of parents on their acceptance of certain accountability measures. No one really disputes that legal parenthood is and should be conditional; what people disagree about is what the conditions should be, with some champions of parental entitlement insisting that the conditions should be the barest minimum—for example, that one must only avoid severe physical or sexual abuse of the child. As a matter of constitutional law, the answer regarding state oversight of education is clear; the Supreme Court decisions described in chapter 3 affirmed over and over again the power of the state to regulate all schools; the state could prescribe a detailed curriculum, establish qualifications for teachers, mandate periodic assessment, and require periodic reporting to school-district officials. But we are focused here primarily on moral rights, which can provide a basis for supporting or criticizing the constitutional doctrine.

From the parents' standpoint, homeschooling is an "other-determining" practice, not a self-determining one, so it is not a matter of moral right for the parents but rather a privilege. The founding generation was correct in viewing parenthood this way; as John Locke expressed it, parental power "so little belongs to the father by any peculiar right of nature, but only as he is guardian of his children."[3] It should be a legal privilege parents enjoy only if they commit to meeting children's needs as the state sees them, just as a guardian for an incompetent adult enjoys the privilege of controlling the ward's life only by promising faithfully to serve the ward's interests as the state sees them. Put differently, a law compelling attendance at a regular school fails the necessity prong of our constitutional test *only if* parents in fact provide the other education-related goods to a child at home. If particular parents are unable or unwilling to provide those other goods, then attendance at a regular school is in fact necessary to serve the state's compelling interest in ensuring those basic goods for the child of those parents.

From the children's standpoint, it is not clear they have any right *against* their parents' being constrained per se in the homeschooling methods that are used. Extreme forms of state oversight and constraint of parents (e.g., posting a state employee in the home around the clock and watching the parents' every move) could undermine the parents' ability to care for a child, by making them feel miserable and harassed and incapable. But the types of homeschool regulation that states have attempted and that might suffice to ensure children's developmental needs are met do not come anywhere close to such extremes.

Conversely, it seems children do have a right *in favor of* state oversight and legal constraint on parental freedom with respect to homeschooling, if the state must in fact permit homeschooling. We might view this as a basic (as opposed to equal-treatment) right: the state, having placed children in the custody and control of certain persons, and implicitly reaffirming that decision every day by continuing to confer legal-parent status and custody on those persons, bears an ongoing obligation to the children to ensure that those custodians meet the children's basic needs and respect the children's natural or moral rights—the rights to learn, explore, associate with others, think independently, ask questions, respectfully express opinions, reach their own conclusions on matters of faith, and more. Otherwise the state would have no justification for continually renewing the adults' legal status as parents and their state-protected custody of the children. Similarly, the state bears an obligation to incompetent adults whom it has placed under guardianship to make sure the guardians are not neglecting the wards' basic needs or violating the wards' rights. Knowing, as it does, that some parents are unwilling or unable to provide what the state views as children's basic needs, the state presumptively would have to exclude those parents from homeschooling or somehow induce them to comply with the state's expectations for children's schooling.

In addition, and more straightforwardly, children have an equality right against the state; the state must provide to all equally the government benefit of a guarantee of adequate education. To declare a right to education, as many states do in their constitutions or statutes, but then implicitly say, "Except for those children whose parents want to deny it to them," constitutes a prima facie violation of children's equality right, which is embodied in the equal protection clause of state and federal constitutions.[4] It is so just as much as if the state declared a right against physical abuse but then added the qualification "Except those whose parents belong to church X, Y, or Z, because those churches endorse what we regard as abuse." Or as if the state declared a general right of adults against domestic violence but then added, "Except women whose husbands don't want them to have that legal benefit."

III. Is Regular School Attendance Necessary to Protect Those Interests of Children?

This question, then, is the crux of the policy analysis. There is little or no disagreement that children have developmental needs that necessitate some form of schooling. There can be no rational disagreement that the state, so long as it presumes to place children under the legal custody and state-protected control of particular private caregivers, to the exclusion of other potential caregivers, bears a responsibility to ensure children's basic needs, as the state understands them, are met. When it selects people to serve as legal parents, whether those persons are biological parents or not, the state must insist that they accept that the child will receive an education that the state deems adequate. If they are not willing to accept that, then the state should choose other parents for the child from among the millions of people wishing to adopt a child, because receiving an education is of fundamental importance to a child's life.

Moreover, the state cannot be agnostic about the content of children's temporal welfare, else it would have no moral justification for placing them into legal family relationships in the first place. There is no conceptual or moral distinction between a law prohibiting parents from burning a child with cigarettes and a law precluding parents from depriving a child of the schooling-related basic goods identified in chapter 6. On the other hand, there can also be no rational disagreement that once the state has placed children into a (presumptively healthy) parent-child relationship, it must respect the children's fundamental interest in being secure in that relationship and the children's right to remain home absent strong justification for demanding that they leave it.

The state's stance toward homeschooling therefore boils down to this set of questions: First, is compulsory attendance at a regular school necessary to ensure children's developmental needs are met, or is there a less restrictive means of accomplishing that? Second, if regular-school attendance is not the only way to serve the compelling interest in children's proper development, should the state impose conditions on parents' election to homeschool? There is no right of parents or children that creates a presumption against conditions, but rather rights of children that create a presumption in favor of conditions, if homeschooling is in fact an acceptable alternative to regular schooling.

A. Prohibition or Permission?

Courts' means-ends analysis of state infringement of individual liberty is typically fact-intensive. Whether the infringement is justifiable as necessary to serve important state interests (in this case, parens patriae interests) is a practical question. It essentially asks, "In light of actual present-day circumstances, could the state serve its interests by some other means, or is this really the only feasible way of accomplishing its aims?" With respect to homeschooling, we (or a court) should ask, "In light of what we believe to be true about the abilities, ideologies, and inclinations of persons who are legal parents in our society, can the state ensure that children acquire the basic goods even while being homeschooled, or is regular schooling necessary for children to acquire them?"

Two complications yet unaddressed loom large at this point. First, "regular schooling" is a broad concept in our society, encompassing a great range of types of public, quasi-public (e.g., charter), and private schools. One can imagine a society in which the regular-school universe is much more homogeneous, with intensive state oversight ensuring little variation from one school to the next. Some European countries might be this way. The United States, though, has been far more laissez-faire, resulting in a proliferation of different school types. Of particular relevance here, private schools are, like homeschools, currently virtually unregulated in the United States. Some states are quite explicit and adamant about the complete freedom of private schools; Mississippi's compulsory schooling statute, for example, says,

> Nothing in this section shall ever be construed to grant, by implication or otherwise, to the State of Mississippi, any of its officers, agencies or subdivisions any right or authority to control, manage, supervise or make any suggestion as to the control, management or supervision of any private or parochial school or institution for the education or training of children, of any kind whatsoever that is not a public school according to the laws of this state; and this section shall never be construed so as to grant, by implication or otherwise, any right or authority to any state agency or other entity to control, manage, supervise, provide for or affect the operation, management, program, curriculum, admissions policy or discipline of any such school or home instruction program.[5]

As a result of this complete freedom, social scientists have documented immense variation in the structure, aims, instructional content, and treatment of pupils in private schools in America—in particular, among religious schools, which constitute nearly 90 percent of all private schools. In short, American states are doing nothing today to ensure that private schools are supplying rather than denying basic goods for children. That in itself makes it very difficult to argue that the state must prohibit homeschooling and require attendance at a regular school. Any parents prohibited from conducting homeschooling could easily find or create a small private school, even one located in some family's house, that provides almost exactly the same experience for children.

What regular schools might ensure is children's exposure to people from other families, and that might provide some protection against undetected physical maltreatment and extreme forms of intellectual confinement. This will not always be true; a private school might have only a couple of families as clients and a single administrator/teacher who is utterly lacking in qualifications for educating children and is adamantly opposed to any state restriction of how parents or schools treat and train children. Many private schools are created and staffed by ideologues more extreme in their divergence from the state's view of children's interests than many parents who patronize them—for example, scolding parents who "spare the rod." A large portion of church schools were founded by a local pastor who wanted the school to serve in part as a model for parents on how best to raise children, and for many congregations the model entails breaking children's will and "sinful" tendency to question and imposing on children an orthodoxy that includes a subordinate role for women.[6] But prohibition of homeschooling likely would save many children from educational neglect or physical maltreatment—namely, those who are suffering these things at home and whose parents are not part of a community that condones their approach to child-rearing or that would create a private school if a state eliminated authorization to homeschool.

In any event, the state *should be* imposing academic accountability and maltreatment prohibitions on private schools. States have never had good reason to assume all parents would make choices for children that are consistent with what the state regards as children's educational interests. In fact, there is ample documentation of children attending private schools that from the state's perspective are horrible (just as there are children attending public schools that are horrible).[7] The explanation is much more about legislative capitulation to aggressive advocacy and even violent resistance on the part of ultraconservative religious groups, in a context devoid of strenuous countervailing advocacy in behalf of children whose legal parents are members of those groups. This is a general problem with child-welfare legislation; young children cannot advocate for themselves, and very few people care about other people's children enough to advocate for them. The same problem explains why nearly every state has a "spiritual treatment" exception to medical neglect laws, an act of deference to the Christian Science lobby in the absence of substantial pushback in behalf of the children at risk of death from religious medical neglect. Unsurprisingly, legislators do not always act on principle, and sometimes they act on tragically misguided principles.

We therefore proceed to analyze the prohibition versus permission question with the assumption that the state should be regulating private schools to ensure that what they provide is, from the state's perspective, an adequate education, and that even in the current regime of state indifference to what private schools do, requiring that all children attend some regular school would spare many children from educational neglect and physical maltreatment.

A second complication is that there could be conflicts of interest across children. Homeschool advocates generally concede that some ostensibly homeschooling parents are actually committing educational neglect, but they insist it is only a small number and take the position that it is unreasonable to constrain the many for the sake of the few. Suppose that currently 99 percent of homeschooled children are acquiring the basic goods but 1 percent are not, and suppose the state could not feasibly identify the 1 percent so as to compel just the parents of those children to enroll them in a satisfactory regular school. Would it be justifiable to order all children to leave their homes for schooling, even though this is not necessary for 99 percent of them, because that is the only way to ensure no child incurs educational neglect?

Because we concluded in chapter 4 that homeschools *can* provide the basic goods and that, in fact, homeschooling can be superior to regular schooling in several ways, inherently or in light of local circumstances, a blanket prohibition of homeschooling would undoubtedly make some children worse off. But on the other hand, the current prevailing legal regime of unconstrained homeschooling freedom for any parents who wish to do it is, everyone concedes, resulting in some children being worse off than they would be if they attended a regular school (one that is at least minimally adequate, as we assume for sake of analysis). Thus, there appears to be a conflict of interest among children as to a potential policy of compulsory regular-school attendance, *if* we assume the state cannot identify and eliminate inadequate homeschools. We do not think that assumption true, but some people do, so we will consider this apparent conflict of interests further.

Our first step in answering this question of how to resolve a conflict of interests is to recognize one very important point that pro-homeschool extremists willfully fail to acknowledge: we now have *no idea whatsoever* what the actual percentages are of how many children would be made worse off by prohibition and how many better off. Homeschool advocates' routine assertion that the latter group contains few children is abject and irresponsible speculation utterly lacking in evidentiary support. On this score, it is fair to accuse these homeschool advocates of being disingenuous. Not a single one of them has even met more than a small percentage of the two million or so homeschoolers in the United States, let alone observed their homeschooling or the educational attainment of their children, and they know that.[8] Presently homeschoolers in most US states report to no one and submit to no oversight. There are not even reliable estimates of how many children are being homeschooled, because many states do not even have an enforced notification requirement. There is thus no basis for reliably estimating how many children have never attended regular school. And for the vast majority of homeschooled children in the United States, the state has no basis for determining whether their homeschooling is minimally adequate. As discussed further in the next subsection, the state and onlookers like ourselves could know the extent and quality of homeschooling generally *only if* states began assiduously overseeing the practice and requiring periodic assessment.

Moreover, there are reasons to believe that the percentage of home-schooled students failing to receive what the state regards as an adequate education—that is, one that provides the basic goods identified in chapter 6—is substantial. The main reason is that surveys and ethnographic studies suggest a great number of parents choose to homeschool because of religiously based disapproval of what goes on in public schools, and for a substantial percentage of religious objectors the disapproval arises from a fundamental disagreement with the state's aims for education. In other words, we have reason to believe that a large number of homeschooling parents reject in principle for their children some of the basic goods identified in chapter 6, which almost surely means they fail to provide those goods through their homeschooling.

In particular, many reject the objective of independent thinking about values and aims in life, oppose instruction in scientific methodologies that might enable children to challenge religion-based claims about human and natural history and about contemporary society that parents want them to believe without question, and/or want to constrain their daughters' lives to a single occupation—housewife.[9] To the extent that such parents do value secular learning, they treat it—even basic literacy—as of little importance relative to unflinching acceptance of religious doctrine and reactionary political views.[10] Reading comments on HSLDA's online blog gives one a clear sense of the anti-intellectualism and authoritarian disposition that pervade the ideologue camp of homeschoolers. In addition, some homeschooling mothers in evangelical Christian households do not want to be homeschooling, but their husbands order them to do so.[11] States' inclination to be *more deferential* to parents with a religious objection to child-rearing legal duties, whether pertaining to education or medical care or something else, is tragically perverse from a child-welfare perspective. Children need for those parents to be *more constrained* than others, not less. In addition, published ethnographic work and testimonials by former homeschool students provide ample anecdotes of grossly academically deficient and abusive homeschooling environments.[12]

So suppose the state's defense of a categorical prohibition were that it is necessary to ensure that some inestimable, but probably large, number of children does not suffer educational neglect. The state, we are supposing for the moment, cannot identify and eliminate inadequate homeschools by some system of oversight, and for all it knows, they could be a majority of all homeschools. We are also supposing (counterfactually) that all regular schools are educationally adequate from the state's perspective. Based on those assumptions, the state could plausibly say prohibition is necessary to ensure no children suffer educational deprivation or denial of basic goods. Further, such prohibition would not cause "harm" to any children; even if homeschooling would have been better for some, regular school is good enough to meet the child's developmental needs, and though it amounts to an infringement of the right to remain home, it is a justifiable infringement because it is (we are supposing for the moment) the only way to guard against deprivation of several other basic goods. Every child receives the benefit of that guarantee against deprivation, even if it is not in reality needed by some, just as health insurance is a valuable good even if one never gets sick or injured.

We believe this conclusion would hold even if we did somehow happen to know (perhaps by divine revelation) or justifiably believe (perhaps based on studies of the dispositions, knowledge, and teaching capacities of adults in general) that only a small percentage of homeschools in any given time period are unacceptably poor in quality (despite the posited impossibility of identifying particular homeschools as inadequate). The value of the guarantee must be affected by the probability of needing it, just as insurance is less valuable (and premiums therefore lower) the lower the risk of needing it. But the harm of grossly deficient schooling is sufficiently great that the value of the guarantee remains sufficiently high. Reasonable people can disagree about that; it rests on subjective valuations. But the point is largely academic anyway because the percentage of current homeschools that are grossly deficient is likely, as explained above, substantial, and because, as discussed below, it certainly is possible to identify clearly inadequate homeschools.

In sum, in an actual society like that in America where private schools are unregulated, the state cannot justify prohibiting homeschooling. Only if the state did ensure that all regular schools are adequate yet at the same time were incapable of identifying inadequate homeschools could the state show that a blanket prohibition of homeschooling is necessary to secure basic goods for children. Because we believe the state is and always will be capable of identifying inadequate homeschools and of prohibiting homeschooling only for those parents found irremediably deficient, that hypothetical situation would never be an actual situation. Thus, blanket prohibition is not morally or constitutionally permissible. As to at least some children, perhaps most of those now being homeschooled, the state lacks sufficient justification for infringing their moral and constitutional right to remain in their homes with their families. It is not the least restrictive means of promoting the state's compelling interest in ensuring children an adequate education, because the state does have the capacity to ensure homeschooled children receive an adequate education.

But the state must exercise this capacity; it owes a moral (and arguably constitutional) duty to children to begin overseeing private schooling of all kinds, including homeschooling, as well as public schools and doing what it reasonably can to eliminate inadequate or harmful schooling of all kinds. It cannot justify giving parents the power to waive children's state-law right to a public-school education unless and until it institutes effective measures to ensure parents' exercise of such power does not result in serious educational deprivation or other developmental deficits or harms.

B. On What Conditions?

That leaves the final question of what conditions the state should attach to its legally empowering parents to choose homeschooling for a child. Homeschool advocates say the answer is none. But their argument for this rests in important part on the supposition about percentages that we showed above to be entirely groundless, disingenuous, and irresponsible. Their assertion that the existence of a few bad homeschools is not sufficient reason to monitor or restrict or burden all homeschooling parents suffers not only from a lack of evidence as to what the vast majority of homeschools are like and from ignoring evidence that permissive homeschooling laws facilitate child labor, maltreatment, and complete neglect of some children's education, but also from a mischaracterization of state oversight as presenting an intervention versus nonintervention choice and a reliance on the bankrupt notion of parental entitlement.

An adequate regulatory regime should entail a meaningful initial qualification process, subsequent periodic review, and remedial action when homeschooling proves deficient.

I. INITIAL QUALIFICATION   All public schools and many private schools scrutinize the qualifications of prospective teachers; they do not presume that every applicant, or even every applicant with a teaching certificate, is competent, let alone the best available teacher for children. Yet only a small number of states make any effort to screen out parents presumptively incapable of providing an adequate home education. Certainly all states should at least deny parents who are patently incapable of teaching, or who for other reasons are likely to disserve their children's welfare by homeschooling, the power to keep children out of school. But how to identify them?

States generally require that applicants for teaching positions in public schools have secured a state-issued teaching license, but this seems inappropriate for homeschooling. Licensure is neither a necessary nor a sufficient condition for being a good teacher. People who become state-licensed as teachers are on average only modestly above average in intelligence and academic success, so it could be that 40 percent of a society's population is of higher intelligence than most licensed teachers. (Some licensed teachers are brilliant; we are not suggesting otherwise.) Licensure reflects training as well as intelligence, but homeschoolers rightly point out that much of the training provided in university schools of education is about controlling and dividing time among a group of twenty or thirty children, a skill that is unnecessary for the typical homeschooler, and highly intelligent people can today readily find and digest information about pedagogy on the internet. Schools of education are widely regarded as one of the least rigorous components of American universities today (though some are quite rigorous), and we know that a significant percentage of people with state-issued teaching credentials are bad teachers, so the credential is also not a sufficient condition for being a good teacher.

The small number of states that require any sort of academic credential of homeschoolers ask only for a high school diploma or GED. This seems easily justifiable as a minimum requirement. A parent who herself or himself lacks sufficient aptitude, academic ambition, or practical ability to make it over the extremely low bar of a high school diploma or GED has no business controlling the education of a child. Ask yourself, if you were going to be born again someday, and to parents who dropped out of high school for whatever reason, whether you would want them to be your sole teachers during your childhood. It is not impossible for someone lacking a high school diploma to be an adequate teacher; there are historical examples of self-taught persons becoming highly accomplished (e.g., Ben Franklin), and such persons might be especially good teachers for their children. But if someone today who dropped out of school at age fourteen or sixteen wants the state to empower them to be a child's sole teacher, that child has a right that the state demand that the parent make some demonstration of academic aptitude and a capacity to apply themselves to an academic challenge by doing what is necessary now to get a high school diploma or GED. The state should wonder about the motivations and dedication to their children's welfare of anyone who refuses to do that, to go finish basic schooling themselves, in order to meet this very low qualification for homeschooling. Yet the highest rate of homeschooling, among parents grouped by their own educational attainment, is among those whose "highest educational level" is "less than high school."[13] States should require these parents to send their children to a regular school unless and until they themselves complete a high school education.

Requiring that a parent obtain a bachelor's degree and master's degree in teaching, on the other hand, which are commonly necessary to obtain a state-issued license, and which would disqualify most current homeschoolers, seems too much, at least for homeschooling in the primary grades. This requirement would exclude too many parents who could be good homeschoolers for younger children, simply because these parents cannot devote the much greater time it would take to complete those degree programs. Something in between those two levels of academic qualification might be optimal—for example, a high school diploma or equivalent plus completion of a homeschooling training program (something one-fourth of current homeschoolers have done voluntarily),[14] of perhaps one hundred hours. And it might be that a college degree should be required for anyone wishing to homeschool a child at the high-school level. There is evidence that homeschooled children experience deteriorating performance in the later grades if their parent has only a high school diploma.[15]

In addition to requiring that homeschoolers themselves have some minimal amount of learning, states should require demonstration of some aptitude for teaching. Even some of the most academically accomplished people are clueless about how to teach anyone else anything. But how could a parent who has never been a schoolteacher demonstrate such aptitude?

We suggest that for parents whose child has never attended a school full-time before reaching the compulsory-schooling age (i.e., has not gone to full-day preschool), and who wish to homeschool instead of enrolling the child in a regular school at that point, school-district employees simply assess their child, in person, at the time the child reaches that age. On the basis of that assessment, district employees can gauge what sort of instruction the parent has already been providing in the home and what social experiences the parent has been arranging for the child. There is a tendency to think education begins only at age five or six, whatever a state has set as the age when children must attend some sort of school. But, of course, children start learning from early infancy, and competent parents do a great deal of teaching at home and in the community before a child reaches "school age." The state, in its parens patriae role as agent for the child, should expect that parents who indicate a desire to homeschool their child can show that they have already been promoting the child's cognitive development, social and communication skills, literacy and numeracy, and knowledge. In effect, this would treat the time before the child reaches school age as "preschool time" and would treat the parents as the preschool teachers. This would test whether the parents are competent at that early stage when teaching might be easier in some ways than it will be in later years, both because the skills little children should be acquiring are relatively basic and because there is a wealth of how-to information and enrichment programs (e.g., at local libraries) available to parents of preschoolers.

This initial assessment should include an evaluation of a child's native abilities (e.g., an IQ test), so that achievement can be measured on that basis. It would not make sense to fault a parent for a child's performing below average if the child has a genetically created learning disability that makes higher achievement impossible. But if the school district assesses a child who has just reached school age and finds that he or she is already lagging developmentally well behind the level of which he or she is capable, that should be as clear an indication as any that the parent is not competent to homeschool. If, on the other hand, the school district finds that a child is at or above the expected level, it should feel sufficiently confident that the child's parents are capable of homeschooling, at least provisionally until the first assessment of academic progress beyond this baseline is conducted. (One necessary caveat is that, because IQ tests measure a developing ability, not a fixed, genetically determined ability, a low IQ score should also trigger further evaluation to diagnose the cause of slow development.)

Once this approach were adopted, all parents would be on notice as to what they must do in order to qualify to be homeschoolers; they must engage in preschool home instruction and succeed sufficiently at it. When parents first apply to homeschool an initial assessment of a child should occur anyway in order to identify any learning disabilities of which parents might be unaware and to ensure the child is not suffering from physical maltreatment.

With respect to parents who decide to begin homeschooling after a child has already attended a regular school for one or more years—for example, a child who is kindergarten age but has had substantial preschool experience outside the home, or a preadolescent whose parents want to spare him or her from the notorious travails of middle school—there is also a way for parents to demonstrate teaching aptitude in advance. Parents could meet with school-district officials in the spring before the school year in which they wish to commence homeschooling, accompanied by the child, and propose a modest course of summer study (perhaps just one or two subjects) that can serve as a basis for showing-by-doing that they are capable of adequate home instruction. They could present the results of the summer instruction before the next school year begins and receive approval if the results are sufficient. A socialization component could also be included; parents could be required to present at the end of the summer evidence that the children have participated during the summer in a significant number of activities or programs with children outside the family, such as a sports team, a scouts group, or a sleepaway camp.

In addition to excluding parents whose prior instruction of their children has been substantially deficient, states must guard against homeschooling's serving to hide abuse in the home. Children have a right against the state's placing them in legal parent-child relationships where the parents are legally empowered to keep them secluded from all outside observation; that is simply too dangerous a thing for the state to do to a child. One thing the state does in many contexts to prevent child abuse is a background check on potential custodians; it does this when considering applications for adoption or for many jobs involving direct contact with children. When a parent signals a desire to homeschool, the school district or some other state agency should consult state databases to see whether any household member has any relevant criminal history (i.e., something that might suggest a danger to children) or any civil record of child maltreatment. Given the motivation abusive parents (and abusive intimate partners of parents) have to keep maltreated children away from outsiders' observation, the state should be extremely wary of any parents with an official record of founded child maltreatment or felony convictions purporting to homeschool a child.[16] HSLDA characterizes criminal-background checks as "draconian," but in reality they are no imposition on nonabusive homeschoolers. Such information is already in state databases, so school officials simply need for parents seeking approval to homeschool to provide a list of all household members. Anyone who contends that requiring homeschoolers to list the people in their household or excluding from homeschooling those applicants with a household history of child abuse or felony convictions constitutes an unbearable incursion on freedom cannot possibly genuinely care about children. Any such child maltreatment or serious criminal history should trigger an in-depth individualized review to determine whether homeschooling is an appropriate choice for the child in question. At present, Pennsylvania appears to be the only state requiring any kind of background check, and its review is limited to convictions for certain crimes against persons and relies on reporting by parents rather than an official check of the state's criminal and child-maltreatment databases.[17] Yet when a parent with a history of maltreatment communicates an intention to homeschool, this is an obvious sign that a child might be at high risk of serious maltreatment, and states' empowerment of such parents as homeschoolers implicates the states in any further abuse or death these children subsequently suffer.[18] It is worth noting in this context that there is an emerging trend in the United States, now instantiated in four states (Maryland, Michigan, Minnesota, and Texas), to conduct such a background check on all biological parents when any child is born, as a means of preventing maltreatment.[19] The trend reflects increasing acceptance of the notion that, as with other profoundly important responsibilities, if we seek to assume control of a child's life, even if the child is our biological offspring, we have to expect that our histories might disqualify us from doing so.

2. PERIODIC REVIEW   After initial approval, the school district should reassess the homeschool every six or twelve months, as described below, to ensure the child continues to progress as he or she should. As many homeschoolers acknowledge, instructing a child becomes more difficult for most parents as the child gets older, because the content of courses becomes more complex and challenging, and so it cannot be safely assumed that a parent successful in the preschool years will remain successful at teaching all the way through elementary, middle, and high school years. (Of course, with some parents, the opposite could be true; they might find it easier to teach physics than phonics.) In fact, even in the current legal environment of nonregulation, a third of parents who start homeschooling voluntarily give it up after one year, and a large portion of the remainder give up after the early grades, presumably after finding it too difficult or burdensome.[20] This provides some support for a contention that most parents can be trusted to judge, at least after a period of trial

and error, whether and when homeschooling is best for their children. But we do not know whether all or even most who abandon the effort do so based on a disappointing assessment of their children's academic progress or instead based on their own fatigue. If the former, then that suggests a substantial percentage of parents who decide to homeschool are mistaken in their initial judgment of whether it will be best for their child. If the latter, then we have to worry that many of those who persist might simply have more determination or might be doing so little by way of instruction that they have nothing to feel burdened by. The mere fact of continuing after beginning is not, in and of itself, sufficient assurance that the child is progressing well academically and is not suffering from maltreatment or social deprivation or out in a field picking tobacco twelve hours per day.

The most straightforward form of ongoing oversight is a reliable periodic assessment of each child's educational progress and physical and psychological well-being. This can be accomplished by meetings, perhaps twice yearly, between a family and someone who is properly trained to conduct educational assessments and who is employed by the local school district. Ideally, these assessors would be people who have themselves homeschooled successfully, so that they are both supportive of homeschooling and sufficiently knowledgeable about its particular advantages and challenges to provide constructive feedback. But it might be difficult in some communities to hire such people. An assessor could review a portfolio of the student's work brought in by the student or parents, interview the child without the parents present, and ask the child to perform certain tasks on the spot (e.g., writing, performing mathematical operations, explaining how to test a scientific hypothesis, and displaying substantive knowledge).[21] These tasks need not all be the same ones that children of the same age in public schools are required to perform for assessment; the assessment could, as a general matter, be individualized to allow for various curricular approaches and ordering of subjects (e.g., trigonometry before geometry, second language before state history). But it should measure progress for all with respect to the basic goods of critical thinking, methods of inquiry in a variety of disciplines, and social skills, as well as literacy and numeracy.

This would be analogous to periodic well-child checkups with the doctor, only focused more on cognitive development than physical development (though entailing some observations about that as well) and conducted by a school-district employee or contractor rather than a private party picked by parents. Implicitly, notice to parents of what progress will be expected would give them some guidance in advance in choosing or developing a curriculum. And, needless to say, the state would conduct the same progress review for girls and boys, which would implicitly rule out gender-discriminatory treatment of homeschooled students.

This evaluation must be done by someone employed or chosen by the school district, because homeschoolers have, as noted in chapter 4, made a mockery of legal requirements for assessment in states that permit parents to submit an assessment by a private party of their choice; it is quite easy to find someone (e.g., a church pastor or a for-profit, online homeschool-approval agency) willing, perhaps for a fee, to submit a positive statement about a child's progress without actually performing any competent assessment.[22] So this would distinguish our proposal from existing law in the few states that ostensibly require periodic assessment; farcical statements of completed evaluation would no longer suffice. The assessor, though, ideally would also be familiar with the quality of education in the local public schools and therefore able to compare a child's progress to what is normal in those schools, given that the ultimate question is whether the homeschool is an adequate substitute for alternatives practically available to a given child.

Such an assessment system would be effective, we think, in identifying children suffering from educational neglect, physical or psychological maltreatment (including sexist subordination of girls), or a severe socialization deficit. An important incidental benefit of face-to-face academic evaluation is the opportunity to ensure homeschooling is not serving as a cover for abuse or neglect or child labor, as it appears to have been in the *Jonathan L.* case in California. This seems preferable, at least from a political standpoint, to mandatory home visits made solely to check for maltreatment (an approach proposed in Iowa).[23] And it would not be extraordinarily costly for states to do; certainly it is less costly for the state than educating the children themselves in public schools. Complaints historically about the cost of monitoring homeschooling falsely compare that cost to the state's not spending any money whatsoever on the education of some children,[24] which is an indefensible baseline; the comparison should be to what the state spends on other children, including those in public schools.[25] In addition, the practical burden on families would be slight, at least so long as the time and location of the meetings are not terribly inconvenient. Assessing by review of portfolio rather than by standardized testing preserves the valuable parental freedom to individualize the curriculum in accordance with an individual child's interests and home circumstances. Public-school systems rely on standardized testing rather than portfolio review in part because of cost but also because the latter makes precise assessments and comparisons across students quite difficult, there being significant subjectivity inherent in portfolio review. But precise assessment and comparison is not needed with homeschooled children; it should suffice that a portfolio shows the child is progressing academically well enough in light of his or her native abilities.

Homeschool advocates who oppose state oversight generally do not point to the burdensomeness of record keeping to support their opposition. Instead some predicate their opposition on assertions that curricular or testing requirements would unduly constrain parental freedom, and many simply make categorical and unsupportable claims about absolute parental sovereignty over children and about state incompetence. Many betray their own lack of sophistication in scientific reasoning by ascribing pervasive incompetence to all state employees based on evidence as to a small percentage of bad public schools or public-school teachers (while conversely insisting that a small percentage of bad homeschools should not tar all homeschools).

Yet this periodic individualized review need not be the singular required form of oversight; it need not be the only means the state gives parents to demonstrate that a child is not suffering from educational deprivation or maltreatment. The state might offer parents a choice among several means. Randall Curren and J. C. Blokhuis suggest mandatory part-time enrollment in a public school.[26] That could instead be simply one alternative offered to homeschooling parents; "dual enrollment" (e.g., two classes taken at the local high school, or a few hours a week at the elementary school) could spare parents from having to meet periodically with an academic assessor, as it would enable teachers to assess the child's reading and writing ability, intellectual and social development, and health. There has been resistance in many localities to homeschoolers' participating in public-school activities, but it has mostly been in connection with sports, where parents whose children attend public school full-time are unhappy about their children losing a spot on a team to a homeschooled child, and the motivation appears to be selfishness rather than any defensible principle. Public-school systems should create every possible opportunity for homeschooled students (whose parents presumably are paying taxes that fund the public schools) to participate in the schools' activities, instructional and otherwise. This can be beneficial not only for the homeschooled students but also for children and adolescents attending the public schools full time; the homeschooled students might offer their peers a different perspective on the school, on the team or club, or on many other things.

Still another possibility for fulfilling the aim of periodic review might be partial enrollment in a private school that the state has "accredited" on the basis of rigorous examination of its academic quality, coupled with a requirement that a teacher in that private school who has a state teaching credential submit a report on the (mostly) homeschooled child's academic progress, interpersonal communication abilities, and apparent health. Other approaches might also work, but it is essential that someone able *and inclined* to conduct an informed and objective assessment of the child do so for review by state education officials. Giving any parent monopoly control over a child's life and over access to the child is absolutely unacceptable; the state cannot plausibly justify its doing that to children.

The current regime of no state oversight of homeschools is therefore immoral; it is a dereliction of a duty the state owes to children—importantly, a duty that arises not simply out of a general societal responsibility to protect helpless people but also from the state's action of placing each child into the legal custody of particular persons and continually renewing that placement. The state must include among the conditions it establishes for people becoming legal parents that they accept periodic professional assessment of their child's development, just as the state imposes conditions on people who wish to adopt a child or to serve as guardian for an incompetent adult and on people to whom it entrusts many other important responsibilities. If you wish to enjoy the role of legal parent to a child, you must agree to accept this modest burden, in addition to the other legal duties that states already impose on all parents.

Again, this way of thinking about parenthood, as a fiduciary role with substantial duties dictated by the state, was the norm for most of American history. As eminent nineteenth-century jurist Joseph Story expressed it, "Why is the parent by law ordinarily entrusted with the care of his children? Simply, because it is generally supposed, that he will best execute the trust reposed in him; for, that it is a trust, and of all trusts the most sacred, no one can well doubt." Industrialization and cultural diversification turned the American consciousness toward a more individualistic and rights-based way of thinking of citizens' relationships to each other and to the state, and children's welfare and personhood to some extent got lost in the process. Yet even at the turn of the twentieth century, legal-treatise author Lewis Hochheimer would write that "the American cases may be characterized as an utter repudiation of the notion, that there can be such a thing as a proprietary right of interest in or to the custody of an infant." Instead, they reaffirmed "the idea of trust as the controlling principle in all controversies in relation to such custody. . . . In true legal conception, [the parent] is simply the agent or trustee of the government."[27] In this light, the Supreme Court's endorsement of the notion of parental entitlement as against the state in the 1920s was an implicit rejection of the traditional conception of parenthood, *not* resting on tradition as most people today suppose. If states in this country had continued to adhere to the traditional trust and fiduciary conception of parenthood, then it would simply be accepted, just as many other legal expectations for parents are simply taken for granted, that states may and should hold homeschooling parents accountable, or could ban homeschooling if necessary for children's well-being. If the states returned to this conception, it would eventually again become accepted and taken for granted.

We think other potential forms of state oversight, compliance with which could be a condition on parents' election of homeschooling, are unnecessary. One common proposal is that homeschool students take the same standardized tests that children in public schools take. Homeschoolers rightly object that forcing their children to take and pass such tests effectively forces them to adopt, to a substantial degree, the same content and schedule of instruction as in public schools, which largely eliminates the flexibility and individualization of instruction that are core virtues of homeschooling. One might add to this the substantial legitimate criticisms of the standardized testing regimes that legislatures have in recent decades foisted on public schools,[28] regimes that some suspect are driven by conservatives seeking to sabotage public schooling so that parents and taxpayers will shift their attention to private schools.[29] Many education experts recognize portfolio assessment—that is, review of a compilation of student work demonstrating a variety of cognitive skills—as superior in many ways to standardized testing, despite the greater subjectivity it entails.[30]

Notably, the periodic assessment should not only provide some assurance that children are developing well cognitively and acquiring knowledge that will prepare them for college and life in mainstream society (should they choose that as adults), but should also enable the state to get some sense of whether a child is receiving adequate socialization and is not being maltreated. Every child has a right against the state that the state makes at least such minimal effort to guard against the possibility that the adult custodians of the child are denying the child the basic goods of socialization and physical and mental security. Socialization can be gauged to some extent by how children behave in the personal interview—for example, whether they appear comfortable interacting with the assessor, what they say about people outside the family, and what activities they report participating in. Being able to converse with an adult is not necessarily indicative of an ability to interact fluently with peers, and the latter is important, but evidence of participation in activities and programs with other children can provide some reassurance as to the latter. In thinking about such assessment, one should not exaggerate the extent to which regular schooling serves as a positive socialization experience; children in schools spend many hours sitting near other children but forbidden to socialize with them, and in the short periods when they are permitted to talk with each other they remain under adult supervision, or, if they can escape adults' gaze, their interactions might reflect pent-up frustration and rebelliousness more than the idyllic civil discourse that critics claim homeschooled children miss out on.

C. Remediation

What is to be done if an assessment reveals that a child is lagging in one or more areas? Should the state immediately pull the plug and insist that the child immediately begin attending a regular school?

States have a great deal of experience working with students and parents to overcome poor academic performance and parental neglect. Public-school teachers and administrators address this routinely with students attending public school, and they apply a sliding scale of remedies, depending on the severity of the deficit and the inclination of student and of parent to cooperate. Child-protection agencies and juvenile courts respond to parental neglect of many kinds on a daily basis, and they likewise apply a range of strategies to improve children's situations, from offering services and assistance to removing a child from parental custody. State reaction to assessments of homeschooled children should likewise be calibrated to the magnitude of any deficit.

A common case might be one in which a child is doing well on every measure but one or two because the parents are weaker in teaching some subjects than others. A parent with a PhD in English might struggle to teach math and science, and a parent with a PhD in chemistry might not have a firm command of grammar and punctuation. This situation becomes increasingly likely as a child progresses from elementary school to middle and high school, where subject matter is more advanced. The state's first response to poor progress on certain subjects naturally should be to simply help the parent make up for that weakness—for example, by suggesting (and perhaps supplying) instructional materials and strategies the parent can use, or by providing a list of tutors or homeschool networks. If the problem persists in subsequent reviews, the state might have to shift from suggesting to mandating additional assistance—for example, by insisting the child attend a regular-school class in the weak subjects or receive tutoring (for which the state might pay). All children are entitled to a share of state education funding if this would improve their secular education, so states, having chosen to empower parents to waive their children's state-law right to a public-school education, should direct some education funding toward ensuring homeschooled children receive the instruction they need.[31]

Although the initial qualification process should minimize this, it is possible—again, more so in the upper grades—that an assessment will find a child of normal ability substantially deficient across the board in terms of academic progress, including intellectual skills and knowledge. In such a case, school officials might first see whether there is a "management" problem that might be fixable—for example, by assisting parents to create a daily schedule and set up a space conducive to learning (e.g., without a television on all the time). More likely, the parents are simply incapable of facilitating their children's learning, and the children need to receive instruction from someone else. The state might first allow parents to attempt improvement by joining a homeschool network, hiring tutors, and partially enrolling a child in a regular school. If less severe options appear unpromising, however, the state should immediately revoke the parents' qualification to homeschool and mandate that the child attend a regular school. This is something juvenile courts regularly order parents to do, typically in cases where a child is enrolled in public school but chronically truant, with the threat of removing the child from parental custody if the parents fail to comply. In all child-protection cases in which an agency worker or judge threatens to remove a child, parents might be very upset, and there is the danger they will do something even worse with the child, but the state cannot dismantle the child-protection system generally for this reason; instead it attempts to convince parents to comply, by explaining the needs of the child and by attaching more severe consequences to any further harmful behavior. Educational neglect is no different conceptually in this regard from physical neglect.

What might be especially difficult to address is a perceived deficiency in social development. In the first place, such a deficiency is difficult to measure; the judgment is inherently highly subjective. In addition, a lack of socialization that is sufficient to be apparent to an assessor likely reflects a parental aversion to contact with almost any persons outside the family, an aversion that likely causes the parent to instill paranoia in the child. In that case, any forced association could be counterproductive if the child is fearful or hostile. Other parents might not want their children interacting with such a child. If parents have made their children so terrified of the outside world that the children appear seriously disturbed to the assessor, then the state should probably treat the situation as one of psychological abuse and initiate the child-protection process, which could result in removal of the child or in parents' agreeing to receive treatment for mental illness, if that is the underlying cause. But in more modest cases, where the child is simply unpracticed and wary, the state's only reasonable remedy might be simply encouraging the parents to broaden the child's social universe as much as the parents comfortably can, explaining to the parents why this is important to the child's well-being. Perhaps the state could give parents a list of programs of various sorts for children in the community and require them to produce at the next review evidence of having attended a certain number of programs each month. This is similar to what child-protective caseworkers might do in a case of medical neglect—provide a list of clinics or doctors and require proof of the parents having taken the child to a doctor.

Also difficult to address during childhood is a deliberately induced deficit in knowledge of various conceptions of the good, of the various faiths and political ideologies to which people in America and elsewhere subscribe. Ultraconservative religious parents are not likely to shield their children from awareness of ideological difference; to the contrary, they are wont to warn children about it regularly. They are likely, though, to characterize other worldviews inaccurately and unfairly so that people who hold them appear unreasonable and threatening. This is a significant problem for children because it is likely to diminish their ability and inclination to pursue higher education and a career in mainstream society that might best fit their talents and abilities. As a general matter, though, deficits in knowledge are easier to address later in life than developmental delays are. Certainly many people who have grown up in an ideologically homogeneous community are able to succeed in the larger world and as adults become familiar with other belief systems. In college or in the workplace, they encounter people of other races, cultural backgrounds, and religions, and they come to appreciate that those people are reasonable and decent. More problematic is homeschool instruction that renders a person incapable of civil discourse and inclined to caricature, demonize, insult, and even threaten anyone with whom they disagree on political issues. The reaction among homeschoolers to early publicity about this book suggests there is a lot of this kind of instruction of children going on.[32] To the extent that knowledge about other worldviews is really important during childhood, a deficit in this area might be partially addressed by having the assessor who identifies it spend a little time with the child talking about it. If parents have trained a child to react in terror to mention of other worldviews or to the prospect of interacting with people who have them, then the problem is also one of socialization and possibly psychological abuse, which we addressed just above.

Ultimately, oversight of homeschooling cannot alleviate every concern one might have about the deficiencies or inclinations of some parents, just as state oversight of public-school teachers will never produce perfect, or even uniformly good, public education. In part this is because we cannot identify or do not know how to address particular problems, at least not without unacceptable cost to the core parent-child relationship, and this might be true regardless of what sort of schooling a child receives. What can the state do, for example, for a middle-school or high-school student who is developing a sense that he or she is gay, and whose parents have a religious conviction that homosexual persons should be stoned to death? Perhaps if the child attended public school, he or she could find a support group to help deal with this acute conflict, but such parents are more likely to send their children to a religious school if they do not homeschool, and in any event such a youth might suppress the awareness rather than admit it to him- or herself or others.

SUMMARY   Our policy conclusion, therefore, is that states should empower parents to keep children at home for schooling, but only upon the condition that the parents accept two requirements. First, by way of prequalification, the parents would have to possess at least a high school diploma (or GED) and would have to demonstrate to school-district officials that they have previously successfully educated their child ("home preschooling" or "home summer schooling"), taking into account the child's native abilities. Second, they must accept periodic assessment of each homeschooled child, ideally twice per year, by one of the means described above (i.e., personal interview and individualized portfolio review, partial attendance at a public school, or partial attendance at a state-accredited private school and assessment by a certified teacher there), so the state can ensure the child is progressing adequately. Progressing adequately includes not only learning to read and do mathematical operations but also developing analytical abilities commensurate with age, understanding and applying methodologies in a variety of disciplines, learning to communicate and interact harmoniously with persons outside the family, and acquiring substantial knowledge. The assessment should leave ample freedom, however, for parents to emphasize some disciplines and bodies of knowledge rather than others, so long as the choices are not unduly narrow. But the state must stand prepared to apply a range of remedial measures if an assessment shows that a child is substantially underperforming in one or more areas, in light of his or her native abilities.

Notes

1. We leave aside here interesting incidental questions that ascribing this right raises, such as whether there is a corresponding right of children to leave home when they wish to do so—for example, if they decide at some point they want to attend a regular school—a right that operates against parents as well as against the state. With young children, we have in mind an interest-protecting rather than choice-protecting right. The focus here is the permissibility of laws requiring children to attend a regular school.

2. See, e.g., Brown v. Bd. of Ed. of Topeka, Shawnee Cty., Kan., 347 U.S. 483, 493, 74 S. Ct. 686, 691, 98 L. Ed. 873 (1954) ("Education is perhaps the most important function of state and local governments. . . . In these days, it is doubtful that any child may reasonably be expected to succeed in life if he is denied the opportunity of an education. Such an opportunity, where the state has undertaken to provide it, is a right which must be made available to all on equal terms."); Rothner v. Chicago, 929 F.2d 297, 303 (8th Cir. 1991) ("Government has few interests more compelling than its interest in insuring that children receive an adequate education."); Crites v. Smith, 826 S.W.2d 459, 466–67 (Ct. App. Tenn. 1991); Murphy v. State of Ark., 852 F.2d 1039, 1041 (8th Cir. 1988); and Jonathan L. v. Superior Court, 165 Cal. App. 4th 1074, 1103, 81 Cal. Rptr. 3d 571, 593 (2008) ("California also has recognized that the 'welfare of a child is a compelling state interest that a state has not only a right, but a duty, to protect.'").

3. John Locke, *Second Treatise of Government*, ed. C. B. Macpherson (Hackett, 1980; orig. 1690), sec. 65.

4. See Dwyer, "Children We Abandon." The state would also violate this equality right by failing to ensure that some public schools are adequate.

5. Miss. Code. Ann. § 37-13-91.

6. See, e.g., Joyce, *Quiverfull*, 3–10, 217–34; Edward T. Babinski, *Leaving the Fold: Testimonies of Former Fundamentalists* (1995); Albert J. Menendez, *Visions of Reality: What Fundamentalist Schools Teach* (1993); Susan D. Rose, *Keeping Them Out of the Hands of Satan: Evangelical Schooling in America* (1988); Paul Parsons, *Inside America's Christian Schools* (1987); and Alan Peshkin, *God's Choice: The Total World of a Fundamentalist Christian School* (1986).

7. See, e.g., sources cited in note 6, supra, and "School Vouchers: The Emerging Track Record," National Education Association, last visited September 18, 2018, http://www.nea.org/home/16970.htm (listing instances of grossly deficient or sham private schools receiving state funding).

8. See, e.g., VaHomeschoolers, "Responsibility, Trust, and Virginia's Religious Exemption," previously available at http://vahomeschoolers .org/blog/2012/09/responsibility-trust-and-virginias-religious-exemption/, on file with the authors. This post contended that "the vast majority of the 7000 or so parents" who claim Virginia's religious exemption from compulsory schooling "take their children's educations extremely seriously and dedicate themselves to ensuring the quality of those educations," a statement based only on "our interactions with" an unspecified number of people who happened to have joined or contacted the organization or attended a homeschooling event, without acknowledging that parents might fail to provide an adequate education despite taking their children's schooling seriously, and asserted that the religious exemption is "not being misused" based solely on the fact that the number of parents claiming the exemption has not increased greatly in recent years, a glaring non sequitur.

9. See, e.g., Joyce, *Quiverfull*, 3–10, 217–34; Kristin Rawls, "Barely Literate? How Christian Fundamentalist Homeschooling Hurts Kids," Alternet, March 14, 2012, http://www.alternet.org/story/154541/barely _literate_how_christian_fundamentalist_homeschooling_hurts_kids.

10. Joyce, *Quiverfull*, supra.

11. See Kunzman, *Write These Laws on Your Children*, 144.

12. See, e.g., the Homeschoolers Anonymous website, http://home schoolersanonymous.org/; the Recovering Grace website, http://www.re coveringgrace.org/category/personal/; Catherine Wagley, "The Duggars: Sexual Abuse in the Christian Homeschooling Movement," JSTOR Daily,

January 13, 2016; Katherine Stewart, "The Dark Side of Home Schooling: Creating Soldiers for the Culture War," *Guardian*, May 8, 2013; Michelle Goldberg, "Homeschooled Kids, Now Grown, Blog Against the Past," *Daily Beast*, April 11, 2013; and Kunzman, *Write These Laws on Your Children*, 43–61, 64–65, 78–87.

13. Sarah Grady, Meghan McQuiggan, and Mahi Megra, *Parent and Family Involvement in Education: Results from the National Household Education Surveys Program of 2016: First Look* (Washington, DC: National Center for Education Statistics, 2017), 18.

14. Grady, McQuiggan, and Megra, *Parent and Family Involvement*, ii.

15. Kunzman and Gaither, "Homeschooling," 18.

16. See, e.g., R. L. Stollar, "When Homeschool Leaders Looked Away: The Old Schoolhouse Cover-Up," Homeschoolers Anonymous, October 8, 2014, http://homeschoolersanonymous.org/2014/10/08/when-homeschool -leaders-looked-away-the-old-schoolhouse-cover-up/ (discussing concealment of sexual abuse among homeschoolers).

17. 24 Pa. Stat. Ann. § 13-1327.1 ("The affidavit shall contain a certification to be signed by the supervisor that the supervisor, all adults living in the home and persons having legal custody of a child or children in a home education program have not been convicted of the criminal offenses enumerated in subsection (e) of section 1115 within five years immediately preceding the date of the affidavit."). Arkansas's education code states that parents may not elect to homeschool a child if there is a sex offender living in the household (Ark. Code § 6–15–508), but it does not direct anyone to conduct a background check to see whether any parent is violating this dictate.

18. See, e.g., Lyz Lenz, "Raashanai's Story: The Dark Side of Home-Schooling," *Guardian*, October 19, 2015.

19. See Dwyer, *Liberal Child Welfare Policy*, 130–36.

20. See Isenberg, "What Have We Learned About Homeschooling," 398, 406.

21. See Alexandra Beatty, *Best Practices for State Assessment Systems* (Washington, DC: National Academic Press, 2010).

22. See Kunzman, *Write These Laws on Your Children*, 174, 219.

23. Senate Bill 138 in the 2017 Iowa legislative session would have ordered, with homeschooling families only, "school districts to conduct quarterly home visits to check on the health and safety of children." The bill made no progress in the state legislature.

24. See, e.g., Fineman and Shepherd, "Homeschooling," 98.

25. For an explanation of why parents' choice to keep a child out of public schools does not obviate children's right to an equal share of state education funding, see Dwyer, *Vouchers within Reason*, chap. 6.

26. Curren and Blokhuis, "*Prima Facie* Case against Homeschooling," 14.

27. See Shulman, *Constitutional Parent*, 4.

28. See generally Schneider, *Beyond Test Scores*, supra.

29. See, e.g., Harvey Siegel, "High Stakes Testing, Educational Aims and Ideals, and Responsible Assessment," *Theory and Research in Education* 2, no. 3 (2004): 219–34; Randall R. Curren, "Educational Measurement and Knowledge of Other Minds," *Theory and Research in Education* 2, no. 3 (2004), 235–54.

30. See Linda Fernsten, "Portfolio Assessment," Education.com, December 23, 2009.

31. See Dwyer, *Vouchers within Reason*, chap. 6.

32. Readers might still find on the HSLDA website or on CRTV's Facebook page a "discussion" about this book. HSLDA is perennially sounding the alarm about the slightest suggestion that legislators might consider requiring something of homeschoolers, and demonizing anyone behind or supporting such proposals. One might reasonably suppose HSLDA's nearly hundred thousand paying members and countless nonpaying subscribers share the organization's embattled mentality and uncivil disposition and pass these on to their children.

Conclusion

Past, Present, and Future in the Real World

Homeschooling in America has come almost full circle in terms of being viewed as normal and a fulfillment of parental duty. The rise of public schools and proliferation of compulsory-schooling laws made homeschooling something aberrational and requiring defense for nearly a century. But today it is again, as it was in the colonial era, something quite familiar, even if it is today practiced by a far smaller percentage of the population. And it is becoming again a source of pride, garnering admiration even from many people who do not homeschool their own children but recognize its potential virtues and the dedication to one's children that it reflects. What is dramatically different today, relative to the colonial era, are the educational demands that the modern economy and contemporary social and civic life impose, which make it much more likely that homeschooling today will be inadequate in terms of what the state views as in each child's best interests, despite the best of parental intentions. And so our normative analysis recommends continued acceptance of homeschooling but condemns states for failing to exercise meaningful oversight and thus abandoning children to the risk of serious educational deprivation and abuse.

Our analysis of what oversight states should exercise might be pointless politically. Defenders of unsupervised homeschooling are among the more powerful political forces in America, whereas there is no advocacy organization pushing in the other direction that has substantial heft and makes homeschool regulation a central concern. There are several groups of former homeschooled students that protest what was done to them,[1] some of which publicly advocate for increased state oversight of homeschooling, but they are no match politically for HSLDA. Teachers' unions are powerful, but the regulation of competitors to public schools is at best a secondary concern for them. Since its founding, HSLDA has successfully eliminated or prevented the passage of numerous laws aimed at prohibiting, limiting, or overseeing homeschooling. The organization is hypervigilant and hypersensitive to any initiatives that in any way constitute or could lead to state oversight of homeschooling, so there is no chance of "sneaking one by them" or getting them to agree to some halfway measure. Even when homeschooling parents kill their children, there is little public outcry demanding greater oversight.[2] To homeschool extremists, these children are no one's concern except the parents who killed them. And there is no reason to expect the political landscape to change. If anything, power on the side of unregulated homeschooling will only increase as the number of homeschoolers continues to swell. One might think this political reality should lead to a conclusion in favor of prohibition, but that is even more unrealistic politically.

What we hope to have accomplished here is in part simply to have demonstrated the strength or weakness of the arguments made by those for and against prohibiting or regulating homeschooling, and to have arrived at a conclusion about the appropriate legal regime that is theoretically sound—namely, that states must permit homeschooling but also must oversee it, at least to the extent of imposing a meaningful prequalification procedure and subsequent periodic assessment of the homeschooled children's academic progress and basic well-being. We cannot convince legislators that they will be reelected if they act in accordance with our conclusion, but they should see that homeschool advocates' arguments against state oversight are invalid, making the failure to oversee and insist on academic accountability for homeschooling parents a gross dereliction of the legislators' moral and legal duty to children. As ultimate protectors of children's basic welfare, the legislators are failures. We have also suggested, though, some ways in which the state might make a new legal regime of genuine oversight more palatable—for example, by offering parents a menu of options for assessment and by making offers of assistance the preferred first response to any deficiencies identified through assessment.

We close, though, with two more realistic recommendations for improving state oversight of homeschools to save the unknown number of children who now are receiving little or no education of value or who are subject to maltreatment at home severe enough that parents are fearful of exposure should they send their children to school.

First, states could take a carrot rather than stick approach to regulation and offer financial support to parents who agree to comply with prequalification and periodic-assessment rules. This is the unrealized potential of school voucher programs that already exist for regular private schools; states could attach regulatory strings to the receipt of vouchers, and this would influence the private-school market, inducing more schools to accept and attempt to effectuate the state's aims for children's education. If taxpayers in voucher jurisdictions knew what sort of fanatically illiberal schools can be state funded, they might insist that legislators amend the voucher-program rules. Homeschooling expenses are generally far less than private-school tuition, so there might be less potential for financial inducement, but states could offer to reimburse homeschoolers not only for the costs of (approved) curricular materials, equipment (e.g., computers), and supplies but also for the costs of purchased classes, tutoring, museum memberships, social experiences for children (e.g., a scouts group, sports teams), and anything else that the state deems valuable for homeschooled children and that can be targeted sufficiently to avoid fraudulent fabrication of expenses. Some school districts in Alaska are doing this today with many homeschooling parents; in exchange for funding of educational supplies, parents register in one of the state-run correspondence schools (parents have a choice among curricula and pedagogical approaches) and accept school officials' ongoing review of their children's academic progress. In California, homeschoolers receive state funding for secular and religious materials and fee-based classes in the community by associating with and reporting to a form of "charter school" that is essentially an overseer of home-based instruction.[3] HSLDA opposes vouchers for homeschooling precisely because it fears regulation will follow funding (even though that has not happened with vouchers for private schools), but this has not stopped legislators from introducing homeschool-voucher bills at state and federal levels (e.g., H.R. 610 in the 2017–18 congressional session).

Second, there is a yet-unexplored possibility of using litigation to force legislative action. Chapter 2 described litigation efforts to eliminate regulations. No one has yet attempted, as far as we know, litigation to force the adoption of regulations, but there are viable legal claims to be made. The state's empowerment of parents to keep their children out of school, with no meaningful effort to ensure that the children still receive an adequate education and are not subject to maltreatment, effectively denies some children important state benefits that other children receive. States thereby run afoul of the US Constitution's equal protection clause, which requires states to have rational justification for refusing a public benefit to some persons that the states give to other, similarly situated persons. States infringe the equality right not only when they themselves decide that some individuals will not receive a benefit otherwise generally available but also when they empower some private parties to decide that some individuals will not receive the benefit. Space does not permit presentation here of the full legal argument,[4] but this brief suggestion provides some sense of its basic contours. In addition to the federal equal protection clause, many states have in their own constitutions a guarantee of education for all children,[5] upon which advocates for children might also be able to ground a legal claim. Moreover, in addition to the denial of verified education to homeschooled children generally, which might trigger only rational-basis review (which is highly deferential to legislatures), the current regime of nonoversight inflicts particular harm on girls, given that ultraconservative religious homeschools typically impress a sexist ideology on children and discourage girls from any aspiration other than domestic service to a man.[6] This disparate impact might inspire courts to be less deferential to legislatures. Litigation also depends on some advocacy organization's caring enough and devoting resources but typically requires far less in resources than does swaying a majority of legislators.

Our principal purpose in this book, however, has been not to chart a path to legal reform but rather simply to inform and inspire further thought about a growing phenomenon in our society that many find intriguing and that has a profound impact on the lives of millions of children. We hope this book will accomplish this with all readers, regardless of their predisposition to support or disparage homeschooling, and improve everyone's understanding of alternative perspectives.

Notes

1. These include Homeschoolers Anonymous, Homeschool Alumni Reaching Out, and Homeschooling's Invisible Children. For a description of the membership, aims, and creation of these organizations, see Kathryn Joyce, "The Homeschool Apostates," *American Prospect*, February 9, 2014, http://prospect.org /article/homeschool-apostates. Another group founded and run by homeschool alumni is the Coalition for Responsible Home Education, which advocates for greater state oversight of homeschooling. One group, No Longer Quivering, is actually run by former homeschool parents.

2. See Associated Press, "Tragic Deaths of Home-Schooled Kids Rarely Lead to New Rules," MSN, December 6, 2015, http://www.msn.com/en-us/news/us /tragic-deaths-of-home-schooled-kids-rarely-lead-to-new-rules/ar-AAg5UCD.

3. Calif. Educ. Code § 47612.5(d)(1).

4. For the full argument, see Dwyer, "Children We Abandon."

5. See, e.g., N.C. Const. art. I, § 15 ("The people have a right to the privilege of education, and it is the duty of the State to guard and maintain that right.").

6. See Kunzman, "Homeschooling and Religious Fundamentalism," supra, at 20.

Bibliography

Abbott, Edith. "A Study of the Early History of Child Labor in America." *American Journal of Sociology* 14 (1908): 15–37.

Abbott, Francis E. *Compulsory Education*. Boston: Index Association, 1878.

Andrade, Albert. "An Exploratory Study of the Role of Technology in the Rise of Homeschooling." PhD diss., College of Education of Ohio University, 2008.

Angulo, A. J., ed. *Miseducation: A History of Ignorance-Making in America and Abroad*. Baltimore: Johns Hopkins University Press, 2016.

Baldwin, Neil. *Edison: Inventing the Century*. Chicago: University of Chicago Press, 2001.

Barfield, Rhonda. *Real Life Homeschooling: The Stories of 21 Families Who Make It Work*. New York: Fireside, 2002.

Bennion, Janet. *Polygamy in Primetime: Media, Gender, and Politics in Mormon Fundamentalism*. Lebanon, NH: Brandeis University Press, 2012.

Bestor, Arthur. *Educational Wastelands: The Retreat From Learning in Our Public Schools*. Champaign: University of Illinois Press, 1953.

Brighouse, Harry. *School Choice and Social Justice*. New York: Oxford University Press, 2000.

Bumstead, Richard. "Educating Your Child at Home: The *Perchemlides* Case." *Phi Delta Kappan* 61, no. 2 (October 1979): 97–100 (quoting Holt).

Butterworth, Michael. "The Passion of the Tebow: Sports Media and Heroic Language in the Tragic Frame." *Critical Studies in Media Communication* 30, no. 1 (2013): 17–33.

Callan, Eamonn. *Creating Citizens: Political Education and Liberal Democracy*. New York: Oxford University Press, 1997.

Carper, James C. "The *Whisner* Decision: A Case Study in State Regulation of Christian Day Schools." *Journal of Church and State* 24, no. 2 (1982): 281–302.

Carper, James C., and Neal E. Devins. "Rendering unto Caesar: State Regulation of Christian Day Schools." *Journal of Thought* 20, no. 4 (1985): 99–113.

Carper, James C., and Thomas C. Hunt. *The Dissenting Tradition in American Education*. New York: Peter Lang, 2007.

Carter, Stephen. *The Culture of Disbelief: How American Law and Politics Trivialize Religious Devotion.* New York: Anchor Books, 1994.

Cayley, David. *Ivan Illich in Conversation.* Toronto: House of Anansi Press, 1992.

Chiu, Elaine M. "The Culture Differential in Parental Autonomy." *University of California Davis Law Review* 41 (2008): 1773–828.

Curren, Randall, and J. C. Blokhuis. "The *Prima Facie* Case against Homeschooling." *Public Affairs Quarterly* 25, no. 1 (January 2011): 1–19.

Cutler, William. *Parents and Schools: The 150-Year Struggle for Control in American Education.* Chicago: University of Chicago Press, 2000.

deMause, Lloyd, ed. *The History of Childhood.* New York: Psychohistory Press, 1974.

Devins, Neal. "State Regulation of Christian Schools." *Journal of Legislation* 10 (1983): 351–81.

Diamond, Sara. *Spiritual Warfare: The Politics of the Christian Right.* Boston: South End Press, 1989.

Duvall, Steven, Joseph Delquadri, and Lawrence Ward. "A Preliminary Investigation of the Effectiveness of Homeschool Instructional Environments for Students with Attention-Deficit/Hyperactivity Disorder." *School Psychology Review* 33, no. 1 (2004): 140–58.

Dwyer, James G. "The Children We Abandon: Religious Exemptions to Child Welfare and Educational Law as Denials of Equal Protection to Children of Religious Objectors." *North Carolina Law Review* 74 (1996): 1321–478.

———. *Liberal Child Welfare Policy and Its Destruction of Black Lives.* New York: Routledge, 2018.

———. *The Relationship Rights of Children.* New York: Cambridge University Press, 2006.

———. *Religious Schools v. Children's Rights.* Ithaca, NY: Cornell University Press, 1998.

———. *Vouchers within Reason.* Ithaca, NY: Cornell University Press, 2001.

Ensign, Forest Chester. *Compulsory School Attendance and Child Labor.* Iowa City, IA: Athens Press, 1921.

Fineman, Martha Albertson, and George Shepherd. "Homeschooling: Choosing Parental Rights Over Children's Interests." *University of Baltimore Law Review* 46, no. 1 (2016): 57–106.

Freire, Paulo. *Pedagogy of the Oppressed: 30th Anniversary Edition.* New York: Continuum, 2005.

Gaither, Milton. *Homeschool: An American History.* New York: Palgrave, 2008.

Galston, William. *Liberal Purposes: Goods, Virtues, and Diversity in the Liberal State.* New York: Oxford University Press, 1991.

Goldstein, Joseph. "Medical Care for the Child at Risk: On State Supervention of Parental Autonomy." *Yale Law Journal* 86 (1977): 645–70.

Guterson, David. *Family Matters: Why Homeschooling Makes Sense.* New York: Harcourt, 1992.

Gutmann, Amy. *Democratic Education*. Princeton, NJ: Princeton University Press, 1987.

Hall, David D. *Cultures of Print: Essays in the History of the Book*. Amherst: University of Massachusetts Press, 1996.

Harding, Kip, and Mona Lisa Harding. *The Brainy Bunch: The Harding Family's Method to College Ready by Age Twelve*. New York: Gallery Books, 2014.

Hartman, Andrew. *A War for the Soul of America: A History of the Culture Wars*. Chicago: University of Chicago Press, 2015.

Hasson, Mary Rice. "The Changing Conversation around Homeschooling: An Argument for More Data and Less Ideology." *University of St. Thomas Journal of Law and Public Policy* 7, no. 1 (2012–2013): 1–23.

Heimlich, Janet. *Breaking Their Will: Shedding Light on Religious Child Maltreatment*. Amherst, NY: Prometheus Books, 2011.

Holt, John. *Instead of Education: Ways to Help People Do Things Better*. Boulder, CO: Sentient Publications, 2004.

Holt, John, and Patrick Farenga. *Teach Your Own: The John Holt Book of Homeschooling*. Chicago: Da Capo Press, 2003.

Hunt, Thomas C., and James C. Carper, eds. *The Praeger Handbook of Faith-Based Schools in the United States, K–12*. Vol. 1. Santa Barbara: Praeger, 2012.

Illich, Ivan. *Deschooling Society*. New York: Harper and Row, 1971.

Isenberg, Eric J. "What Have We Learned About Homeschooling." *Peabody Journal of Education* 82, no. 2–3 (2007): 387–409.

Jernegan, Marcus Wilson. *The Laboring and Dependent Classes in Colonial America, 1607–1783*. New York: Ungar, 1960.

Jowett, B., ed. *The Dialogues of Plato: Translated into English*. Vol. 5. Oxford: The Clarendon Press, 1792.

Joyce, Kathryn. *Quiverfull: Inside the Christian Patriarchy Movement*. Boston, MA: Beacon Press, 2010.

Katz, Michael. *A History of Compulsory Education Laws*. Bloomington, IN: Phi Delta Kappa Educational Foundation, 1976.

Kent, James. *Commentaries on American Law*. 9th ed. Vol. 2. Boston: Little, Brown and Company, 1858.

Klicka, Christopher. *Home School Heroes: The Struggle and Triumph of Home Schooling in America*. Nashville: B&H Publishing Group, 2006.

Knowles, J. G., S. E. Marlow, and J. A. Muchmore. "From Pedagogy to Ideology: Origins and Phases of Home Education in the United States, 1970–1990." *American Journal of Education* 100, no. 2 (1992): 195–235.

Knox, Barbara L., Suzanne P. Starling, Kenneth W. Feldman, Nancy D. Kellogg, Lori D. Frasier, and Suzanna L. Tiapula. "Child Torture as a Form of Child Abuse." *Journal of Child and Adolescent Trauma* 7, no. 1 (2014): 37–49.

Kunzman, Robert. "Homeschooling and Religious Fundamentalism." *International Electronic Journal of Elementary Education* 3, no. 1 (2010): 17–28.

———. *Write These Laws on Your Children: Inside the World of Conservative Christian Homeschooling*. Boston: Beacon Press, 2009.

Kunzman, Robert, and Milton Gaither. "Homeschooling: A Comprehensive Survey of the Research." *Other Education: The Journal of Alternative Education* 2, no. 1 (2013): 4–59.

Laats, Adam. *Fundamentalism and Education in the Scopes Era: God, Darwin, and the Roots of America's Culture Wars*. New York: Palgrave Macmillan, 2010.

———. *The Other School Reformers: Conservative Activism in American Education*. Cambridge, MA: Harvard University Press, 2015.

———. "Religion." In *Miseducation: A History of Ignorance-Making in America and Abroad*, edited by A. J. Angulo, 161–83. Baltimore: Johns Hopkins University Press, 2016.

Laing, Jacqueline A., and Russell Wilcox, eds. *The Natural Law Reader*. Hoboken, NJ: Wiley-Blackwell, 2013.

Levinson, Meira. *The Demands of Liberal Education*. New York: Oxford University Press, 1999.

Lois, Jennifer. *Home Is Where the School Is: The Logic of Homeschooling and the Emotional Labor of Mothering*. New York: New York University Press, 2012.

Lombard, Ellen C. "The Home Reading Courses of the United States Bureau of Education." *Annals of the American Academy of Political and Social Science* 67 (1916): 267–69.

Lupu, Ira. "Home Education, Religious Liberty, and the Separation of Powers." *Boston University Law Review* 67 (1987): 971–92.

Macedo, Stephen. *Diversity and Distrust: Civic Education in a Multicultural Democracy*. Cambridge, MA: Harvard University Press, 2000.

Mazama, Ama, and Garvey Musumunu. *African Americans and Homeschooling: Motivations, Opportunities, and Challenges*. New York: Routledge, 2015.

McDowell, Susan A., Annette R. Sanchez, and Susan S. Jones. "Participation and Perception: Looking at Home Schooling Through a Multicultural Lens." *Peabody Journal of Education* 75, no. 1/2 (2000): 124–46.

Mead, Margaret. *Blackberry Winter: My Earlier Years*. New York: Simon and Schuster, 1991.

Mendenhall, Dorothy Reed. "Research Is a Passion with Me." In *Written by Herself: Autobiographies of American Women*, vol. 1, edited by Jill Kerr Conway, 171–99. New York: Vintage, 1992.

Messerli, Jonathan. *Horace Mann: A Biography*. New York: Knopf, 1972.

Miller, Ron. *Free Schools, Free People: Education and Democracy after the 1960s*. Albany: State University of New York Press, 2002.

Monaghan, E. Jennifer. *Learning to Read and Write in Colonial America*. Amherst: University of Massachusetts Press, 2005.

Montgomery, Zachariah. *Poison Drops in the Federal Senate: The School Question from a Parental and Non-Sectarian Standpoint*. Washington, DC: Gibson Brothers, 1886.

Moore, Raymond, and Dennis Moore. "The Dangers of Early Schooling." *Harper's*, July 1972, 58–62.

Moore, R. Jonathan. *Suing for America's Soul: John Whitehead, the Rutherford Institute, and Conservative Christians in the Courts.* Grand Rapids, MI: William B. Eerdman's Publishing Company, 2007.

Morgan, Edmund S. *Benjamin Franklin.* New Haven, CT: Yale University Press, 2003.

Morris, Edmund. *The Rise of Theodore Roosevelt.* New York: Random House, 2001.

Murphy, Joseph. *Homeschooling in America: Capturing and Assessing the Movement.* Thousand Oaks, CA: Corwin, 2012.

Parsons, Paul. *Inside America's Christian Schools.* Macon, GA: Mercer University Press, 1987.

Payne, George Henry. *The Child in Human Progress.* New York: Putnam's, 1916.

Pearl, Michael, and Debi Pearl. *To Train Up a Child.* Pleasantville, TN: No Greater Joy Ministries, 1994.

Perrin, John William. *The History of Compulsory Education in New England.* Meadville, PA: The Chautauqua-Century Press, 1896.

Peters, Shawn Francis. *Judging Jehovah's Witnesses: Religious Persecution and the Dawn of the Rights Revolution.* Lawrence: University Press of Kansas, 2000.

———. *When Prayer Fails: Faith Healing, Children, and the Law.* New York: Oxford University Press, 2007.

———. *The Yoder Case: Religious Freedom, Education, and Parental Rights.* Lawrence: University Press of Kansas, 2003.

Quigley, Patrick Francis. *Compulsory Education: The State of Ohio v. Patrick Francis Quigley.* New York: Robert Drummond, 1894.

Ramsay, David. *Memoirs of the Life of Martha Laurens Ramsay.* Charlestown, MA: Samuel Etheridge, 1812.

Ray, Brian. "Academic Achievement and Demographic Traits of Homeschool Students: A Nationwide Study." *Academic Leadership Journal* 8, no. 1 (2010): 1–32.

Reagan, Michael. *The New Reagan Revolution: How Ronald Reagan's Principles Can Restore America's Greatness Today.* New York: Thomas Dunne Books, 2010.

Reed, Jean, and Donn Reed. *Lifetime Learning Companion: The Best of the Home School Source Book.* Bridgewater, ME: Brook Farm Books, 2009.

Reich, Rob. *Bridging Liberalism and Multiculturalism in American Education.* Chicago: University of Chicago Press, 2002.

Rendleman, Douglas R. "Parens Patriae: From Chancery to the Juvenile Court." *South Carolina Law Review* 23 (1971): 205–59.

Robertson, Pat. *The Collected Works of Pat Robertson.* New York: Inspirational Press, 1994.

Rothbard, Murray. *Education: Free and Compulsory.* Auburn, AL: Ludwig von Mises Institute, 1999.

Rushdoony, Rousas. *The Messianic Character of American Education: Studies in the History of the Philosophy of Education*. Nutley, NJ: Craig Press, 1968.

———. *The Philosophy of the Christian Curriculum*. Vallecito, CA: Ross House Books, 2001.

Scherman, Rita. *A Mother's Letters to a Schoolmaster*. New York: Knopf, 1923.

Schlafly, Phyllis. "Child Abuse in the Classroom." In *Landmark Speeches of the American Conservative Movement*, edited by Peter Schweizer and Wynton C. Hall, 94–104. College Station: Texas A&M University Press, 2007.

Schneider, Jack. *Beyond Test Scores: A Better Way to Measure School Quality*. Cambridge, MA: Harvard University Press, 2017.

Schoff, Hannah. "The National Congress of Mothers and Parent-Teacher Associations." *The Annals of the American Academy of Political and Social Science* 67 (1916): 139–47.

Schoff, Hannah Kent. *The Wayward Child: A Study of the Causes of Crime*. Indianapolis: The Bobbs-Merrill Company, 1915.

Shulman, Jeffrey. *The Constitutional Parent: Rights, Responsibilities, and the Enfranchisement of the Child*. New Haven, CT: Yale University Press, 2014.

Skocpol, Theda. *Protecting Soldiers and Mothers*. Cambridge, MA: Harvard University Press, 1995.

Steffes, Tracy. *School, Society, and State: A New Education to Govern Modern America, 1890–1940*. Chicago: University of Chicago Press, 2012.

Stevens, Mitchell. *Kingdom of Children: Culture and Controversy in the Homeschooling Movement*. Princeton, NJ: Princeton University Press, 2003.

Tanenhaus, David. "Between Dependency and Liberty: The Conundrum of Children's Rights in the Gilded Age." *Law and History Review* 23 (2005): 351–85.

Tebow, Tim. *Know Who You Are: Live Like It Matters*. New York: WaterBrook, 2017.

Thomas, Mason P. "Child Abuse and Neglect, Part I: Historical Overview, Legal Matrix, and Social Perspectives." *North Carolina Law Review* 50 (1972): 293–349.

Tozer, Steven E., Bernardo P. Gallegos, and Annette Henry, eds. *Handbook of Research in the Social Foundations of Education*. New York: Routledge, 2011.

Van Galen, Jane. "Explaining Home Education: Parents' Accounts of Their Decisions to Teach Their Own Children." *The Urban Review* 19, no. 3 (1987): 161–77.

Wilhoit, James. *Christian Education and the Search for Meaning*, 2nd ed. Grand Rapids, MI: Baker Academic, 1991.

Williams, Heather Andrea. *Self-Taught: African American Education in Slavery and Freedom*. Chapel Hill: University of North Carolina Press, 2005.

Wright, Danaya C. "Policing Sexual Morality: Percy Shelley and the Expansive Scope of the Parens Patriae in the Law of Custody of Children." *Nineteenth Century Gender Studies Online Journal* 8, no. 2 (Summer 2012).

Yuracko, Kimberly. "Education Off the Grid: Constitutional Constraints on Homeschooling," *California Law Review* 96 (2008): 123–84.

Zimmerman, Jonathan. *Whose America?: Culture Wars in the Public Schools.* Cambridge, MA: Harvard University Press, 2002.

Index